MODERN PORTUGUESE POETRY
ESSAYS, POEMS & TRANSLATIONS

Published by the Modern Humanities Research Association
Salisbury House, Station Road, Cambridge CB1 2LA

ISBN 978-1-83954-107-0

First published 2020

This book appears also as a special issue (volume 36 no. 2) of
Portuguese Studies, a journal published by the
Modern Humanities Research Association

Disclaimer: Statements of fact and opinion contained in this book are those
of the author and not of the editors or the Modern Humanities Research
Association. The publisher makes no representation, express or implied, in
respect of the accuracy of the material in this book and cannot accept any
legal responsibility or liability for any errors or omissions that may be made.

Trademark notice: Product or corporate names may be trademarks or
registered trademarks, and are used only for identification and explanation
without intent to infringe.

Copy-Editor: Richard Correll
Production Editor: Graham Nelson

Modern Portuguese Poetry

Essays, Poems & Translations

Edited by
Paulo de Medeiros and
Rosa Maria Martelo

MODERN HUMANITIES RESEARCH ASSOCIATION
2020

Contents

Introduction

Rosa Maria Martelo and Paulo de Medeiros

'Is poetry important?' asks Bernard O'Donoghue right at the beginning of his recent *Poetry: A Very Short Introduction*.[1] This questioning, and self-questioning, of poetry is so common as to probably qualify as one of poetry's hallmarks. Suspicions of poetry, as well as grand claims about it, abound. From Plato's (in)famous banishment of the poets from the ideal city, to Shelley's equally well-known and often cited assertion that '[p]oets are the unacknowledged legislators of the World',[2] poetry, it seems, can stand for anything. Adrienne Rich has often questioned what the role and function of poetry is, and, more to our point now, what poetry's standing in the world is. In a short essay printed in *The Guardian*, Adrienne Rich took this in her incomparable way, and commented ironically on the 'free market view' of poetry that would render it redundant: 'There's actually an odd correlation between these ideas: poetry is either inadequate, even immoral, in the face of human suffering, or it's unprofitable, hence useless. Either way, poets are advised to hang our heads or fold our tents. Yet in fact, throughout the world, transfusions of poetic language can and do quite literally keep bodies and souls together — and more'.[3] The imbrications of poetry in society as well as poetry's aesthetic claims, as Rich points out, do not constitute a paradox at all, and certainly are not mutually exclusive: 'we can also define the "aesthetic", not as a privileged and sequestered rendering of human suffering, but as news of an awareness, a resistance, which totalising systems want to quell: art reaching into us for what's still passionate, still unintimidated, still unquenched'. This is also, in a sense, what Emily Dickinson expressed so well, as O'Donoghue reminds us: 'I dwell in Possibility — | A fairer House than Prose — | More numerous of Windows — | Superior — for Doors –'.[4] Without claiming any universality for poetry, and mindful of the historical specificities that always inform any cultural expression, we would like to affirm much the same qualities, the same degree of introspection and critical self-reflection, of engagement with society in all of its variants, and the same exalted claims on

---

[1] Bernard O'Donoghue, *Poetry: A Very Short Introduction* (Oxford: Oxford University Press, 2019), p. 1.

[2] Percy Bysshe Shelley, 'A Defence of Poetry' [1821; 1840], in *The Major Works* (Oxford: Oxford University Press, 2009), p. 701.

[3] Adrienne Rich, 'Legislators of the World', *Guardian*, 18 November 2006, <https://www.theguardian.com/books/2006/nov/18/featuresreviews.guardianreview15> [accessed 29 February 2020].

[4] Emily Dickinson, 'I dwell in Possibility', in *The Complete Poems of Emily Dickinson*, ed. by Thomas H. Johnson (Boston, New York, and London: Little, Brown and Co., 1961), p, 327; here as quoted by O'Donoghue, p. 47.

the aesthetic and the emphasis on form, from within the very multiplicity of voices and shapes, as marking contemporary Portuguese poetry.

This book, which first appeared as a special issue of the journal *Portuguese Studies*, wants to focus on this poetry, from the latter part of the twentieth century to our actual present. This poetry figures here in various ways, most directly with the section containing a brief anthology of texts from some of contemporary Portuguese poetry's most significant authors. And of course the collection of critical essays that engage with the various issues and problematics that have marked this poetry, including a continuous experimentation in terms of form, media, and intermediality. Added to this we also have six reviews of recent books and journals that allow for yet another view of our subject's vibrancy. As organizers we refused any illusions or aspirations to exhaustive coverage, which would in any case always be impossible, even if we had more than the space of any one volume. Nonetheless we think that the current special issue, in both its critical and anthological components, allows for a productive reflection concerning the main lines that have been structuring contemporary Portuguese poetry, without dismissing in any way its modernist foundations. Indeed, it is not haphazardly that the critical essays, when read in sequence, make abundantly clear the fact that the relations between poetry, ethics, and politics, constitute a shared concern of all the poets and critics assembled in this issue.

Those relations are analysed right from the start by Silvina Rodrigues Lopes. She begins addressing some of the modern formulations of an indirect relation between the poetic and the political and then follows them noting how 'reason and imagination unfold each other to move away from the aesthetics of appearance and establish a space of response and solicitation which opens aesthetics to the ethical-political'. In the essays that follow it is possible to see some permutations of this question, with special attention given to the ways in which it figures in the work of Ana Luísa Amaral, here read by Marinela Freitas and Paulo de Medeiros; and also in the writing of authors whose texts are marked by a complex mixture of irony and dysphoria, as in the case of José Miguel Silva, here analysed mostly by Pedro Eiras. These are visions of crisis and a questioning of the ways of the world which, in some cases, might lead towards a re-valorization of the lyrical mode, but which also lead towards other forms of problematizing subjective experience, and even to a search for ways to experience kinds of dissolution, such as shown by Manuel Portela.

Referring to an announced abandonment of poetry by the poet José Miguel Silva, whose most recent book of poems is significantly entitled, *Últimos Poemas* [Last Poems], Pedro Eiras asks: 'Should we identify a coherent gesture in José Miguel Silva's work? Or is there a sort of ironic resistance in this farewell to poetry and to the world of the *polis*?' One can also speak of an ironic stance in Ana Luísa Amaral's poetics, inasmuch as, to follow Marinela Freitas, the poet 'questions gendered assumptions embedded in language and explores new ways of articulating difference', making us question the formulation of rigid identities. Paulo de Medeiros's essay, in turn, focuses on Amaral's most recent book, which is profoundly marked by biblical intertextuality and by ekphrasis, combining both so as to put forth an urgent and very actual political critique.

The various modes of intermedial and intertextual writing, as well as some means of reconceptualizing, or even questioning, the relation between poetry and image, and between poetry and representation, guide the essays of Rosa Maria Martelo and Joana Matos Frias. The former takes on a panoramic shape as it ranges over various poets and their creation; whereas the latter focuses on one of the greatest poetic voices of all time, Fiama Hasse Pais Brandão, a poet for whom the processes of representation and the verbal modes of creating images were always central in what was a most rigorous deployment of poetic thought. Other poets directly studied in the various essays will be present again in the brief anthological second part of this issue. And not only those, as we also include some poets only briefly alluded to in the essays, who would also deserve fuller critical attention if there were space for more, such as Gastão Cruz, António Franco Alexandre, or Manuel de Freitas. As such, and still very much aware of our limitations, we hope to provide for varied readings of contemporary Portuguese poetry across generations.

*   *   *   *   *

The editors wish to thank the Instituto de Literatura Comparada and the Fundação para a Ciência e a Tecnologia for their financial support of this project.

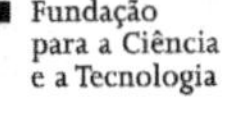

UIDP/00500/2020

Of Literature as a Composition of the Disparate and its Political Implications

Silvina Rodrigues Lopes

Universidade Nova de Lisboa

1

My intent is to investigate the relationships between literature and politics, with the aim of understanding how these terms become entwined in vortices of change, without resorting to one of them to justify what supposedly lies within the scope of the other, and without negating the asymmetry that results from the impossible task of assigning political action and thought to literature. Politics presupposes the intent to question and persuade, which predominantly makes discourse a chain of sentences — of questions, reasons, examples, prescriptions, etc. — while the precondition for literature is the suspension of meaning, the usual meaning of words, phrases and their connections.

As they do not address a specific pre-determined audience, literary texts lend themselves to providing answers not entirely subordinated to a particular intention or interest, answers which are immutable and non-hierarchical. What cannot be measured cannot be put on a scale. Whether writing another literary text, a philosophical text mysteriously inspired by a literary text, in connection with a new problem, or as a means to obtain answers regarding a perspective found during reading, writing always assumes a certain lack of embarrassment. That which we freely accept as meaning based on themes, motives, words and affections is 'recognized' as an event for its power to create something new: answers displace that which they 'recognize'. When the resulting text is literary, the affirmation of that which is singular is decisive (as, obviously, being expressed through language, it is open to universal reason). If the answer is 'non-literary', philosophical, it increases displacement to root itself in reason, without becoming bound by it. Therefore, the figure of the reader cannot exist, as the underlying specialization is instantly lost to philosophy, that dedicated to the search for ultimate reasons or the construction of systems.

Ethical and political implications arise at the intersection. Free from what preceded them, they claim their place in history with their demand for the right to literature as a right to indeterminacy — in line with the obligation of not standing in the way of the future, given that conscious perception represents insufficient situational comprehension. This implies the conjunction of a double movement, that of safeguarding the unexpected, *pharmakon* (medicine or poison), and that of concern for the justice of shared experience.

In the nineteenth century, several poets presented themselves as 'educators of humanity', an expression thereof, its mentors, tutors and guides. This stance, laden with misconceptions — that of genius, emancipation and universality — was based on literature as a means of communication and propaganda, which allowed books regarded as the exponents of such ideas to be written and to mobilize people around ideals professed by their authors, who were considered geniuses given their capacity to mobilize others. Based on circularity — if it is ingenious, it will produce an effect; if it has an effect, it is therefore created by a genius — the defence of political literature presents not only the dangers of all propaganda, which rests on the exacerbation of feelings, but also those of creating the nationalist figure, the genius as an undisputed authority. In addition, it negates literature by supposing its instrumentalization.

Placing someone in a position of untouchable genius, and espousing their words without limits, can give rise to situations such as Victor Hugo's *Speech on Africa*. At that event, the writer was presented as belonging to 'the race of giants [...] and a powerful defender of all the dispossessed, the weak, and the oppressed in this world, a glorious apostle of the sacred right of human beings'.[1] Hugo himself stated that 'in the 19th century, whites made men of the blacks; in the 20th century, Europe will make a world out of Africa [...] Go forth! Take over this land. Take it. From whom? Nobody. Take this land from God. God gives the earth to men. God offers Africa to Europe. Bet on this Africa, and in one stroke solve your social issues, transform your proletarians into owners.'[2]

Transposed as social and political intervention, authority which comes from recognizing someone as a poet reveals nothing but obscurantism, be it by suturing poetry to politics, as in the case of Victor Hugo, or suturing politics to poetry, as explicitly postulated in Heidegger's philosophy. The latter relationship, theorized and advocated by English and German Romantic tradition, integrated the idea of 'literary autonomy', and carried over into 'modernism' and other 'vanguards' without major setbacks, reaching the present as a kind of 'spontaneous philosophy' of poetry.

Therein, autonomy is identified as a space for manifesting a form of writing (about the sacred, or being) that, as the object of poetry, makes poetry the nature of politics. Literature has this status because it is a supreme language: it postulates the existence of a higher power, revealed and heralded by the poet in a fundamental language, that of an 'us nation' or an 'us universe'. Accidentally, poets compete for the right to make this 'us' statement. This is the case with Fernando Pessoa and his pretention as an über-Camões. Beyond that spirit, on the more serious side of things, lies the pretention of founding new ways of feeling (a new era of feeling), so that, to quote Wordsworth, 'every author, as far as he is great, and at the same time *original*, has had the task of creating the taste

---

[1] Introductory words by M. Victor Schoelcher, preceding Victor Hugo's *Speech on Africa*, Kindle edn, 22197.

[2] Ibid. 22199–22204.

by which he is enjoyed; so it has been, so it will continue to be'. The quotation is in perfect harmony with the idea of avant-garde aesthetics: poets carve out the path followed by others, which justifies the caesura between politics and poetry. The latter's value lies in its eternity and power to interfere with history, which it creates as a stream of feelings. It lies at the root of the relationship between ethics and politics, not as a singular statement, but as a priori politics: literally the 'politics of literature', assigning literature the power to determine the feeling of people living in society.

A more recent version of the 'politics of literature' can be found in this excerpt from a book by Jacques Rancière: 'What literature opposes in usurpations of democratic literacy is another scale of meaning and literary action [...]. It is, in sum, a different *sensorium*, a different way of linking the power of affection and the power of significance. Now, a different communion of sense and sensibility, a different relation between words and beings is also a different shared world and a different people.'[3] According to the author, the competence of literature to create 'a different communion of sense and sensitivity' stems from 'writing as a machine through which life can speak, writing that is simultaneously more mute and talkative than democratic speech'. The writing machine perfectly replaces the sacred, since both are concerned with talking about life — prophetic speech that lays the ground for understanding what is yet to come, by stating that which we (still) do not understand.

Speaking of the prophetic, Maurice Blanchot said it best: 'The possibility of escaping prophetic intolerance is the possibility of creating a poem' (The Beast of Lascaux). This hypothesis does not prevent poets from engaging in politics. Very much in the way nobody is exclusively engaged in politics, nobody can be reduced to being nothing but a poet, or a fisherman, a painter, a teacher or a bookkeeper's assistant. To paraphrase Karl Marx, it is acceptable for anyone to teach in the morning, go fishing in the afternoon, write poems in the evening, etc. What is not acceptable is for someone to be indifferent to injustice, to refrain from standing up against tyranny. As Deleuze said: 'the business of men, in situations of tyranny and oppression, well, it's actually to become revolutionary, because there is nothing else to be done'.[4] René Char speaks of his active involvement in the French Resistance to Nazism in similar terms: 'I don't want to forget that they forced me to become — for how long? — a monster of justice and intolerance, a confined simplifier, an arctic character disinterested in the fate of those who do not join him in slaughtering the dogs of hell.'[5]

At times, or throughout a lifetime, many poets found themselves in situations that compelled them to engage in politics — in extreme ways,

---

[3] Jacques Rancière, *Politiques de la littérature* (Paris: Galilée, 2007), p. 23 (my translation).
[4] Gilles Deleuze and Claire Parnet, 'G *comme gauche*', *l'abécédaire de Gilles Deleuze*, DVD dir. by Pierre-André Boutang (Editions Montparnasse, Paris, 2004).
[5] Cit. in Maurice Blanchot, *Les Intellectuels en question (mars 1984)* (Paris: Fourbis, 1996), p. 23.

joining resistance movements against invaders or by other means, fighting the usurpation of individual freedom and communal life. However, their writing is not a reflection or an extension of this activity. Even when poems include verses that raise political issues, this does not make them political poems. There is no direct mapping between political action or discourse and poetry or vice versa. There is also no parallel between the two. On the one hand, as Wittgenstein clarified, language games are not watertight, there are always relationships between them. On the other hand, the 'creative' dimension of poetry undoes or erases limits and rules, to the point that it no longer makes sense to speak of language games, meaning that the possibility of discourse is eroded,[6] with all its implications for stable organization and thus for a centrist view, even if ignored.

By emphasizing its passive nature and associated interruptions, literature takes form as a composition of disparate parts, which implies that it persists outside of any identifiable pocket of reality. To conceive that literature has political implications therefore concerns the worldly role of that which is irreducible to any kind of discourse, although it is constituted by many, and, as such, presents itself as an interruption. Thus, none of this is related to what some consider 'political literature' or what others term the 'politics of literature'. These latter two expressions assume that literature can be defined, an identifiable discourse. 'Political literature' refers to a type of literature, whereas the 'politics of literature' either assumes that politics can be extracted from literature or advocates the use of literature in the service of politics.

2

In Portuguese literature, the poetry of Fernando Pessoa is an extraordinary example of the refusal of the centrist view, figuring in his heteronyms and the insurmountable drama faced by each of them. As Bernard McGuirk writes: 'Pessoa's textual assemblage can always also be read as mobile and instrumental. For, across the panoply of his heteronyms, he is able both to enter and to keep a distance from a multiplicity of aesthetics, a plurality of postures, a heteroglossia of poetic experimentations.'[7]

If we dwell on the role of clouds and mist as protagonists in *The Book of Disquiet*, we can find that several of their appearances suggest a refusal of triumphalist aspects in the definition of Western culture, namely the prime importance of action and, with it, the thirst for power. On the other hand, one should pay attention to the lightning that sometimes flashes across them, favourably lighting up the sublime like a feeling that suddenly punctuates life. Escaping from the dream also creates episodes: 'Even though I am a prolific dreamer, there are times when dreams escape me. Then things appear clearer.

---

[6]   In this regard cf. Bernard McGuirk, *Erasing Fernando Pessoa* (London: Critical, Cultural and Communications Press, 2017).

[7]   Ibid. p. 18.

The mist I surround myself with dissipates. And all the now visibly rough edges wound the flesh of my soul. All the hard surfaces bruise the part of me that knows them to be hard'.[8] In this case, the episodes bring clarity, the horror of the familiar, the feeling of the sinister takes the place of the 'I', preventing it from living its life, and affording it nothing but suffering. It can be said that for Bernardo Soares the sinister is a form of boredom.

But, in *The Book of Disquiet*, existence is not solely composed of clouds, dreams, mysteries and episodes — by the erasure or syncope of the subject. Subjectivity, as a form of external awareness, interruption without loss of the self created through abstraction, brings to life that which boredom and its horrors destroy: sensitivity. Not as refuge in a definitive state, but as a transient link and a 'brief intermittent breeze'. Consider the fragment beginning with the following excerpt: 'An uncertain evening breeze touches my brow and my consciousness with something like a vague caress, all the gentler for not being a caress. I know only that suddenly, just for a moment, my tedium feels more comfortable, like an item of clothing that stops chafing against a sore' (p. 219). The change brought about by the 'fitful afternoon breeze' induces a state of consciousness where the lightness of life is embodied in the brief, intermittent passage that creates some distance from boredom, making the latter more bearable. The breeze attenuates, and sweeps away the obsession that allows boredom to infiltrate the skin, making it more bearable. And it passes by. It passes by ever so lightly and fitfully.

Literary dynamics that they are, dispersion, erasure, and passing by with events are forms of engaging with the world, in its instability and unpredictability, but also forms of escaping the boredom that threatens to dissolve the 'I'. Not because poetry restores self-possession, or is a form of presenting a truth (or truths), but because of its refusal to be limited by the 'I', preconceptions, that which can be deduced from them, or to representations of the world, poetry presents itself as a space for the fragile and discontinuous birth of subjectivity as a creative power. If subjectivity could repeat itself, like a repeated model, it would negate itself. It comes into existence by diverging, breaking with what has already been said, and what is already known, every time unique, and exposed to testimony of itself. Literary autonomy is not sympathetic to enclosing texts within a confined space, a tradition, a history, a canon, etc. It is fulfilled by affirming some prior event beyond subjugation (technical or poetic), in a manner that cannot be reduced to facts.

---

[8]   Fernando Pessoa, *The Book of Disquiet: The Complete Edition*, ed. by Jerónimo Pizarro, trans. by Margaret Jull Costa (New York: New Directions, 2017), pp. 16–17.

3

There are passages in poems by Sophia de Mello Breyner Andresen where the refusal of political tyrannies becomes evident to a greater or lesser degree. This fact, and the political positions she held, are often considered exemplary elements of a poet's personality, and justify the possibility of alternating between both politics and poetry, while considering poetry the main activity, sometimes the determinant, foundational activity. This is a mistake, for the reasons I presented above: the nature of political intervention is discourse and action, while the nature of poetry is radical indeterminacy. Poetry is not imbued with discursive consistency, since it does not compose a meaning and suspends any chance of a conclusion. Thus, any implications regarding thought or action are perpetually deferred, and cannot be taken as exemplary or superior. Any postulation of this kind would be based on the worst of the emancipation paradigm: the existence of an emancipating role assigned to the genius as the embodiment of someone who does not have to justify themselves, whose expression alone is sufficient to ensure they are right and just. But as the poet is neither at the top of a scale of values, nor do they precede it through a privileged relationship with the world, or make use of words with definite objectives, the place of the poet in each poem is that of the abyss, meaning the sublime, where representations fail. The erasure of the poet in each poem is a mark of the broken discourse that takes on a paradoxical, dispersive consistency. Thus, political implications always come later, in readings, which are dispersive by nature, many yet always unique, always approaching failure by restricting themselves to a pocket of reality.

In the poem that I transcribe below, the desolation of war and the affirmative dimension of confidence in human beings hint at the possibility of linking the characteristic confidence of human beings with the imperative of refusing violence. The poem makes no such statement, but its composition leaves room for this suggestion:

The Dead Soldier

The infinite heavens gaze upon his face
Absolute and blind
And the breeze now kisses his mouth
Which will never kiss anyone again.

Both hands still cupped
From possession, impulse, promise.
A weight is lifted from his shoulders
Scattered, it is lost in the afternoon.

And the light, the time, the hills
They are like tears around his face
Because his life was gambled and lost
And in the sky, birds suddenly fly by.[9]

---

[9] Sophia de Mello Breyner Andresen, *Mar Novo* (Lisbon: Caminho, 2003), p. 45 (my translation).

The poem presents itself as a picture where a soldier killed in war stands out in the landscape. While it continues along the same lines as Rimbaud's 'Le Dormeur du val' or Fernando Pessoa's 'Mother's Little Boy', the poem written by Sophia immediately confronts the death of the soldier in the title, thus abruptly exposing the horror of war, the hopeless sadness that death spreads over the world. As a reminder of war, the title immediately conjures up images of how, in the First World War, technological progress and industrialization were used to increase the power of destruction, which has since grown exponentially. The poem, which exposes how a life came to an end, reveals absolute irreversibility and suffering in the face of another's death. The pain of nature is a pain mirrored by human beings, and is thus captured by tears: 'And the light, *the time*, the hills | They are like tears around his face' (my emphasis). The tears cloud our gaze and create space for memory that is not a mere archive, but concern for the earth and the world, for our home. In this landscape, 'time' is human, writing a distant memory in space and time. And in turn, the tears trigger reflection: 'Because his life was gambled and lost.' The recognition of those who are responsible, whose consent has enabled some to gamble away the lives of others, as if they were things, is political in nature. The poem does not make this explicit. The important thing about the poem is that it captures the tears. The tears are an appeal to vigilance, just like the gambling reference is a condemnation of official humanism, which requires sacrifice and war, pitting us versus them, the enemy, to reinforce itself.

Beyond this type of humanism, the indeterminacy of human experience is coded in the division that is each individual, in their humanity insofar as they can experience sensations, which is not incompatible with indestructible freedom. Faced with the extreme inhumanity of war, the poem neither argues nor proposes. Its most luminous point, humanity's safeguard, that of promise: 'Both hands still cupped | From possession, impulse, promise. | A weight is lifted from his shoulders | Scattered, it is lost in the afternoon.' Promise is indestructible: it encapsulates that which is reasoned and felt, that which is carried by the breeze of words that keep the overwhelming weight of reality at bay, dispersing it and allowing the lightness of all early life to keep on passing by. The breeze appears in the second verse of the poem by Pessoa ('The warm breeze') and in the third verse of the poem written by Sophia ('And the breeze now kisses his mouth'). This image carries the memory of a life that is no longer life, but the image would negate itself if nothing could break free from it, if it failed to conjure up the weight that is scattered, not the terrifying spectre, but confidence without justification, without figuration. This is an ethical and political gesture implied by the poetic word, a pauper addressing others.

4

In the novel *Finisterra: Paisagem e Povoamento*, by Carlos de Oliveira, the contiguity between the possible (more or less probable) and the impossible is a form of conjugating both, in gradations that make them indiscernible, a way of approaching events, of approaching that which cannot be captured by history as it cannot be measured and ordered in a sequence, but which nonetheless interferes with history. The 'man', as he is referred to by one of the protagonists, studies the architecture of a house as if seeking to understand the world in the process as well as through the documents attesting to the history of the house. But the man's childhood (everyone's, always unique) gets in the way, as he also seeks to understand and find truth in his childhood. Childhood, which presents itself in marks, signs and drawings, has many allies: the clouds, the reflected light shining through them which opens up space, attention, the fever, the chaos of the garden, the ability to describe and invent stories, the myths, the landscapes, the mist, and the halo that protects the house, marking and preserving a transition zone between the internal and the external, family and the vast world. The character of the 'child' is presented as an unfolding of the man through memory, which takes shape through the action of remembering, deciphering, and reliving that which was lost in indecipherable marks, causing it to be re-written, and thus surrounding the entire novel in mystery. The 'child' does not have dilemmas, and this is how it figures in connection to events, where differences are erased under the imminence and premonition of the new, which is a request for hospitality.

The obstinate relationship between childhood without measure — which persists as the creative power behind images, the ability to float among the clouds while confined to the abandoned (chaotic) garden, disconnected from reality — and the architect's reason, which kept the house closed off to outside threats, weaves a space open to events without subjugation to history, but which nonetheless follows in the multiple and incomplete history, beginning with man's origin and settlement, definitely lost and impossible to trace. Pilgrimage and the many types of fire may be a reminder of times immemorial, which can be accessed through 'the (irreparable) breach in memory' made by imagination.[10] The difficult transition to a sedentary way of life, and the mixture of desire and violence that settled among and persists in cultures, is the basis of duplicity. Narration exposes the core of this duplicity, which, without resolution, precludes conclusions. By design, through memory and imagination triggered by himself, as an extension of space and time, the 'man' journeys towards childhood, and, conversely, the 'child' journeys towards maturity. In turn, the final note reveals that the author of the book imitates 'one of the narrators', showing that duplication is an act, an act that does not intend to capture reality but to emphasize imagination, not as a matter of being

---

[10]   Carlos de Oliveira, *Finisterra: Paisagem e Povoamento* (Lisbon: Livraria Sá da Costa, 1978), p. 4 (my translation).

measured, but of creating precise images through the power with which they are incessantly interchanged, proven inadequate, and made undecipherable, removing them from the dilemma.

Notice the clouds and the mist; without them there would not have been reflection or mystery. However, the clouds are also a threat, which is contained by the halo that protects the house and provides a transition zone between the internal and the external. In this zone, light and dreams are possible. If the threat came from outside, the outside would be one of the poles in a dilemma — cultivate the garden and expand the dream, or check the house's foundations, doors and windows to resist the external invasion? But the scattered clues (including economic) lead to an illogical conclusion: the outside erupts from within the house (world) and its foundations are therefore crumbling. The difficult task of naming this event is given by a made-up word. This word, 'gisandra', is a complete enigma (pp. 4, 170, 171). In the novel, it is the name of a gelatinous plant, suggesting it is related to the voracious force that is Gisekia (a plant of the Portulacaceae family that grows among the dunes and is known for its destructive 'competition' with other species), and is also suggestive of instinct (semen production) and persistence, a nocturnal, hidden force of nature. 'Gisandra' does not name nature, but rather a multiplicity of combined forces (theology, habits, ethical and political backgrounds) that threaten life on earth. The insistence on its vegetable nature is aligned with an image of the end of the world as a regressive movement: the end of humans and other animals, the return to the beginning of life on earth. There is no good or evil in nature, the latter exists in memory through symbols impregnated with conceptions, the foundations of cultural metamorphoses, which during the transition to a sedentary way of life dissolved nomadism into the rituals of pilgrimage and attention to nature into their obsession. With this, nature became naturalized, that is, it became a simple force that man intended to place at his disposal.

In *Finisterra*, the relationship with nature is a paradigm into the problem of the 'moral character of the search' (p. 65): the violence exerted on nature turned against humanity, who inherited this perpetration and (consequently?) distinguishes in itself those who were subject to suffering by fire and those who imposed it as terror. The technique of mastery of nature based on cruelty is not separable from the dream of progress. *Finisterra* asks: dream or preconception? As Baudelaire wrote in *Fusées*, the 'defiling of hearts' is the foundation of the progress by which *Le monde va finir*. *Finisterra* also opposes technical progress that brings non-differentiation, 'the serene catastrophe' (p. 134) — in the form of the 'gisandra', in tune with the winning force that designs and conceives in techno-scientific terms and on behalf of the Great Architect or his 'opposite' (*Gallerte*, gelatine, appears in a writing by Marx as 'a figure of undifferentiated human labour')[11] — writing that gives the word to sharing the duplicity of

---

[11] Cf. Jacques Derrida, *Spectres de Marx* (Paris: Galilée, 1993), p. 265; Karl Marx, *Le Capital*, vol. I (Paris: PUF, 'Quadrige', 1993), p. 43.

the world unfolded into given words and acts with the capacity to suffer with
the suffering of others, and not consider it a mere detail in the accounting of
progress.

Finisterra's attention to life in the contingency of the world (that which
theological and political perspectives ignore) makes this book an invaluable
counterpoint to any ready-made politics and any attempted technological and
scientific explanation of the world: man engages with the world so that he may
exist in it (reducing violence, with the demand for justice as a guide), poetically,
diverse and disperse in freedom, responsibly. Decisively, the refusal of the (me
or you) dilemma is delivered in the affirmation of irreducible multiplicity: the
existence of subjectivity free of chronological linearity within space-time, of a
foundation or an ideal; subjectivity which occurs by differentiation from itself,
inseparable from feeling and premonition that give purpose to reason.

5

With Luiza Neto Jorge, the affirmation of subjectivity as a relationship with
external facets and the unexpected passages that the poem finds, shows it is
above all a statement of *pathos* without tears. Writing where tears, a reflexive
expression of feelings, would cover the sharp edge of the verses. This edge,
or fire, was carved from deep memory fragments (where personal experience
is built from mnemotechnics and their excess in poetry, song, sharing, etc.):
'blind', 'in the dark', a clear and hermetic statement, as in this, the first of '5
poems for the unchanging night'.

I

> I may be here
> I may be here perfectly poor
> a candle I lit myself a sharp spur
> murdered by the dark rhythm of the wind
>
> I may be here
> – the moss is as slow as darkness –
> and I know the blind voice of the songs by heart
> (wake me up silent viola)
>
> I may be here a perfect insomniac
> Stone
> A long impersonal secret
> Embroidering my solitude[12]

Here, the use of the word 'may' is a clear shift away from the paradigm of power,
the will to dominate, because it does not suppose qualities or riches, but rather
the construction of a space in which one is 'perfectly poor'. Between 'I may
be here perfectly poor' (in the first stanza) and 'I may be here a perfect stone'

---

[12]   Luiza Neto Jorge, *Poesia* (Lisbon: Assírio & Alvim, 1993), p. 23 (my translation).

(in the third), the poem can be understood as a construction of the conscious awareness of taking part in a game that exceeds personal experience, the game of social instinct (which includes politics). A piece in a game divided into many games, both stone and carving material, like subjectivity sculpted into a poem. But not a static statue: the word 'insomniac' suggests wakefulness and openness to that which prevents sleep. But note that 'insomnia' is not a dominant force in the poem. There is the 'dark rhythm of the wind', the 'moss is as slow as darkness', knowledge of 'the blind voice of the songs by heart', the 'impersonal secret'. The latter sculpts the dynamics of the poem, embroidering its limits by embroidering solitude. Each time unique, solitude in the poem is linked to insomnia, irrevocably emanating from it through the continuity that the article 'a' establishes with the word 'insomniac', establishing the second to last verse, and the verses following verses: 'insomniac | a long impersonal secret | embroidering my solitude'.

There is a poem by Luiza Neto Jorge, from which I quote three verses: 'What is hard to know | Is how death is corrected, | or diverted,' in which the title, 'Enchantment', draws attention to the value of song, which can be said to be essential to the poem, making the rawness and cruelty of the world visible in an alleviated death, and leading to two imperatives: 1. not to ignore it, lest it reign; 2. amend the object of writing in writing, because death cannot be tamed. To consider that such imperatives belong to the limiting tangential space between poetry and politics is to see that this space is spectral in nature, and indefinite, a still nature, a simple still nature. Note the poem 'Still Life with Bernardo Soares'. With Bernardo Soares, the still nature is not alone, it exceeds itself in stillness. From this excess, an 'I' is born in the poem, a transient and transitive subjectivity. It also passes through it: 'It wanders the landscape, irradiating me; | the blurry sun finds me, | It is I, it is my table, | my quiet, and it grinds.' As if the poem had in itself a light (a sun) that, blurry, provides a feeling of peace that grinds — the spectral form of existence, restlessness.

6

I find in *Illuminations* (2018) by Théodore Fraenckel, which I will refer to next, an increased spectrality, which amplifies the projections of the disease of poetry to make them share in the pockets of reality normally kept separate by compartmentalization, namely the visions of everyday existence and art. I begin on the subject of name, a supreme irony: how does a name make sense when placed in a book as the author's name, if the writer is born in what he writes, through his writing, without answering for what he wrote except for his writing? If to be born in one's own writing is to be born not only with others, but also of the world and its ruins? This is the ironic, light and tragic learning poetry invites: the writer signs up by differentially repeating what comes to them, spontaneously and through reflection — inseparable forms that underlie the creation of artifices, simulacra, traversed by a metaphysical, melancholic breath which brings death to figurations of themselves. By signing up, the writer agrees to imbue themselves in the poem and in what is staged therein. In another image: they agree to be part of the tomb and the legacy left behind for others, without exerting any power over them. The complexity of the poetic testament stems from the fact that it bequeaths nothing as such, that its legacies are silence passed down in words, which thus awaken other words and other silence, in an 'eternal return', as expressed by Maurice Blanchot.

In *Illuminations*, each poem (or even a verse or part thereof) can be seen as a game where a path is opened up among spectres, without letting them dominate imagination and thought: to find them is to select them and create the distance afforded by thought. The book is made up of various frameworks that shape it into an abyss. The first is provided by the title, the second is presented by the staged irony of authorship, insofar as: 1. it is impossible, for there is no news of there having ever existed a Théodore Fraenckel who 'was born in 1900 and died on 3 July 1950', and even if he had existed, he would never have written a book dated from 2018; 2. impossible, but suggestive of meaning given the choice of name — close to that of Dadaist and surrealist 'author' Théodore Fraenkel, differing only in the addition of the letter 'c'; 3. impossible also given the overlap between birth and death that the referred staging may suggest.

Since death cannot be approximated, the frames outlining the paintings it hangs from go as far as the disease of poetry can take them. The first 'framework' consists of the title *Illuminations*, and its relationship with the medieval book, made and drawn by hand, assigning the creation of the poem a minimal and decisive sense of oscillation between meaning and meaninglessness, which do not complement each other, but mutually disturb each other, as made evident in the poem. In other words, it is a framework that requires openness. According to the framework, the suggestion made by the name of Théodore Fraenkel (1896–1964) reinforces the demand for openness: this poet, a physician, signed a letter jointly with Artaud addressed to the 'Head doctors of insane asylums' (published in *Révolution surréaliste* no. 3), where both revolted against the exclusion methods perpetrated by asylums, comparable to barracks, to prisons, to exclusion in the name of a social dictatorship. Through this name, *Illuminations* specifically denotes the implication of poetry in the face of dictatorship, which judges in the name of reason: the suspension of meaning, the affirmation of the right to uncensored speech.

One is always born 'after death' (in a particular sense, after the death of others, although this is not the only meaning of the expression). If it is true that after the names of saints, it was the names of authors that came to exert the aggregating role of culture, that which is supposed to erase (to what end?) the evils of self-determined existence without a safe representation to hold on to, it is no less true that the thought of the author's death has been removed from the public sphere — and *Disquiet* stands as the title of a book by a Great Author (so great there were several of him); literature naturalizes and writes about things in books: things themselves, that educate the 'elites', which supposedly everyone has the right to become. On the one hand, staging the author's destitution is a way of stating that there is no ready-made 'literature', and, on the other hand, stating that there is responsibility beyond literature, responsibility without fault or sacrifice, which resists the threat of the last to speak, the threat of automated speech, constructed by the coding of feelings.

The word *Illuminations* is both taken and not taken from the title of Rimbaud's testament, *Illuminations*. However, David Scott has noted that the original English title of the book would have been *Illuminations, (Coloured Plates)*.[13] The Portuguese translation, *Iluminuras (Gravuras Coloridas)* [Illuminations (Colour Engravings)] uses 'Illuminations' in the same sense, but raises other pertinent suggestions regarding the book, breaking with the traditional distinction between poem and illustration, claiming for poetry a means of creating visions with words. The importance of the relationship between images and text, in the various meanings ascribed to the word — one of them that poems are composed like canvases — the word 'canvas' is repeated several times, denoting the canvas of memory as it becomes the canvas for the poem, composed by materials ranging from films, poems, paintings and music to other inscriptions, namely those marking historic events, at the crossroads where they find mutual illumination, without cancelling each other out.

It is through the indecipherability and mystery of links — in a symbolic manner, in the awareness that the senses and words form a web of contaminations that cannot be untangled, whereby perceptions are made unstable and fleeting — that contemplation of ruins becomes a disruptive movement in *Illuminations*, hanging on the brink of something else, where allegories falter. The poems illustrate themselves, undoing the distinction between the poem and what lies beyond it, through suggestions made in ways that expose the unstoppable motion of requests placed upon thought. And although the pre-Renaissance and Renaissance writers support melancholic sentiment, providing it with a vehicle into the 'present', it is above all presented as suspension — nothing is ever completely decided.

The disparate is summoned through obscure affinities, such as refusing that destiny should be alien to the person experiencing it, that it comes entirely from outside. Impositions arise externally: there are choices to be made. And making choices is not about order, but rather about making the poem an offering of complexity which does not replace the reader, which hints at the fact that they must untangle the web canvas of discourse, its non-linearity, that there is no substitute for personal effort, in time, whereby historicity asserts itself non-complacent with alleged historical progress. This approaches what, during its inception, the surrealist movement declared insurrection against history.

---

[13]   Quoted in Arthur Rimbaud, *Iluminuras: gravuras coloridas*, trans. and ed. by Rodrigo Garcia Lopes and Maurício Arruda Mendonça (São Paulo: Editora Iluminuras Lda., 2014), p. 148.

By allowing itself to be travelled along multiple paths, the energy of the poem prevents its political implications from being enunciated. In other words, poetry neither replaces theory nor cancels its restlessness for answers, but materializes a means of escaping the theoretical siege of a theological trap:

> [...]
> What good fortune is the inner landscape...
> Because if a flower distracts us,
> The serpent, intimate with theory, burrows
> Under the ruin until it reaches
> The point on the canvas
> Where the fruit becomes undesired
> In our own eyes.[14]

Finding the 'point on the canvas' where absence becomes imminent, the impossible flawless association between sensations and words, is to stop looking deeper among the ruins. Here, the poem breaks with the conclusions, moving away from the relationship between knowledge and permanent debt, in endless displacement. This is about making absence an unrecognizable part of the game of writing, part of its meaning and the suspension of meaning, as in the poem 'Bonnard', which evokes a picture by the painter of the same name in reference to the moment when the painter finishes his work: when the meeting between life and death has been spread in images to such an extent 'that he himself, now, | can no longer dissociate himself from it.' That suspension aims at the limits of idealization is also explicit, for example, in the following verses of 'Allegory', 'Where the fruit becomes undesired | In our own eyes'. There, the stabilizing idealization of meanings and the binding of vision to contemplation (melancholy) supersede the disruptive energy from whence mystery erupts.

Returning to the disparate, it must be said that what the diversity of titles in *Illuminations* points to are not cultural references, but moments in which we share with others that which, lacking in conscious experience, gives way to silence and vertigo. That meeting of absences has titles, a sequence, but each poem is and is not on that page (the pages are not numbered), it refuses to be one, it is divided in time without its own continuity, not an end, but time exposed as a non-geometric thickness, inhabited time, asymmetric.

The spectres can bring terror to life, but they are neither death nor life. The movement of bringing them 'into the light of day' hides that which destroys the multiplicity of times. In this regard, the allusions to the First World War are particularly important, since it is known how many artists have adhered to it or even extolled it. The poem titled '*In the light of day. De Chirico, 1914*' mentions poems by Guillaume Apollinaire and paintings by Chirico, who both took part in this war, and extolled it to an absolutely scandalous extent, as a show with aesthetic value. In calligrams published in 1918, but written during the war, it is nonetheless horror that prevails, as can be seen in the aforementioned poem:

---

[14]   Théodore Fraenckel, *Iluminuras* (Lisbon: Douda Correria, 2018) (my translation).

'[...] Thus, war and death | enamelled, were in undeniably | strong waters, the horror of which we only found | again in De Chirico's paintings, one in particular, | *Mistero e melanconia di una strada* [...]'. This painting is dated 1914, the beginning of the war in which the painter took part. In it, the horror is not directly present: there is a long road, flanked by an architecture of arches that compose order and disorder with one side in the light and the other in the shadow. Mystery envelopes the whole picture, but four aspects are highlighted: the order and disorder of the perspective inferred from the architecture, the shadow cast by an unseen statue, the girl with the arch, and the parked carriage, its open doors indicating it is waiting. The shadow presents itself as a threat that is not totally ignored because it has its own shadow. In the poem, the girl's path is covered in the verse 'Or the resuming the (im)possible joy'. Which, once again, raises the enigma of the possibility and impossibility of joy, itself enigmatic. The painting not only captures the enclosure and terror of an era, but the mystery of the arch and its revolutions, where so much of Nietzschean eternal recurrence can be read, which sacrifices beginnings, such as the lightness of its movement and the possibility of an open future that follows from it. Although the overwhelming shadow appears to be from the future, the girl and the arch make clear that this is not so. Following the abovementioned verse, the poem continues:

> The coldness of the strokes and the shadows
> Allows us no room for doubt, however,
> As to the severity of what the canvas portrays.
> Given the clarity of multiple signs
> Forgotten on the canvas
> On this occasion, no one may be excused
> For missing the train or the time.[15]

In the last two lines there is a passage into the present time, pointing at multiple signs that continue to reflect horror. In a reading, the enigma is transferred from the painting to the allusion of the train (the carriage): it is not necessarily an invitation to enter the path of progress and destruction, ready to swallow up the unwary; or the premonition of extermination trains; it may offer possibility on the roadside, a journey without a predetermined destination. In the poem, on the canvas, that which is imminent is not presented: in the awareness of the unknown, even the past has its enigmas (without which it would become imposition), not by an appropriate choice of rhetoric, but by disowning and suspending rhetoric.

---

[15]   Fraenckel, *Iluminuras* (my translation).

Some Portuguese Poetry from the Past Fifty Years: A Reading through Images[1]

Rosa Maria Martelo

*Instituto de Literatura Comparada Margarida Losa /
Faculdade de Letras da Universidade do Porto*

Poetry is the flip side of painting; it is the voice of the image.

— Claudio Parmiggiani, *Stella, Sangue, Spirito*

[...] if writing and painting are mental means of communication,
it is in the mind that poetry and painting first meet.

— Ana Hatherly, *a reinvenção da leitura*

Historicity, Intersubjectivity and Ekphrasis

Giving an overview of an object of study, whatever that object might be, always implies finding a balance between completeness and legibility, between enumeration and exemplification. It implies making choices, identifying relevant issues and, above all, establishing reading criteria. In this proposal for a reading of contemporary Portuguese poetry, the option is to highlight the articulation between poetry and image. Image here is verbal and intratextual as well as being the object of the intermedial relations established by poetry. It is a particularly relevant topic not only because the manner in which poetry relates to image has changed over the past fifty years, but also because these changes enable us to understand and contextualize other significant shifts in contemporary poetics. It should nonetheless be clear that this paper intends to map an inflection rather than to depict a panorama.

In the last three decades of the twentieth century and in the first two of the twenty-first century, Portuguese poetry has distanced itself greatly from the modernity it had advocated as its essential structural element since the modernism movement and, to a certain extent, ever since the poetics of symbolism. Though in the 1960s no important poet would question the dominant influence of the modern and modernist legacy on the shaping of their personal poetics, this scenario would soon change. Modern and modernist references continue to play a role, but they are now clearly assimilated, they are assessed more critically and some of their limitations are even challenged.

[1] Translated from the Portuguese by Elena Galvão. This article was written as part of research carried out in the ILCML, R&D Unit financed by National Funds through FCT – Fundação para a Ciência e a Tecnologia [Portuguese Foundation for Science and Technology] (UIDP/00500/2020).

Issues such as the significance of the principle of rupture, or the creative resource of metadiscursivity, or the affirmation of the self-referentiality of the poetic text, become regressive when compared to other types of problems.

Within this context, the publication of *Metamorfoses, Seguidas de Quatro Sonetos a Afrodite Anadiómena* [Metamorphoses, Followed by Four Sonnets to Aphrodite Anadyomene] (1963), by Jorge de Sena (1919–1978), anticipates many of the different paths that were to be trodden in the coming decades. The prevalent poetics of Portuguese poetry in the 1960s valued images especially for their verbal and rhetorical force and their use of metaphor. For example, the poet and essayist António Ramos Rosa (1924–2013) defined poetry in relation to how it treated the verbal image. This was a frequent topic in his critical writings, as evidenced by the following statement from a 1959 article: 'Modern poetic image re-establishes unity in multiplicity, restores the richness of the original perception in its various meanings, establishes the identity of the opposites, creates a new reality while at the same time keeping each term concrete and independent'.[2] The poet emphasizes the creative power of the image in a rhetorical sense and the creative freedom of poetic discourse, which he views as not being subject to the rule of the excluded middle; he celebrates the life-giving power of the verbal image and its capacity for concreteness. All these elements have the potential to give rise to new dimensions of reality through commitment to verbal imagination and experimentation with discourse. It is an idea that has taken different shapes in the poetry of Ruy Belo, Herberto Helder, Luiza Neto Jorge, Gastão Cruz, amongst others. It confirms the predominance of a strongly figurative discourse in these authors' poetry, which is otherwise always marked by an uncommon lyrical quality.

Recalling the best achievements of his generation, Gastão Cruz (b. 1941) describes the masters of this modernity:

> And it was on images that poetry fed, we thought, strong and unpredictable images, to use two of Camilo Pessanha's adjectives in his poem 'Branco e vermelho' [White and red]: [...]; images we found in the poems by Cesário, Pessanha, Sá-Carneiro, Pessoa. Images that, in those final years of the 1950s, we were rediscovering in the poems of Sophia, Ramos Rosa, Cesariny, Eugénio.[3]

What do the poets cited by Gastão Cruz have in common? The rhetorical use of images is undoubtedly one of the traits they share. In all these authors, visual and concrete suggestions often occur in contexts of verbal transfiguration that arises from the metaphorical or other figurative treatment of perceptual images. The poets that most impress Gastão Cruz 'in those final years of the 1950s' are Sophia de Mello Breyner Andresen, António Ramos Rosa, Mário Cesariny, and Eugénio de Andrade. All these poets ascribe great importance to concrete perceptual images and to the transfiguration obtained thanks to

---

[2]　António Ramos Rosa, *Poesia, Liberdade Livre* (Lisbon: Ulmeiro, 1986), p. 22.
[3]　Gastão Cruz, *A Vida da Poesia: textos críticos reunidos* (Lisbon: Assírio & Alvim, 2008), p. 294.

image metaphors where very different fields of vision come into contact in surprising ways.[4] They are poets of immanence, who believe that the matter of the world must be lyrically translated into density (and intensity) of discourse and into transfiguring visual suggestion: 'My confident vision is hallucination', clarifies Herberto Helder (1930–2015) in *Photomaton & Vox*.[5] At a different level, another example could be Sophia de Mello Breyner Andresen's treatment of the relation between the visual image and the phonological dimension of poetry, which in her poems appears so strongly connected to each of her poems' themes and their perceptual suggestiveness. In his 1970 essay 'Função e justificação da metáfora na poesia de Eugénio de Andrade', Gastão Cruz writes,

> The greatest specificity in the language of poetry is indeed this capacity for making words and names unique by transforming them into images. There are no *common* nouns in poems. Naming is creating images and one of the fundamental characteristics of poetic images is their uniqueness. Metaphor is an intensification of images (on top of which other images are produced). Or, conversely, an image is already a metaphor.[6]

In *Metamorfoses*, by Jorge de Sena (a poet Gastão Cruz did not cite in the above list), images continue to be present in these terms, but they are also given a different treatment: intermedial reference.[7] In this book, the relation between words and images drawn from the plastic arts play a structuring role, as it is a predominantly ekphrastic work in which almost all the poems thematize a specific work of art (usually a painting or a sculpture), almost always seen in a museum. Sena had even thought of calling the collection *Museu* [Museum], but he ended up putting the idea to the side for fear of the *passé* connotations that the term might have.[8]

Jorge de Sena's interest in intersemiotic transposition, more precisely in intermedial reference to plastic artworks whose reproductions were shown along with the poems, can be better understood if we consider that the poet always kept a critical distance from the excessive sentimentality he saw in Portuguese lyrical poetry. Ekphrasis allowed him to explore forms of

---

[4]   To better understand the concept of image metaphor, a type of metaphor which is structured around the crossing of perceptual images, see Daniel W. Gleason, 'The Visual Experience of Image Metaphor: Cognitive Insights into Imagist Figures', *Poetics Today*, 30.3 (2009), 423–70.

[5]   Herberto Helder, *Photomaton & Vox* (Lisbon: Assírio & Alvim, 2013), p. 22.

[6]   Gastão Cruz, 'Função e justificação da metáfora na poesia de Eugénio de Andrade' (1970), in *A Vida da Poesia*, pp. 134–42 (p. 140, original emphasis).

[7]   Irina Rajewsky distinguishes the notion of intermedial reference from the notions of media transposition and media combination: 'In this third category [intermedial reference], as already in the case of media combination, intermediality designates a communicative-semiotic concept, but here it is *by definition* just *one* medium — the referencing medium (as opposed to the medium referred to) — that is materially present. Rather than combining different medial forms of articulation, the given media-product thematizes, evokes, or imitates elements or structures of another, conventionally distinct medium through the use of its own media-specific means'. Irina Rajewsky, 'Intermediality, Intertextuality, and Remediation: A Literary Perspective on Intermediality', *Intermédialités/Intermediality*, 6 (Autumn 2005), 43–64 (p. 53).

[8]   Jorge de Sena, 'Post-fácio 1963', *Metamorfoses* (1963), in *Poesia II* (Lisbon: Moraes, 1988), pp. 157–58.

intersubjectivity through which he implemented the poetics of testimony he had so meticulously described in the Preface to *Poesia I*. Testimony, he suggested, should be a compromise between the projective dimension of lyrical subjectivity (as an exercise in liberating one's identity) and memory and what it implies in terms of ethical compromise (a way of living in History, in time, also in relation to poetic and aesthetic tradition). Hence, Sena's description of the poet as someone who is able to 'suffer all in one's conscience or affections': 'testimony is, first and foremost, language' he clarified.[9]

This is not the place to delve into the complexity of the nineteen 'applied meditations' which constitute the body of Sena's *Metamorfoses*,[10] or to address the reasons why the invention of a lightly allusive language in *Quatro Sonetos* [Four Sonnets] constitute a (radical) way of freeing images and eroticism from the semantic straitjacket imposed by language. It is essential, however, to highlight his innovative treatment of images, which must be considered together with the importance Sena attributed to historicity for comprehending human experience. In a 1961 text entitled *O Reino da Estupidez* [*The Kingdom of Stupidity*], Sena describes himself as follows: '[...] serei sempre, a menos que o demónio íncubo do academismo se apodere de mim, inimigo da cantiga dormente, da lamúria pessoal, ou da convicção apenas intelectual com que os novos mundos são apenas invocados' [[...] unless the nightmarish demon of academicism takes hold of me, I shall always be an enemy of numbing tunes, of personal moaning, and of the merely intellectual conviction calling for new worlds].[11] This description, which is not devoid of a certain element of caricature, enables us to understand an important element: in Sena's poetry, the three dimensions of historicity, intersubjectivity and ekphrasis are all related to a poetics that reacts to what is considered an excessively figurative and intimate lyricism.

In this sense, *Metamorfoses* can be viewed as the first step in the changing relation between poetry and images. At a time when the poetic image no longer inspired the same euphoria with its creative power, new forms of dialogue between poetry and image (as well as image conception) were to appear. Although ekphrastic poetry had not been unknown in Portugal up to that point, it would gain in popularity in the last decades of the twentieth century. Much of this popularity is due to João Miguel Fernandes Jorge (b. 1943), another great proponent of intermedial relations between poetry and the visual arts. He was eventually the one to use the word *museu* [museum] in the title of one of his books, *Museu das Janelas Verdes* (2002) [Museum of the Green Windows], a volume which was entirely conceived as a dialogue with the artworks of the Museum of Ancient Art in Lisbon. But there are many other interart dialogues

---

[9]   Jorge de Sena, 'Prefácio' [Preface to 1st edn of *Poesia I*, 1960], *Poesia I*, 2nd edn (Lisbon: Moraes, 1977), p. 26.
[10]   Sena explains that he regards the ekphrastic poems in *Metamorfoses* as applied meditations 'in much the same way as we use the expression "applied science" in opposition to "pure science"'. See Jorge de Sena, 'Post-fácio 1963', p. 158.
[11]   Jorge de Sena, *O Reino da Estupidez* (Lisbon: Moraes 1979), p. 40.

in João Miguel Fernandes Jorge's poems. In 1980, for instance, he published *Uma Exposição* [An Exhibition], a fascinating book produced in collaboration with Jorge Molder and Joaquim Manuel Magalhães. In the volume, Molder's photographs and the two poets' texts enter into dialogue with Edward Hopper's paintings, giving rise to several narratives. Another relevant example of João Miguel Fernandes Jorge's poems interacting with museum collections is *Mirleos* (2015), which is based on works exhibited in the Machado de Castro Museum, in Coimbra.

A poet who should also be mentioned within this trend is Al Berto (1948–1997), author of *A Secreta Vida das Imagens* (1991) [*The Secret Life of Images*], a collection of twenty-six poems which establish dialogues with paintings and sculptures by various authors, from Giotto to Rui Chafes, including a large number of contemporary Portuguese artists.

What can be observed in Jorge de Sena's and João Miguel Fernandes Jorge's poems is a relation between their interest in poetry and the lesser importance attributed to images of a metaphorical origin. Ekphrasis appears clearly linked to forms of restraining abstract lyricism and reviving narrativity in poetry, thus frequently generating texts whose blurriness makes them a mixture of lyrical poems and narrative poetry. It is also possible to establish a connection between a greater use of ekphrasis and the presence of other creative processes of narrativity, such as the treatment of historical themes. In Al Berto's book, we can see a relation between ekphrasis, narrativity and otherness. It is important to note that Al Berto had been a student of plastic arts, which allowed him to create outstanding ekphrases thanks to his deep understanding of the colours, the shapes and the materials used in the works he describes.

The revaluation of narrativity and otherness obtained through ekphrasis can also be found in works such as *Movimentos no Escuro* [Movements in the Dark] (2006) by José Miguel Silva (b. 1969), or, more recently, *Ágora*, by Ana Luísa Amaral (2019). The former establishes dialogues with feature films, sometimes thematized with great freedom, but always restraining the lyrical element through narrativity. The latter finds inspiration in biblical elements which the poems share with the paintings whose replicas are printed alongside the texts. This last book will be addressed later on. For the time being, it is important to underline that in both volumes ekphrasis provides access to multiple perspectives and circumstances, often historical and political, which enable the poets to reach more complex forms of intersubjectivity as well as to make their stand and social critique. Regardless of the timeframe they adopt, both José Miguel Silva and Ana Luísa Amaral resort to ekphrasis to denounce violence and injustice in our contemporary world. Moreover, the growing importance of intermedial references to plastic arts in contemporary poetry is clearly visible in the number of poems and the variety of authors included in the anthology *Passagens: Poesia, Artes Plásticas* [Passages: Poetry, Plastic Arts].[12]

---

[12] Joana Matos Frias, *Passagens: Poesia, Artes Plásticas* (Lisbon: Assírio & Alvim, 2015).

Ekphrasis thus appears to be a writing strategy which, much like allegory (to the detriment of metaphor) or the mixture of lyricism and narrativity, serves to restrain and reorient the lyrical register. Ekphrasis, genre hybridity, and the greater use of allegory in contemporary poetry can be related to the gradual rise of what Marjorie Perloff has called unoriginal genius. 'Já não é possível dizer mais nada | mas também não é possível ficar calado' [It is no longer possible to say anything | but it is equally impossible to stay quiet], summarized Manuel António Pina (1943–2012) in his first book, *Ainda não é o fim nem o princípio do mundo calma é apenas um pouco tarde* [It is not yet the end or the beginning of the world keep calm it's only a little late].[13] The title clearly shows a rejection of the idea of a rupture with the past, though still admitting the possibility of creation and innovation. It was a little late (but not too late), because the assimilation of modern tradition made it difficult for poetics of rupture to establish themselves. This tradition, however, had at the same time become an endless source that could be quoted and elaborated upon. Indeed, this situation allowed for creating in a new and different way, namely by resorting to intertextuality and intermedial reference much more systematically. As Fiama Hasse Pais Brandão put it, in *Era* (1974), '[o] progresso dos textos | é epigráfico. Lápide e versão, indistintamente' [the progress of texts | is epigraphic. Headstone and version, indistinguishably].[14] The awareness that writing is always a way to revisit past literature and past arts in general, though clearly not a new idea, gained more and more relevance and became a predominant element in the poetry produced from the 1970s onwards.

Revisited Legacies

Many are the names that could be cited in relation to this growing awareness, but Manuel Gusmão (b. 1945) is one that should be given special emphasis, considering the importance of intertextuality and intermediality in his poetry. According to Gusmão, a writer is always also 'alguém que leu, que lê; que recorda e esquece parcialmente aquilo que leu' [somebody who has read, who reads; and selectively remembers and forgets what they have read], as he asserts in one of the essays in *Uma Razão Dialógica* [A Dialogical Reason].[15] Historic time is the great protagonist in his poetry, more specifically human historicity (just consider the suggestive title *Teatros do Tempo* [Theatres of Time], from 2001). Gusmão describes such a concept by emphasizing the complexity of 'tempos sobrepostos' [overlapping times], which have been inherited in the (dis)order of History also in the guise of overlapping texts. Marx and Benjamin are clearly present in his perspective, and this can be seen in Gusmão's

---

[13]   Manuel António Pina, *Ainda não é o fim nem o princípio do mundo calma é apenas um pouco tarde* [1974], *Todas as Palavras — Poesia Reunida* (Lisbon: Assírio & Alvim, 2012), p. 71.

[14]   Fiama Hasse Pais Brandão, *Era* (1974), in *Obra Breve* (Lisbon: Assírio & Alvim, 2017), p. 173.

[15]   Manuel Gusmão, *Uma Razão Dialógica* (Lisbon: Edições Avante!, 2011), p. 137.

demand for justice, which he describes as a 'promise': a transgenerational, transtemporal, intertextual and intermedial appeal which neither history nor poetry can possibly ignore. Within this perspective, the poet establishes a sequence of dialogues with a certain literary tradition in which this 'promise' and the demand that it be fulfilled are especially alive (consider the importance given to the intertextual dialogue with Carlos de Oliveira's *oeuvre*, all of which is imbued with calls for social justice).

Understanding the importance of interart references in contemporary poetry implies regarding intermediality with the parallel use of intertextuality as the driver of writing and not as more or less occasional creative circumstance. It is indeed important to make this distinction. Here is an example. Some of the most renowned female writers of the second half of the twentieth century and of the current century, such as Maria Teresa Horta, Luiza Neto Jorge and Ana Luísa Amaral, have used intertextual dialogue as a way of questioning and subverting the poetic canon. As mentioned above, Ana Luísa Amaral's *Ágora* (2019) is structured around biblical themes which inspire meditations on cruelty and injustice in today's world. The book highlights the female figures in the Bible by intersecting intertextual and intermedial references. Thus, in 'Anunciação' [Annunciation], Maria — depicted before the open Book as in the painting by Gerard David which is featured alongside the poem — dares to question the Angel, who commands her to accept God's order in a reply filled with irony: 'resta-te só dizer | *em mim se faça* || (E fecha o livro | porque os livros | não prestam)' [what is left for you to say is | *in me be fulfilled* || (And close the book, | because books | are no good)].[16] In another poem, Veronica sees in Jesus's face 'o rosto de todos os | que habitam os restos | e o rasto da justiça' [the face of all those | who inhabit the scraps | and the wreckage of justice].[17] This intertextual revision had already played an important role in Ana Luísa Amaral's poetics in previous books. In *Génese do Amor* [Genesis of Love] (2005), the muses inspiring Dante, Petrarch and Camões acquired their own voice and critical distance, while in *Escuro* [Dark] (2014), Pessoa's poetics or, more precisely, the epic references in *Mensagem*, were summoned and quoted.

Intertextuality serves the double function of paying homage and being subversive also in other authors, such as Adília Lopes (b. 1960), Margarida Vale de Gato (b. 1973) and Golgona Anghel (b. 1979). Adília Lopes, in whose more recent books there is a greater hybridization of lyricism and autobiography, has always used intertextuality as a driving force for writing and as a form of subversion and appropriation of the canon, combining erudition with references to advertisement and popular culture. Margarida Vale de Gato offers the best summary of the complexity of this type of hybridization when she states, in *Lançamento* [Launches]: 'Não existe relação entre poesia e comunicação ou entre poesia e intimidade que não seja equívoca' [No relation between poetry

---

[16] Ana Luísa Amaral, *Ágora* (Lisbon: Assírio & Alvim, 2019), p. 17.
[17] Ana Luísa Amaral, *Ágora*, p. 118.

and communication or between poetry and intimacy is unequivocal].[18] Author of *Mulher ao Mar* [Woman at Sea], a book *in progress* which she adds to in each new edition (2010, 2013), Margarida Vale de Gato places herself in a line of women poets who value intertextuality. Among others, she highlights Christina Rossetti, Emily Dickinson and Sylvia Plath. As for Golgona Anghel, Romanian by birth but living in Portugal and writing in Portuguese, her ironic and disconcerting style has involved intertextual dialogues with texts as emblematic as the famous ode by Álvaro de Campos which starts 'Vem, Noite antiquíssima e idêntica' [Come, ancient and identical Night]. Golgona Anghel revisits Campos's poem in a provocative lowering of the tone, with lines such as these: 'Vem, noite de copos, noite de loucos, | estou só e sem inspiração' [Come, night of drinking, night of follies, | I am alone and at a loose end].[19]

Intertextuality and intermediality are often a euphoric way of interacting with tradition and the other arts in the above-mentioned writers. In other cases, however, these interactions become more dysphoric. Examples of this are the unique poetry by António Franco Alexandre (b. 1944), which, despite resorting to irony and humour, reinforces dysphoria and scepticism, and, more recently, the work of Luís Quintais (b. 1968), where intertextuality and intermediality are also extremely relevant. Nevertheless, dysphoria becomes more manifest when poets use allegory in Benjamin's sense of the concept, i.e., when they regard it as a creative process and a way to express a lack or a failure. This is what happens in the poetry of Manuel de Freitas, José Miguel Silva and Rui Pires Cabral. More recently, Elisabete Marques (b. 1982) makes use of allegory with a much lesser degree of scepticism in *Animais de Sangue Frio* [Cold-blooded Animals] (2017), a book in which speaking animals remind us of human beings and allow this young woman poet to criticize the world we live in.

Rui Pires Cabral is a poet to be discussed when talking about the relation between allegory and intermediality. His work, however, will be addressed at the end of this study. What should be stressed now is the existence of a functional parallelism between the systematic recourse to intermediality and intertextuality and the way in which both are elements of a new paradigm of aesthetic creation in which the idea of originality peacefully interacts with revisitation, citation and rewriting. At the same time, as the borderlines amongst the arts become more diffuse, intermedial and interart porosity turn into privileged means of creation.

Between Writing and Images

At a different level, one that was perfected by surrealist poets and Portuguese experimental poets, the anti-lyrical reaction of Portuguese poetry enhanced the iconicity of verses and poetic forms through intermedial dialogues between

---

[18]   Margarida Vale de Gato, *Lançamento* (Lisbon: Douda Correria, 2016), no pagination.
[19]   Golgona Anghel, *Nadar na piscina dos pequenos* (Lisbon: Assírio & Alvim, 2017), p. 28.

poetry and the plastic arts. Authors like the surrealist Mário Cesariny, or other authors like Ana Hatherly, among writers and artists belonging to experimental poetry (PO.EX), tested transmedial ways of conceiving lyrical and non-lyrical poetry. Within these, the idea of poetry and, more specifically, of 'texto-acto' [action-text], as Ana Hatherly called it,[20] liberated itself from a strict verbal matrix and integrated transmedial or more performative dimensions. Alberto Pimenta's work is equally essential in this respect, due to the interaction between verbal experimentation, humour and social critique. Pimenta, who was working as a lecturer at Heidelberg University at the time of Portugal's Carnation Revolution in 1974, returned to his home country in 1977 and made himself known with an art happening entitled *Homo Sapiens* (1977), in which he occupied one of the chimpanzee cages at the Lisbon Zoo. This action was meant to expose the human condition of living behind more or less symbolic bars, in a society which ensnares us with the illusion of choice and a false impression of freedom.[21]

The 1970s and 1980s also produced relevant contributions to the exploration of the images associated with the iconicity of poetry.[22] Examples of this are Ana Hatherly's pioneering books *O Escritor* [The Writer] (1975) and *a reinvenção da leitura* [*The Reinvention of Reading*] (1975), which explore the visual dimension of writing — print, in the former, and calligraphy, in the latter.[23] These books can be linked to the definition of image quoted and subscribed by Ana Hatherly herself in *a reinvenção da leitura*, when she explains how to read concrete poetry:

> If you see it for the first time do not try to read it as poetry; better, do not even try to read it at all, just look at it. Examine the spaces between the letters, the typographical variations, the spaces around the words. Look at it as an image. Then see what ideas come out of that image associated with the letters and the words in it.[24]

Ana Hatherly created the images contained in *O Escritor* during Salazar's dictatorship, and the elements of resistance in the book are clearly visible in its apparent illegibility, in requiring an active reader, an interpreter who can make sense of the surface jumble of letters, numbers and lines which are drawn, rather than written, by the poet. In an interview on Portuguese national

---

[20]   Ana Hatherly, 'O texto-acto: a futura operação das palavras' (1988), in *Um Calculador de Improbabilidades* (Coimbra: Quimera, 2001), pp. 388–89.

[21]   The records of this *happening* were turned into a book, *Homo Sapiens* (1977), in which the poet's goal is clearly visible.

[22]   More information on this period can be found in the pivotal work by Sandra Guerreiro Dias, particularly her doctoral dissertation, *O corpo como texto: poesia, performance e experimentalismo nos anos 80 em Portugal* (Coimbra University, 2016), online at <https://eg.uc.pt/bitstream/10316/29608/1/O_Corpo_como_Texto_Vol1.pdf> [accessed 20 August 2020].

[23]   Almost all the quotations from this essay are taken from Ana Hatherly, *The Reinvention of Reading*, adapted and trans. by W. C. Watt, *Visible Language*, 11.3 (Summer 1997), 307–20. The Portuguese edition was used only when the quotation was not available in the English version.

[24]   Ana Hatherly, *The Reinvention of Reading*, p. 309.

television when the book came out,[25] Hatherly talked about a story told through images, a narrative revolving around the relation between the writer and the text and between the text and the reader. At the same time, the tension between conventional reading and perceiving the page as an image was essential, as the book challenges the reader, page after page, to become aware of just how vague and blurred the borders are between writing and visual images.

O Escritor addresses the relation between the printed word and drawing, whereas *a reinvenção da leitura* explores and relocates the boundaries between calligraphy and drawing so as to highlight the ambivalence of cursive lettering, which in itself is also a type of drawing. The experimental nature of this book is immediately revealed through its form: a long essay followed by nineteen visual texts. In the essay, Ana Hatherly regards the relation between writing and painting as the founding principle of poetry. She advocates that all poetry originates in drawing/painting or, in other words, all writing is a form of painting. '[A] evolução histórica do texto-visual ou texto-imagem fundamenta, cimenta a sua espécie de necessidade ancestral' [the historical evolution of the visual-text founds, cements its sort of ancestral need], writes Hatherly.[26] What the writer proposes is, indeed, 'uma nova pluralidade da leitura da imagem' [a new plurality in the reading of images], one which pays attention to the iconic nature of the visual poem. Reading and seeing thus become, to a certain extent, interchangeable actions, or at least complementary ones: 'While inviting attention to handwriting as drawing, as painting of signs (making it illegible in order to jolt people out of the habit of content-reading) I was trying to restore writing and handwriting to the semiotic, iconic, autonomously semantic power that it had at its origin'.[27] In the same essay, Hatherly states that, 'The visual poem — visual-text, image-text — is literally silent'.[28] To put it differently, it requires a constructive exercise on the part of the reader. This exercise starts with becoming aware of the iconicity of the poetic text. This is, undoubtedly, one of the ways in which work on images has developed in contemporary Portuguese poetry.

Words and Images, Disjunctions and Conjunctions

It is undisputable that in the time period considered in this study there were doubts as to the social role of poetry. Together with other forms of art, poetry suffered from the process of massification which inevitably accompanied the democratization and industrialization of culture. In an interview published in the journal *Sibila* in 2018, under the title 'Poesia e crítica na grande confusão

[25]   See the interview with Ana Hatherly, by Joaquim Manuel Magalhães, RTP Archives, 3 May 1973 <https://arquivos.rtp.pt/conteudos/entrevista-a-ana-hatherly/> [accessed 20 August 2020].
[26]   Ana Hatherly, *a reinvenção da leitura, breve ensaio crítico seguido de 19 textos visuais* (Lisbon: Futura, 1975), p. 10.
[27]   Ana Hatherly, *The Reinvention of Reading*, p. 311.
[28]   Ana Hatherly, *The Reinvention of Reading*, p. 312.

contemporânea' [Poetry and criticism in the great contemporary confusion], Alfonso Berardinelli remembers the publication of the anthology *Il Pubblico della Poesia* [The Public of Poetry], which he edited in 1975, and states, 'the number of poets increased so much that the only readers of poetry were poets themselves, whether real or potential: there was no longer a separate readership, only poet readers were willing to take an interest in poetry, and this readership was becoming larger and larger'.[29] Berardinelli maintained that the proliferation of poetry had not occurred in the best possible way, and that many of the poets 'lacked their own poetics, their own personal idea of what poetry should be'.[30]

Concomitantly, however, some of the most original poets of the twenty-first century were looking for alternative paths. This is how the poet, critic and editor Manuel de Freitas (b. 1972) describes the poetry of Rui Pires Cabral (b. 1967), characterized by media combination and use of collage:

> Rui Pires Cabral found in collage — or in collage poems, if you wish — another form of strength, when maybe strictly verbal poetry no longer appealed to him. 'Who cares about poetry': that is what we hear day in and day out. But that's not exactly the case: poetry is important, aesthetically speaking; it can be said and done in (a) different way(s). [...] Rui Pires Cabral's productive and consistent work undoubtedly shows that a poet need not be held captive by words to become a great poet. This is proven by books such as *Biblioteca dos Rapazes, Broken, Álbum, Oh! Lusitania* or *Elsewhere* [...].[31]

The books listed by Manuel de Freitas were followed by *Manual do Condutor de Máquinas Sombrias* [Manual for the Driver of Sombre Machines] (2018) and *Simple Science — Things around us* (2019). These volumes, often written directly in English, are also devoted to collage. The former involves 'provas fotográficas de autores anónimos, editadas e reproduzidas sobre papel branco ou de cor' [photographic proofs by anonymous authors, edited and reproduced on white or coloured paper], as described in the colophon; the latter uses clippings and montage of words and images taken from its homonymous book (Blackwell, 1936), a popular science book for youngsters written by a zoologist and a physicist. In *Simple Science*, the lyrical effects of fragmentation, displacement, decontextualization and recontextualization of words and images are particularly evident.

Since 2012, the year in which he published *Biblioteca dos Rapazes* [Boys' Library], Rui Pires Cabral has worked on assembling, collating and then producing collages from a variety of materials, such as book illustrations, old postcards, prints, photographs and texts taken from books (not necessarily

[29]   Alfonso Berardinelli, 'Poesia e crítica na grande confusão contemporânea', *Sibila*, ano 18 (2018), no pagination, online at <http://sibila.com.br/critica/poesia-e-critica-na-grande-confusao-contemporanea/13299> [accessed 20 August 2020].
[30]   Alfonso Berardinelli, no pagination.
[31]   Manuel de Freitas, 'Para Sérgio Lima, em forma de abraço', *eLyra*, 7 (June 2016), p. 335. Online at <https://elyra.org/index.php/elyra/article/download/127/123/> [accessed 20 August 2020].

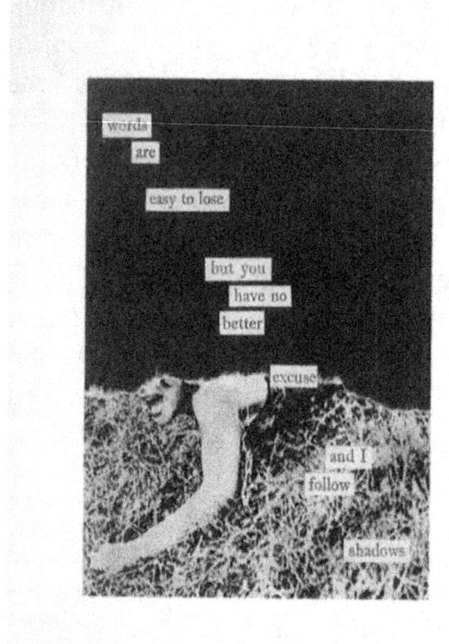

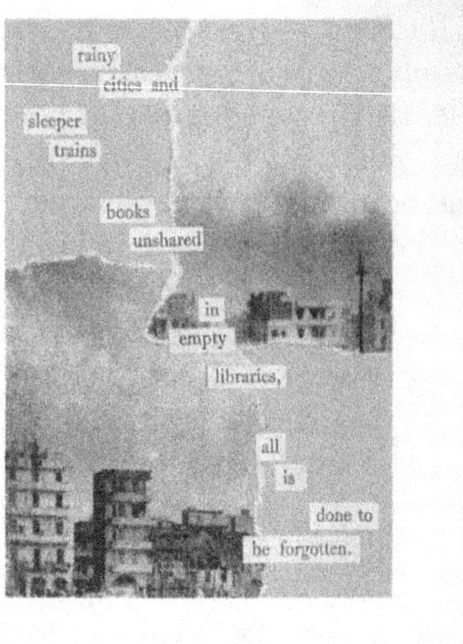

FIG. 1. Rui Pires Cabral. *Oh! Lusitania* (Lisbon: Paralelo W, 2014)

literary). It is a creative process in which words and verbal images are juxtaposed to create a tension with visual images in compositions that call for a reading that will make them converge into a single narrative. This is clearly a case of citationality, which Marjorie Perloff considers essential in twenty-first-century poetics, 'with its dialectic of removal and graft, disjunction and conjunction, its interpenetration of origin and destruction'.[32] Above all, however, it is a way of reacting to the critical situation described by Berardinelli. It is a poetics that rejects spectacle and velocity and retreats into the creative spaces of manual work and re-assemblage of shards, which represent or exemplify the state of the ecologically endangered world we live in.

Concluding Remarks

Resorting to verbal poetic images of metaphorical origin has always been one of the most productive processes in poetry. At the other end of the spectrum is the dissociation between words and images that Rui Pires Cabral obtains by superimposing verbal text onto illustrations, photographs and other visual images. Between these two extremes, however, there are a number of different relations between verbal text and visual image in contemporary Portuguese poetry, and these relations are characterized by both interart porosity and

[32] Marjorie Perloff, *Unoriginal Genius: Poetry by Other Means in the New Century* (Chicago, IL, and London: University of Chicago Press, 2010), p. 17.

tension. This is not to say that more literal uses of visual images and iconic visuality suppress the use of figurative strategies such as metaphor. When, in *Simple Science*, Rui Pires Cabral overlays the caption 'Fig. 126 — Some inhabitants of the deep sea' onto the image of a multitude of people against a black background, the shock effect achieved is caused by the partial juxtaposition of distinct visual domains. Such juxtaposition is a hallmark of the imagetic metaphors so dear to the modernists. Other such examples can be found in other types poetry, such as Ana Hatherly's, mentioned above. Nevertheless, a clear element of novelty is the greater number of works based on intermedial reference and the combination of various media, which clearly search for lyrical restraint through the inclusion of narrative registers.

Indeed, the greater exploration of intermedial relations in poetry seems to rise in parallel with a greater reliance on audiovisual elements in today's world. This is a creative reaction to the decline of the heuristic function of poetry, traditionally grounded in metaphor and figurative discourse. It seems that the current crisis of civilization and its hallmark, relativism, dictate a breaking away from the intrinsic relation between word and image, which has often been considered intensely heuristic and inextricably linked to the language of poetry. This does not mean, however, that poetry has altogether abandoned figurative language. This language remains, though in less conspicuous forms.

The inflection of the images of poetry described in this study can be linked to some of the ways in which poets have tried to deal with the current processes of publication, dissemination and commodification of 'that' which is being called 'poetry' in an increasingly audiovisual world, where silence and intimate time for reading have almost disappeared. Poststructuralist theory and criticism questioned the concept of 'poetic language' that advocated the value of figurativism in the mid-twentieth century. They also questioned the notion of autonomy and self-referentiality. In addition, the borderlines between the arts are becoming more and more diffuse, while hybrid genres and arts are on the rise. Against this backdrop, the creative lines described in this study illustrate different manners of understanding images and reflect different concepts of poetry in the contemporary world. Naturally, nothing is utterly new in literature. Some threads become more visible at the cost of others, in a meshwork that is woven, unwoven, and rewoven for ever and ever.

The Chant of Images:
Fiama and Indifference[1]

JOANA MATOS FRIAS

Faculdade de Letras da Universidade de Lisboa

The work of Fiama Hasse Pais Brandão (including poetry as well as short fiction, plays, essays and translation) is amongst the most relevant in Portuguese literature, but also one of the most complex and baffling, despite its extreme clarity. This is probably why it does not lend itself to epigonism, and also why the critics who have written about it have shown a profound respect for its uniqueness. Such respect may help explain why, unlike what has happened to the work of other contemporary poets, her writing has not yet been the victim of hypercriticism, which could smother its undecipherable elements and nullify its inexplicable character.

Fiama is omnipresent in the book *Sol a Sol* [literally, *Sun to Sun*], by poet Armando Silva Carvalho, published in 2005. Some of the verses of the poem which opens the volume, 'Olhando com Fiama' [Looking with Fiama], read:

> Olhando com Fiama o nosso tempo,
> O espaço é um grão de areia
> Nas retinas:
> Mas sobretudo nas dela
> Que as tem como o mais complexo dicionário
> Do Todo.
> [...]
>
> Sempre me espantou o seu frontal acesso
> Às portas do edifício poético como um monumento do real.
> Pois não sei aqui doutra figura viva ou histórica
> Mais destacada nos nomes que se dão aos enigmas
> Da natureza e da sabedoria.
> E ainda mais o seu trajecto — onde o clássico é tratado por Tu
> Como realidade palpável ao olhar
> Contemporâneo.
> Olhando com Fiama à luz dos livros a fusão do tempo,
> As cenas mínimas, os insectos exemplares da vida,

[1] Translated from the Portuguese by Elena Galvão. This article was written as part of research carried out in the ILCML, R&D Unit financed by National Funds through FCT - Fundação para a Ciência e a Tecnologia [Portuguese Foundation for Science and Technology] (UIDP/00500/2020). The first paragraphs of this text are based (with significant changes and additions) on an interview with Fiama given to Hugo Pinto Santos and included in his article 'Fiama: poeta da palavra, poeta do mundo' [Fiama: Poet of the Word, Poet of the World], *Ler*, 149 (Spring 2018), 100–20.

Letras, sons, estados gerais literários,
É como contemplar a energia translúcida em vibração
Surgindo das imagens líricas e íntegras
Atravessando vertical o cívico
[...]²

[Looking with Fiama at our time,
Space is a grain of sand
In our retinas:
But especially in hers
Which she holds as the most complex dictionary
Of the Whole.
[...]

I have always been amazed at her frontal access
To the doors of the poetic edifice as a monument of the real
For I do not know of any personality, alive or from past history,
Who stands out more in the names we give to enigmas of nature and of
knowledge.
And even more her trajectory — where the Classics are treated with familiarity
As a reality palpable to the contemporary eye.
Looking with Fiama, in the light of books, at the merging of time,
At the minimal scenes, the exemplary insects of life,
Letters, sounds, general literary states,
Is like contemplating translucid vibrating energy
Arising from the lyrical and integral images,
Vertically crossing the civic.
[...]]

This poem, the book it announces, and the 'homage-dialogue' proposed by its verses, have an immediate generational effect, which places the existential and literary affinity between the two poets within the sphere of a historical reading that reinforces the decisive importance of the 1960s (that 'memorable decade', in Fiama's words) for contemporary Portuguese poetry thanks to the works created by Fiama, Armando Silva Carvalho, Gastão Cruz, Nuno Guimarães, Luiza Neto Jorge, Ruy Belo, Herberto Helder, Ana Hatherly and António Aragão, to name just a few. What truly matters is the manner in which the author of *Lírica Consumível* [*Consumable Lyric*] flawlessly synthesizes Fiama Hasse Pais Brandão's poetry, identifying those minute strokes that make up the blueprints of one of the most intense and remarkable poetic adventures ever to grace Portuguese literature: 'retinas', 'dictionary', 'real', 'names', 'nature', 'wisdom', 'classic', 'contemporary', 'books', 'minimal scenes', 'exemplary insects', 'letters', 'sounds', 'lyrical and integral images', 'the civic'. Inside this constellation of words lives the indomitable spirit of an opus whose identity is unmistakable and whose force of character demonstrates what turns writing into a trademark style.

---

² Armando Silva Carvalho, *O Que Foi Passado a Limpo: Obra Poética, 1965–2005*, pref. by José Manuel de Vasconcelos (Lisbon: Assírio & Alvim, 2006), p. 491.

Interestingly, an unsuspected elective affinity with a writer like Nabokov could produce the sharpest synthesis of the *intrinsically artistic* nature of this writing, particularly when the author of *Speak, Memory* compares the 'cenas mínimas' [minimal scenes] of the slides he saw projected in his childhood with the 'insectos exemplares' [exemplary insects] he would later study through his microscope:

> Now that I come to think of it, how tawdry and tumid they looked, those jellylike pictures, projected upon the damp linen screen (moisture was supposed to make them blossom more richly), but, on the other hand, what loveliness the glass slides as such revealed when simply held between finger and thumb and raised to the light — *translucent miniatures*, pocket wonderlands, neat little worlds of hushed luminous hues! In later years, *I rediscovered the same precise and silent beauty at the radiant bottom of a microscope's magic shaft.* In the glass of the slide, meant for projection, a landscape was reduced, and this fired one's fancy; under the microscope, an insect's organ was magnified for cool study. *There is, it would seem, in the dimensional scale of the world a kind of delicate meeting place between imagination and knowledge, a point, arrived at by diminishing large things and enlarging small ones, that is intrinsically artistic.*[3]

If *Área Branca* [*White Area*], dating from 1978, is one of the greatest books of Portuguese poetry, and *Cenas Vivas* [*Living Scenes*], from 2000, one of the most crucial Portuguese lyrical works of the twenty-first century, it is because this uniquely fragile intersection of knowledge and imagination throbs within them, born of the perceptive resizing of the infinitely large and the infinitely small. At the heart of these works is a retinal focus on the minute scenes of nature and the vivid scenes of reality. Both are expressed in a singular fashion, through a careful, meticulous observation of the world down to its tiniest details,[4] a process in which everything within is or can be a manifestation of life — and therefore of poetry itself — as Fiama announces at the start of her 'Canto dos insectos' [Song of Insects], so radical in the ethics it puts forward:[5]

---

[3]   Vladimir Nabokov, *Speak, Memory: An Autobiography Revisited* (New York: Vintage International, 1989), p. 144. My emphasis.

[4]   Something Nabokov himself was particularly sensitive to, so much so that he systematically raised his voice against inaccurate depictions of nature in art: 'Only myopia condones the blurry generalizations of ignorance. In high art and *pure* science detail is everything'; Vladimir Nabokov, *Strong Opinions* (New York: Vintage International, 1973), p. 168.

[5]   Eduardo Prado Coelho succinctly summed up the essence of Fiama's work, speaking about the collection *As Fábulas* [*The Fables*], and her geckos: 'Fiama almost always starts from very concrete circumstances, somehow minute, almost imperceptible, and from there, she writes her fable. Better still: she makes these circumstances speak, makes them express the multiplicity of their implicit feelings, usually half a dozen translucent filaments which, in slow, gradual, arachnid movements, build a cosmic web. [...] With acute feeling, a sort of limitless delicacy, Fiama teaches us to be mindful of the insignificant and dignify it through poetry'; Eduardo Prado Coelho, 'O amor em dois olhares', *Público*, 27 July 2002, n.p.; online at <https://www.publico.pt/2002/07/27/jornal/o-amor-em-dois-olhares-173174> [accessed 20 August 2020].

Podia cantar as aves, mas os insectos
são um misto de aves, de astros e de átomos
que giram em órbita como as imagens de atlas
do Universo ou esquissos de átomos.
[...]
Canto o bater das asas mínimo no ar
como um sopro de aragem num rebento
ou o escaravelho que dobra o fio da erva
e nele dança na oscilação.
Estou aqui a amar e a contemplar
o esforço e a força de cada ser.
[...]
Não desisto de cantar os animais
e as plantas que no berço me embalaram
e me ditaram a voz própria dos poemas.
[...][6] (pp. 555–56; my emphasis)

[I could sing of birds, but insects
are a mix of birds, stars and atoms
which circle in orbits like atlas images
of the Universe or sketches of atoms.
[...]
I sing the minimal fluttering of wings in the air
as a puff of wind on a sapling
or a beetle bending a blade of grass
and dancing on its oscillation.
I am here loving and contemplating
The effort and force of each and every being.
[...]
I shall not give up singing of the animals
And the plants that lulled me in my cradle
And dictated to me the unique voice of poetry.
[...]]

In this poem of successive '*imagens líricas e íntegras*' [lyrical and integral images], as in Nabokov's life and work, the butterfly takes centre stage.[7] The butterfly embodies the connection between the bird, the star and the atom, making it an example of pure oscillation — '*ela que é o símbolo visível | da*

[6]   The original Portuguese quotations from Fiama Hasse Pais Brandão's poems are all from *Obra Breve* (Lisbon: Assírio & Alvim, 2008), a collection of all her poetry. All corresponding page numbers are from this volume. The English translations are a literal rendition meant to help readers who are not familiar with Portuguese to access the original texts.

[7]   Nabokov's obsession with butterflies is well known. He began to collect them as a child, gaining an interest in zoology through his fascination, and dreaming of them often — as he confides in the diaristic *Insomniac Dreams: Experiments with Time* — making them a motif in his work (particularly in poetry) from the first instance. He even began planning a book entirely dedicated to the presence of this insect in art, according to Gerard de Vries and D. Barton Johnson in *Nabokov and the Art of Painting*, who emphasize that 'the unfinished *Butterflies in Art* is *Ada*'s ghostly companion' (Amsterdam: Amsterdam University Press, 2006), pp. 19, 99; cf. *Nabokov's Butterflies*, ed. by Brian Boyd and Robert Michael Pyle (London: Penguin, 2000) and Dieter Zimmer, *A Guide to Nabokov's Butterflies and Moths* (Hamburg: Dieter E. Zimmer, 1996).

metamorfose galáctica' [it is the visible symbol | of galactic metamorphosis] (p. 557). Here and in Fiama's poetry, 'visible symbol' is a concept of operational value. In other words, it is an expression of programmatic meaning: a concept that enlightens and synthesizes the performative importance of her statement *'Não desisto de cantar os animais | e as plantas'* [I will not give up singing of animals | and plants]. This speech act seems anti-modernist, and indeed, almost anti-modern, thanks to the highly transitive project it announces — singing of animals and plants, but also welcoming *'a voz própria dos poemas'* [the voice of the poems themselves] — dictated by the same animals and plants the poems sing of.

In truth, we find ourselves before one of the strongest expressions of a path where, in Armando Silva Carvalho's words, *'o clássico é tratado por Tu | Como realidade palpável ao olhar | Contemporâneo'* [the 'classical' is intimately addressed | as palpable reality to the contemporary eye]. Here, 'classical' is not meant in a literary sense (though such an interpretation could be valid),[8] but rather in an ancient, pre-Socratic sense — a staple in Heraclitean thought — in this case very close to Democritus's principle by which, in all important aspects of existence, it is the animal that teaches humanity, which imitates the way the spider weaves, the swallow builds, the swan and the nightingale sing. Thus, we are not surprised by these verses from *Área Branca* (p. 298): *'Escrevo como um animal, mas com menor | perfeição alucinatória. Não sei imprimir as três linhas | convergentes do pé da gaivota, nem os pomos | leves da pata dos felinos'* [I write like an animal, but with lesser | hallucinatory perfection. I am unable to reproduce the three converging lines | of a seagull's foot, or the light pads | of feline paws]. We find ourselves face to face with another modern way of being, perhaps less ostentatious than the aesthetic manner we usually associate with modernity, but one which fully aligns with a literary project that, from the very beginning — and despite an admitted use of oscillation also in enunciation[9] — sees in Nature *'o princípio evidente | de todas as formas'* [the evident source | of all forms] (p. 15), recognizing in its profuse diversity and its internal coherence the building blocks of any creative process. Schelling called this cognizance the 'point of indifference', the point at which, in Laurence Dickey's words, 'genius becomes aware of how unity and diversity are one and the same thing in the creative processes of nature'.[10] That is why the swan song in *Âmago I (Nova Arte)* [*Core I (New Art)*] reads:

---

[8] Cf., for example, Maria do Céu Fialho, 'Fiama Hasse Pais Brandão: escrita poética recriando os clássicos', *Nuntius Antiquus*, 13.1 (Belo Horizonte, 2017), *passim*.

[9] As Rosa Maria Martelo has pointed out, 'From each book to the next, Fiama offers a succession of experimentations, a thinking process [...] built upon successive attempts. Many diverse attempts. [...] Much of what is most beautiful and fascinating in Fiama's writing springs from the authenticity of this moving from one attempt to the next, which produces a non-linear writing, one made of paths that do not fear either contradiction or reassessment.' 'Fiama ou *opensamen-|tovisual*', in *O Cinema da Poesia* [*The Cinema of Poetry*], 2nd edn (Lisbon: Documenta, 2016), pp. 153–54; my translation.

[10] Laurence Dickey, *Hegel: Religion, Economics, and the Politics of Spirit, 1770–1807* (Cambridge: Cambridge University Press, 1989), p. 265.

Quando oiço a voz do cisne não é
um tópico é antes esta quebra do vento
em que se pode ouvir um cântico.

Embora na literatura ele cante mortal
mente foi o vento no fim do
inverno que parou aqui e a voz nova

do cisne começa a escrever que eu canto.
Também água que escorre cantável por si
em certos momentos foi cantada.

E se falei em Senta ela era das vozes
do canto gráfico a que é toda som
sem modo literário e só hoje um cisne

como ela não como ela na morte
esteve a cantar no jardim sem mito.
(p. 422; my emphasis)

[When I hear the voice of the swan it is not
a topic it is rather this lull in the wind
in which a song can be heard.

Though in literature he sings mortal
ly it was the wind at the end of
winter which stopped here and the new voice

of the swan starts writing that I shall sing.
Also water which flows singable on its own
was at certain times sung.

And if I spoke of Senta she was amongst the voices
of graphic song the one that was all sound
without literary mode and just today a swan

like her not like her in death
was singing in the garden without myth.]

In other words, Fiama partakes of an analogue lineage that views symbolic (i.e. invisible) relationships as capable of creating correspondences between distant or disparate elements. At the same time, however, she doesn't abandon the original and primordial bond with what is visible and perceptible — 'tal como sobrenadar ou tocar | em face visual o invisível' [as if fluctuating over or touching | the invisible in a visible face] (p. 152) — and this bond permanently demands an acutely faithful relationship, one that frequently leads her to doubt the very effectiveness of verbalization and to stage this doubt in her poetry. One of Fiama's early poems, from the book *(Este) Rosto* [*(This) Face*], contains a very clear formulation of this aporia, which is an essential feature of both the poet and her poetry:

Árvore?

1

Onde se implanta ou a implanto, a
descrição. Árvore que exorto,
folhagem abrupta, lugar desse
lugar — presença expulsa. Depois
lugar sobre o lugar, presença
de árvore no seu contorno,
excluído espaço, mero lugar.

2

Acaso estava ali, florira? (Ou eu
além da árvore?) Aonde convergia,
defronte de uma árvore ou ausente
dela — ou em que espaço?
(p. 106)

[Tree?

1

Where description plants itself or
where I plant it. Tree that I exhort,
abrupt foliage, place of this
place — expelled presence. Afterwards
place upon place, presence
of tree in its contour,
excluded space, mere place.

2

Was it there by chance, did it bloom? (Or I
besides the tree?) Where did it converge,
beside a tree or in its absence
— or in which space?]

Transplantation. This is the act that spurs on the questioning in these verses, starting from the title: *is this a tree?* Or rather: if the tree undergoes a process of xenotransplantation into the poem, does it mean that the tree is expelled from its own existence? Or does it mean giving it another existence? An existence through contour (drawing) or description (words)? And in what space? As Rosa Maria Martelo noted when linking this aspect of Fiama's poetry with the thesis set forth in a well-known essay on Romantic imagery by De Man, Fiama knows that the tradition she writes herself into 'is profoundly conditioned by the awareness that natural objects cannot be reduced to words'.[11] In this poem, however, there is an almost imperceptible factor which subliminally insinuates itself from the very first verse and thus balances the components of the text, albeit without effecting a true polarization: '*Onde se implanta ou a implanto*', '*(Ou eu além da árvore?)*'. The two alternatives do not seem to suggest a reading of mutual exclusion between tree and poet. In fact, the most

---

[11]   'Fiama ou *opensamen-|tovisual*', p. 158 (my translation).

interesting effect they evoke is created by the almost complete indeterminacy of the morphosyntactic relationship of complementarity characterizing the final verses ('*Aonde convergia,* | *defronte de uma árvore ou ausente* | *dela — ou em que espaço?*'). At a different level, it is worth noting that, in this poem, Fiama signals an impasse that is as fundamental to her writing as it is fruitful to her readers: the *convergence* between poet, nature and poem, i.e., the complex quality of the ties that bind subject, space and presence.

Years later, this same fertile impasse would become the object of another type of formulation, in a brief poem from *Epístolas e Memorandos* [*Epistles and Memoranda*] (1996) entitled 'Nova epístola para os poetas oitocentistas' [New epistle for nineteenth-century poets]:

> Está ali, de costas para Caspar David, no alto
> de um promontório negro, o que significa que ele
> prolonga ainda mais o olhar do pintor
> e sobretudo a respiração, que inspira e expira o Mar. (p. 595)

> [He is there, back turned to Caspar David, atop
> a dark promontory, which means that he
> extends even further the painter's perspective
> and above all his breathing, which inhales and exhales the Sea.]

Here, Fiama clearly expresses her ekphrastic fascination, which identifies the representation of the emancipated spectator — or observer — as the *punctum* in Friedrich's canvas (or canvases). Considering that she is the only Portuguese-language representative of a speculative poetry that drew much of its inspiration from German Romanticism, her enthusiasm with the pictorial enunciation of a crisis of representation combined with a process of dissociation of creative sensibility is not very surprising. Indeed, as Hans U. Gumbrecht observed in his study of the concept of *Stimmung*, Friedrich's images raise questions about the nexus between experience and perception as well as eliciting a movement of self-reflexivity which leads the observer to wonder at the extent to which their position interferes with their view and interpretation of the world; in sum, such images should be understood 'in terms of a spectrum of observer-perspectives extending from the beautiful harmony of properly adjusted figures, on the one hand, to the sublime displeasure experienced at the breaking-off that occurs between nature and observer, on the other'.[12]

The reason why that epistle is 'new' is that one of the most important poems of *Homenagemàliteratura* [*Homagetoliterature*] had already been dedicated, two decades earlier, to nineteenth-century poets, despite there being no indication of this dedication implying an epistolary register (in fact, this indication is only present in the title). There is a clear and natural chain between the two poems, one whose most salient links I would like to retrace, highlighting the following:

---

[12] Hans Ulrich Gumbrecht, *Atmosphere, Mood, Stimmung: On a Hidden Potential of Literature*, trans. by Erik Butler (Stanford, CA: Stanford University Press, 2012), p. 69.

> [...]
> Mesmo que tivessem morrido convictos inocentes
> de que dos olhos desce o declive infinito da chuva
> transcrito depois para o primeiro movimento do
>
>   animatógrafo
> cujas imagens passageiras no écran mudo
> de uma cortina de chuva
> se reportavam imediatamente à imaginação romântica
> [...]
> [...] Mais do que ninguém esses poetas, o bando, me
> transmitem
> a herança do movimento da existência, estática no âmago
>
>   do indivíduo
> e dispersa através dos olhos, não só nos filmes a que se resume
> o redemoinho das paisagens europeias como nas páginas sinceras
> em que a sinceridade é a harmonia das palavras sentimentais
> [...] (p. 225)
>
> [Even if they had died innocent convinced
> that from the eyes the infinite slope of rain rolls down
> transcribed then into the first movement of the
>
>   animatograph
> whose fleeting images on the muted screen
> of a curtain of rain
> were an immediate reference to romantic imagination
> [...]
> [...] More than anybody these poets, the flock,
> transmit me
> the legacy of the movement of existence, static in the core
>
>   of the individual
> and spread through the eyes, not only in the films which are nothing but
> the swirl of European landscapes like in the sincere pages
> in which sincerity is the harmony of sentimental words
> [...]]

Now, here, transplantation is transcription. The tree is rain. The poems are films. The pages, landscapes. The choice of rain as an element of interconnection between Romantic imagination and film imagery is particularly important,[13] as it establishes a historic bond based on an element that moves from nature to technology without losing its core meaning. In the early years of cinema, the words 'rain' and 'fog' designated a common type of visual interference, which was described in the following terms as early as 1916: 'Since [...] a scratch mark in the corner of the picture is rapidly followed by one in the middle or at the

---

[13] It is, in fact, a juncture that instantly points to fundamental critical readings of English Romanticism, particularly those of the well-known essayist Harold Bloom, meaningfully titled 'The Visionary Cinema of Romantic Poetry', in which Bloom starts by highlighting that the creator of the theme is Eisenstein, who saw cinematic elements in Milton and Shelley. Bloom subsequently proposes that 'the Romantics suggest a more imaginative cinema than we can see in our theaters'; Harold Bloom, 'The Visionary Cinema of Romantic Poetry', in *William Blake: Essays for S. Foster Damon*, ed. by Alvin H. Rosenfeld and S. Foster Damon (Providence, RI: Brown University Press, 1969), pp. 18–19.

top, it looks as though they are dancing all over the place, sometimes in dense clusters, sometimes scattered all around the image. If there are a lot of these defects the screen will appear to be covered with a fine veil of flickering white specks, or a shower of "rain".[14] Once again, it is in Nabokov's writings that we find a connotative use of the concept, which, to some extent, synthesizes the value of its presence in Fiama's poem. In *Камераобскура* (literally *Camera Obscura*, now known in English as *Laughter in the Dark*), Albinus waits while his wife is in labour, and when the doctor announces that she has given birth, we read, 'Before Albinus's eyes there appeared a fine rain like the flickering of some very old film...'.[15] Needless to say, 'flickering' is a key word not just for Fiama's poetry, but for the type of reading of Romanticism she proposes, which is closely related to Wallace Stevens' principle described by Bloom in his essay: to 'make the visible a little hard to see'.[16]

In the passage of the study on the first fruits of Russian cinema I have been citing, Yuri Tsivian summed up the itinerancy of this rain, noting that, historically, 'we may be able to visualize a logical trajectory formed by different spheres of application of the "rain effect"'. This trajectory would consist of four stages: 'unintentional optical interference; a reception trope formed within the sphere of film literature; a literary metaphor that refers to this effect; a text (this time, a film script) that aims to reinstate the "rain" within the film image, to simulate intentionally the effect unintentionally produced'. What should be considered, therefore, is the foundational anachronism that anchors Fiama into a lineage — '*esses poetas* [...] *me transmitem a herança*' [these poets have handed me down their legacy][17] — but that, above all, shows other points of indifference: between the Romantic poem, the silent screen, the painting of Caspar David; between the Romantic poet with their imagination, the painter with their gaze and breath, Fiama with her vision; between spectacle and spectator, observer and observation.[18]

---

[14]   See Yuri Tsivian, *Early Cinema in Russia and its Cultural Reception*, trans. by Alan Bodger, foreword by Tom Gunning (London and New York: Routledge, 2005), p. 86.

[15]   Cf. Yuri Tsivian, *Early Cinema in Russia*, p. 86.

[16]   Bloom, p. 18.

[17]   This confession couldn't be more authentic, and the moulds of this Romantic heritage are probably the greatest challenge Fiama's criticism has to face, as Romanticism, especially of the German kind, cuts through her entire bibliography in astoundingly varied and complex forms, more or less subliminal.

[18]   As Hannah Frank notes in an important clarification: 'What distinguishes "snow" from "rain" is that the former has an existence before the camera lens, while the latter is *a mark on the body of the film itself*. One is embedded *in* the surface of the image, the other is *on* its surface. Yet they have attributes in common: in their dispersal across the screen, in their flickering dance, in their veiling of the screen'; *Frame by Frame: A Materialist Aesthetics of Animated Cartoons* (Oakland: University of California Press, 2019), p. 63. Still, it would be challenging to bring to light a reading of fog in Fiama's poetry, particularly in verses like these from 'Tejo saturnino' [Saturnine Tagus] (p. 169): 'Visões são a matéria em fase de configuração. Defumam-se terra, água, zonas fabris, em fumos, | nítidos como contornos, como maior evidência, entre olhos, reminiscentes, | das formas. [...] || A matéria organizo-a na imagem de esboços fumegando. [...]' [Visions are matter in the process of configuration. Earth, water, industrial areas, are being smoked, in billows of smoke, | clear-cut like contours, like greater evidence, between eyes, reminiscent, | of shapes [...] || I organize matter in the image of a smoking sketch.]

That's why 'ele' [he], in 'Nova epístola aos poetas oitocentistas' [New Epistle to nineteenth-century poets], is so essential to her. Fiama's *re*-vision of Friedrich's famous canvas simultaneously explores the verbal representation of the visual representation (*'Está ali, de costas para Caspar David, no alto | de um promontório negro'*) [He's there, back turned to Caspar David, atop a dark promontory] and the connotative reading of the metaphor contained within the title of the painting, *Der Wanderer über dem Nebelmeer* [*Wanderer Above the Sea of Fog*], by highlighting the breathing of the man in the painting, who is inhaling and exhaling the Sea. This would also allow us to include the poem within a current of notional *ekphrasis* suggestive of other paintings as well, such as the famous *Monge à Beira-Mar* [Monk at the Seashore]. This procedure, while producing a sense of ekphrastic indifference[19] within the reader, emphasizes what Fiama finds to be crucial in Friedrich and in the nineteenth-century poets: the impulse to show, to quote Wordsworth, 'both [...] the objects seen, and eye that sees', as well as the 'absolute freedom [...] from the tyranny of the bodily eye', which Bloom identified as the great burden bequeathed by Romantic poetry to future generations.[20] Indeed, this procedure is visible in other passages of Fiama's work promoting an explicit link with pictorial objects, as in 'A *imprecisão das coisas*' [The imprecision of things] from *Era* (p. 168) — 'Tomai as linhas que nos mostram | a imprecisão das coisas; em Botticelli | a que revela que a primavera então flutuava | por detrás do rosto, equidistante | do pólo do outono [...]' [Take the lines that show us | the imprecision of things; in Botticelli | that which reveals that spring was then floating | behind her face, equidistant | from the pole of autumn] — or, more particularly, in that superlative prose piece *O Retratado* [*The Portrayed*] (1979). This is based on the famous portrait of Fernando Pessoa painted by Almada Negreiros, and its opening reads, 'A escrita é uma figura palpável que imita as figurasobjectos' [Writing is a palpable figure imitating objectfigures]; and then, '*Esta escrita é precisamente igual a um retrato*' [This writing is exactly like a portrait].[21]

It is a gesture that ultimately demonstrates the enormous attention given to the act of naming: to put it in Gastão Cruz's very precise words, what is at stake is '*confiança na força da palavra como casa da imagem*' [trust in the power of words as the *house* of imagery].[22] Almost paradoxically, therefore, it

---

[19]   Here, the concept of 'ekphrastic indifference' is used in the specific sense intended by W. J. T. Mitchell in his essay 'Ekphrasis and the Other'. According to Mitchell, ekphrastic indifference 'grows out of a commonsense perception that ekphrasis is impossible. This impossibility is articulated in all sorts of familiar assumptions about the inherent, essential properties of the various media and their proper or appropriate modes of perception. [...] A verbal representation cannot represent — that is, make present — its object in the same way a visual representation can. It may refer to an object, describe it, invoke it, but it can never bring its visual presence before us in the way pictures do. Words can "cite", but never "sight" their objects'; in *Picture Theory* (Chicago, IL: University of Chicago Press, 1994), p. 152.

[20]   Cited in Bloom, 'The Visionary Cinema of Romantic Poetry', p. 20.

[21]   Fiama Hasse Pais Brandão, *O Retratado* (Lisbon: & etc, 1979), pp. 9, 11.

[22]   Gastão Cruz, 'Fiama: Obra Breve ou o som do poeta', in *A Poesia Portuguesa Hoje* (Lisbon: Relógio d'Água, 1999), p. 171.

is thanks to all these points of indifference that Fiama does not dispense with the opportunity for reflection afforded by accessing the inner spaces of memory and imagination — in *Área Branca* (p. 334), one can read: 'Cada dia transponho um lugar, | da realidade para o sonho. | [...] || Quartos, claustros, pátios que estão dentro | de mim como a medula' [Every day I transpose a place, | from reality to dream. | [...] || Rooms, cloisters, patios that are within | me like bone marrow]. In those spaces, individual experiences and memories mix and merge with historical, collective, and literary experiences and memories. This is clear in passages such as 'evocações || livrescas || na pupila da memória' [book evocations in the pupils of memory] (p. 479), or 'pude comparar | a minha vida à dos historiadores. E que soube | como a tudo o *grande evocador do vento evoca,* | evoca, para que qualquer presença assinale as múltiplas ausências' [I could compare my life to the life of historians. The fact is that I knew | like everything the great evocator of wind evokes, | evokes, so that any presence may signal multiple absences] (p. 162).

Resorting once again to the risky but very productive comparison with Nabokov, this is how the exercise of imagination and its associative power as memory form can be exposed: both memory and imagination sculpt time by denial, that is, they offer *new visions of the past,*[23] as stated openly in the introduction to the 1975 book of the same name: 'De Max Reinhardt recebi, uma vez mais, a realidade; | as imagens instituídas para a relação com o irreal | o das imagens que inovam. E, ainda, o terceiro termo | de ambos, o fantástico, irreal histórico' [Max Reinhart gave me, once again, reality; | the images created to form a relation with what is unreal | innovating images. And, in addition, the third term | of both, the fantastic, the historic unreal] (p. 177).[24]

Down, Plato, down, good dog are Nabokov's humorous words when he links imagination to memory: certainly, in *Cenas Vivas*, Fiama also writes her '*Novas aventuras na caverna platónica*' [New adventures in the Platonic cave] (pp. 645–49) to provoke the Greek, showcasing 'a eternal | janela sob as paisagens nas pupilas' [the eternal window | on the pupils' landscapes] (p. 646),[25] and confessing to having described the 'sombras nem sempre reais' [not always

---

[23] Also in *Strong Opinions*, p. 78, the Russian writer says: 'I would say that imagination is a form of memory. Down, Plato, down, good dog. An image depends on the power of association, and association is supplied and prompted by memory. When we speak of a vivid individual recollection, we are paying a compliment not to our capacity of retention but to Mnemosyne's mysterious foresight in having stored up this or that element which creative imagination may want to use when combining it with later recollections and inventions. In this sense, both memory and imagination are a negation of time.' In Fiama's book, one finds, '*Crio, para além da memória, enunciados | sobre novas visões do passado*' [I create, besides memory, enunciations about new visions of the past] (p. 189).

[24] Titled 'O gnomo' [The gnome], the poem certainly evokes Reinhardt's adaptation of Shakespeare's *A Midsummer Night's Dream*.

[25] Honestly, the link to Nabokov's universe seems endlessly pursuable. Note, for instance, the following passage from *Speak, Memory*: 'As far back as I remember myself (with interest, with amusement, seldom with admiration or disgust), I have been subject to mild hallucinations. [...] Perhaps nearer to the hypnagogic mirages I am thinking of is the colored spot, the stab of an afterimage, with which the lamp one has just turned off wounds the palpebral night' (p. 30).

real shadows] as much as 'a Sombra que confina com a luz do Sol' [the Shadow that borders with sunlight] (p. 647).[26] To a certain extent, then, Fiama defends her own vision of poetry, and though she does so within a context and with assumptions which are quite distinct from those found in Shelley's famous essay, the substance of her ruminations is not that different, especially when she says:

> Corpos de luz estão a passar
> pela boca da caverna deste primeiro andar
> que é a varanda virada para o mar.
> Não são os artífices, nem os recentes habitantes hesitantes.
> Sobretudo uma, que não responde à súbita pergunta
> do filósofo mestre de obras.
> Quem sabe onde colocar as lâmpadas,
> para que os olhos enfim vejam
> corpos de luz que certamente passam,
> vindos desterrados do Universo? (p. 647)

> [Bodies of light are crossing
> the entrance of the cave of this first floor
> that is the terrace overlooking the sea.
> They are no artificers, nor the recent hesitant inhabitants.
> Especially one, who does not answer the sudden question
> of the builder philosopher.
> Who knows where to place the lamps,
> so that the eyes might finally see
> bodies of light which certainly pass,
> coming cast out from the Universe?]

Indeed, this is an old dialogue which had already made its crucial appearance in the opening lines of the *Cantos do Canto* [*Songs of Song*], where, just after 'Canto dos insectos' [Song of insects], we find a 'Canto das imagens' [Song of images], where we read:

> Ao princípio era só uma em cada olhar
> após a grande divisão das águas
> e mesmo, segundo disse Baudelaire, a imagem
> até ao seu século do real múltiplo
> era una, única e própria. Dementes
> chamou este cantor aos fotogramas
> que roubavam à alma a unicidade
> e deram aos olhos frívolos as figuras
> plurais, idênticas, dispersivas.
> Era somente uma a imagem mística,

---

[26] This poem has a prose counterpart in the 1988 tome *Falar sobre o Falado* [*Speaking about the Spoken*]: the text titled 'Ex-orbitar,' where one finds: 'O passado de job é o das imagens; estava nas areias bíblicas, via; *há uma corda debaixo da terra*. Descartes faria suas as palavras do Livro e perante os desenhadores do vale ou as sombras platónicas repelidas para o estado uterino na caverna de antígona, o conceito de exterior e de interior entraria em plena crise'; in Fiama Hasse Pais Brandão, *Em cada Pedra um Voo Imóvel e outros textos*, ed. and pref. by Gastão Cruz (Lisbon: Assírio & Alvim, 2008), p. 144.

dos entes naturais aos transcendentes.
Só uma esta vermelha afelandra
embora as suas irmãs se lhe assemelhem
e desassemelhem, cada uma, sempre.
O concreto pulsava neste ritmo
das coisas parcas, poucas, singulares.
E de repente, nos olhos do poeta
cada coisa reproduziu a imagem
inumeradamente, e a ideia
decaíra no banal prolixo.
Antes, podia hesitar-se entre o modelo
e as sombras de Platão, agora as *flores
malignas* podem reproduzir-se no mundo
nítidas, iguais, supérfluas.
Eu ainda vejo o olhar antigo de Baudelaire
e cada coisa vibra no seu mito,
e cada imagem cria o seu espírito,
e cada cópia fotográfica muda
na liminarmente máxima diferença.
Ao crítico e amante da Pintura
as dúbias imagens decerto deram
a cada rosto um só outro rosto,
a cada paisagem uma só tela.
Já os vidros, a água, a prata traziam
a incerteza aos traços, como se os olhos
que nos deu a Natureza nos fossem
infiéis. E o poeta pôde resistir
a esta perda das formas consagradas
e consubstanciais das coisas que ainda
ecoam a Criação como o eco cósmico. (pp. 558–59)

[In the beginning it was only one in each gaze
After the great parting of the waters
And even, as Baudelaire said, the image
until the century of the multiple real
was one, unique and original. Insane
called this singer the frames
that stole the uniqueness of the soul
and gave frivolous eyes figures,
plural, identical, dispersive.

It was only a mystical image,
from natural to transcendent beings.
Just one this red aphelandra
though its sisters are similar
and dissimilar, each one, always.
The concrete pulsed with this rhythm
of rare, few, singular things.
And suddenly, in the poet's eyes,
each thing reproduced the image,
innumerably, and the idea

> plunged into the long-winded banal.
> Before, one could hesitate between the model
> and Plato's shadows, now the flowers
> of evil can multiply in the world,
> clearcut, identical, superfluous.
> I can still see through the eyes of the old Baudelaire
> and each thing vibrates in its myth,
> and each image creates its spirit,
> and each photographic copy changes
> into a literally maximum difference.
> To the critic and lover of Painting
> the dubious images certainly gave
> to each face one face only,
> to each landscape only one canvas.
> But glasses, water, silver would confer
> uncertainty to the outlines, as if the eyes
> that Nature gave us were being unfaithful
> to us. And the poet could resist
> this loss of the consecrated
> and consubstantiated shapes of things which still
> echo Creation like a cosmic echo.]

Imagery in the age of mechanical reproduction. As usual with Fiama, the poem doesn't totally clarify the degree of her solidarity with Baudelaire's known aversion to the sociocultural and artistic impact of photography, fierily expressed in texts like *Le Publique moderne et la photographie* of 1859. But Fiama's verses compose a true song 'of images'. They belt out different problems and inflexions, as if the text were the result of a kind of choral prosopopoeia that lends voice to every meaning of the word *image* and forms a fascinating version of the dramatic tendency Fiama had already proclaimed in '*Oscilo | entre o cénico e o lírico*' [I oscillate | between the scenic and the lyrical], which T. S. Eliot's 'The Three Voices of Poetry' could easily clarify (p. 339).[27] It is a polyphony of images, then, a polyphony from Plato to Baudelaire through Fiama. Fiama's importance cannot be overemphasized, not only because her voice collects and merges the other voices, but especially because three of her verses put a stop to the succession of shadows and models: 'Só uma esta vermelha afelandra | embora as suas irmãs se lhe assemelhem | e desassemelhem, cada uma, sempre.' That is the point of indifference according to Schelling, according to Fiama: nature, as singular and profuse as the images (re)produced by humans, whether technical or not.[28]

---

[27] In fact, the essay contains a reflection by Eliot that thoroughly applies to Fiama's work: 'If you complain that a poet is obscure, and apparently ignoring you, the reader, or that he is speaking only to a limited circle of initiates from which you are excluded — remember that what he may have been trying to do, was to put something into words which could not be said in any other way, and therefore in a language which may be worth the trouble of learning'; in *On Poetry and Poets* (London: Faber & Faber, 1957), pp. 101–02.

[28] We find a different version of this in *Homenagemàliteratura* (p. 238): 'Cair a noite esmaga-me pela cadência com que a Natureza extermina || a minha fantasia e me substitui na sua própria criação'.

Fiama is, undoubtedly, one of the worthiest descendants of those nineteenth-century poets to whom she dedicated a poem so early on, the protagonists of the 'paisagem mental | do romantismo' [mental landscape of Romanticism] (p. 155)[29] and of a very special lyrical landscape of Modernity. The dedication-poem is part of the 1976 dedication-book *Homenagemàliteratura* [*Homagetoliterature*]. It was, as the name indicates, a book with a (self-)reflective purpose, something easily confirmed by the progression of its constitutive poems, like 'Tábua das comparações' (p. 212), 'Glosa menor (de Miranda)' (p. 216), 'Releituras' (p. 217), or the poem that gives the volume its name (pp. 232–35), which contains a synthesis of her own poetics. In it, we find the formulation of principles such as '*tudo é díspar*' [all is different], '*aprender a transformar || as formas entre si é tornar inteligente a linguagem para a História*' [learning how to transform forms into one another is making language intelligible to History] (p. 232), '*o poeta imorredouro || é o que introduz na língua a metáfora mais densa*' [it is the immortal poet that introduces the densest metaphor into language] because '*é a metáfora que constitui a língua pátria*' [metaphor is a native language] and '*cada metáfora é na sua íntegra incompreensível, || o que a torna o fundamento de toda a diferença*' [metaphors cannot be fully comprehended || which makes them the foundation of all difference] (p. 234).

In a few verses, Fiama proposes a very unusual historical rereading of the most prestigious trope of the logico-semantic figurative system associated with poetry. Metaphor is not considered for its traditional power of analogy and condensation but rather for the exact opposite: its power to differentiate and express disparity. This rereading becomes even clearer after Fiama declares that metaphor is her native language, which places her firmly within a line of thinkers — from Vico to Gadamer and Ricoeur — who consider metaphor to be at the very origin of language. In fact, in an earlier poem titled 'Origem da língua' [Origin of language], Fiama confided in an almost Aristotelian register: '*Se até há poucos momentos eu era indiferente à origem da língua portuguesa | foi porque, passando pelo mesmo caminho, seleccionara outros significados*' [If up until a few moments ago I was indifferent to the origin of the Portuguese language, it was because, treading the same path, I had chosen different meanings] (p. 163). This statement unleashes a seism with near-catastrophic consequences, because what follows on from such a proposal is the observation that, for Fiama, metaphor is not, in Kantian terms, a synthetic figure, but rather a synthetic figure with analytic effects, i.e., a figure of the imagination itself, seen as the human faculty for understanding, as already announced in the verses of a prior collection: 'Estou só, na zona das metáforas | (que é todo

---

[29]   In the poem 'Ode ao choro,' from *Era* (p. 155): 'Antigamente ouvíramos (heine), em que | presbitério contra o fundo romântico, contra o volume do vento? A tarde | evocadora com os signos certos, nuvens que desciam | os descendiam de que alto monte ou coincidência | porque sabemos que das razões as mais obscuras são | as que depois coincidem, as que na paisagem mental | do romantismo decalcam a cinza do lago que choravas | lembrando-o e vendo-o na vertigem da margem. | E como eu sentia o vento, oscilava | nos teus ombros e já olhava as marinhas de turner'.

o pensamento)'[30] [I am alone, in the area of metaphors (which is all thinking)] (p. 200). This is a particularly thorny point of indifference, which nonetheless allows us to fully understand why Fiama decided to begin one of the articles she dedicated to Carlos de Oliveira in 1975–76 with the following important suggestion: 'É possível que conhecer seja conhecer as imagens por palavras, as palavras por outras palavras' [Knowing possibly means knowing images through words, words through other words].[31] Above all else, this possibly means we would now have to start again, joining Fiama in her effort *to see what cannot be seen.*[32]

---

[30]   Cf. 'o pensamen-|to visual' [visual think-|ing], in 'Pormenores vivos de Mallarmé e Antero' [Living details of Mallarmé and Antero] from the book *Melómana* [Melomaniac], p. 254. As Rosa Maria Martelo pithily remarked in an essential essay, '[g]rafado num lexema único, irregularmente cortado pela pausa métrica, "o pensamen-| to visual" tornava-se, sem dúvida, mais visual, ao mesmo tempo que a indissociabilidade entre imagem e pensamento era evidenciada na iconicidade deste neologismo' [written as one single lexeme, irregularly interrupted by a caesura, 'o pensamen-| to visual' (visual thinking) became even more visual, at the same time as the neologism highlighted the indissoluble link between image and thought] (*O Cinema da Poesia*, p. 151).

[31]   Fiama Hasse Pais Brandão, 'Nexos sobre a obra de Carlos de Oliveira | I', *Colóquio/Letras*, 21 (Lisbon: Fundação Calouste Gulbenkian, July 1975), p. 57.

[32]   Cf. Harold Bloom, 'The Visionary Cinema of Romantic Poetry', p. 27.

A Selfless Proliferating Language

Manuel Portela

University of Coimbra

Permutational Poetics

This essay starts from the hypothesis that one of the functions of literary art is to explore the material properties of language as a source of signifiers. According to this hypothesis we could think of literary signification as both the product of socially constituted meanings and the product of emergent possibilities derived from verbal permutation at all levels of language structure (phonetic, morphological, syntactic, semantic) and at all levels of the social semiotics of language action (discursive, pragmatic). Considered as a tool for analysing and discretizing verbal language, writing is a powerful means for experimenting with the cognitive and social materiality of language as an open-ended and generative process for the production of signifiers. The externalization of language that occurs through the medium of writing extends our cognitive ability to explore permutability as a source of signifiers, either in their systemic or in their social productivity. The iterability of writing, i.e., the general property of being quotable and recontextualizable, further extends its generative productivity through endless iterations.

Thus the emergence of particular writing styles, genres and forms could be described as the rhythmic, semantic and narrative effect resulting from the patterned use of certain kinds of permutations which are individually and socially invented in and through writing. Literary art could then be described as an institution for simulating the workings of language as a social semiotic signifying system and for extending its perlocutory effects on our ongoing imagination of how to be human. Writing becomes a continuing rehearsal of our humanity through imaginative works. According to this perspective, the verbal experimentation that takes form through particular kinds of literary representation is an attempt both to imagine lived experience and to imagine the potentiality of being through the proliferation of what can be said by means of language permutations.

Emphasis on signifiability — that is, on the possibility of extending our repertoire of signifiers and references, and thus of what can be imagined — contrasts with the dominant and common-sense approach to literary interpretation, which tends to emphasize representationality, that is, the possibility of addressing an extra-linguistic experience — social or psychological in nature — or referencing a particular verbal form — in the case of imitation or parody — through the fictionality of language. Thus, both common readers and expert interpreters tend to look for the referentiality of the fictionality of language either by reference to a particular social or subjective experience or by reference to a particular verbal form or genre. To interpret, in this sense, is to establish the semantic and ideological conditions for representational interpretability.

In this representational understanding of literary art, the exploration of language for expressive effect is constrained by parameters of correspondence between lived experience and literary representation or between literary form and literary representation. Those parameters sustain the readability and interpretability of verbal worlds. In the former non-representational approach, language becomes an abstract malleable engine for the proliferation of signifiers. Language expresses itself as a living organism whose genome is independent of any sort of representational adequacy. This proliferative generation of signifiers — motivated by the internal logic of verbal association through factorial permutations — enhances the disconnectedness between signifier and signified (and between signifier and referent). This disconnectedness foregrounds the disjunctive relation between language as a structured and formal system, on the one hand, and its situated agency as social practice, on the other.

Although both practices originate in the same symbolic process — i.e., the ability of language to signify both the world and itself — the first set of practices is based on the notion that literary expression consists of producing a unique and motivated form. Reading and interpreting is the act of coming to terms with the uniqueness and motivation of that form, that is, with the particular occurrence of its material instantiation as a written verbal artefact that embodies the subjective conditions of its coming into existence, including the intentionality of a particular arrangement of words.

However, for the second set of practices, the potentiality inherent in a given form turns into the main focus of attention since the form itself is experienced as a generative programme for expanding the writable and the sayable. So the act of producing signifiers is no longer constrained by the drive to produce a self-sufficient and autonomous verbal artefact (filled with subjectivity and intentionality) that we can contemplate, but it becomes infused with the procedurality that generates further signifiers by virtue of the signifying programme itself. The text becomes a witness of the constraint that makes it possible to generate further alternative forms of itself, being both a textual instance and a textual programme for producing further instances. Through this conflation between data and instruction, that is, between output and programme for producing further output, the text opens itself up to an endless series of permutations.

The development of procedural writing practices has intensified over the last decades, since many of these rule-based forms of writing under constraint can now be formalized as computer programmes.[1] For this article, I have

---

[1]   For an extensive discussion of the relation between writing constraints and programmed

chosen two contemporary Portuguese poets whose work may be described as explorations of the signifying potentiality of language through processes of permutation that suggest the exhaustion of the possible combinations of a set of words when arranged according to a given syntactic template. This type of literary experiment could even be called ambient literature, in an analogy with ambient music or ambient video. Texts become a continuous flow that we encounter randomly according to our own shifting and changing attention. The fact that Rui Torres has sometimes presented his work under the form of literary installations is a further indication of the changed ethos of attention and modes of interaction required by these works. Luís Serguilha's work is equally significant because he has not automated his permutational processes, despite the fact that his work is equally factorial in terms of its operational and algorithmic linguistic principles. Textual permutation can be automated, but the generative effect of factorial permutations is independent of algorithmic automation.

My reading of their particular poetics will look at how permutation operates and what its effect is in terms of our experience of the text. I will argue that one of the effects is to provide us with an emulation of the differential workings of language as a living organism. In each case, we are called upon to bear witness to the workings of language (and writing) as a continuous stream of signifiers and an endless chain of substitutions. This means that our experience of the text shifts from attending to a reified form in which each individual element can only be what it is to an open virtualized form in which individual elements can always mutate into other signifiers. This substitution of signifiers results in the multiplication of textual variations, with the ensuing probabilistic distribution of meaning along a syntactic matrix that brings together discrete lexical items. Through the improbable association of lexical items, meaning is experienced as a fuzzy intersection among those items. Because of the visibility of the set of rules that may be said to constitute their textual programmes, readers experience the process of textual production at the same time that they pay attention to specific textual instances.

•

Poems as Data and as Instructions: The Inexhaustibility of Signifiers

Rui Torres has been publishing web-based multimedia poems for two decades. His work builds on the experimental poetics begun in the 1960s in the context of the programmable networked digital media enabled by the arrival of the World Wide Web. He has recreated several print-based texts by twentieth-century Portuguese-language writers through explicit programming of their

computational writing, see Manuel Portela, 'Writing under Constraint of the Regime of Computation', in *The Bloomsbury Handbook of Electronic Literature*, ed. by Joseph Tabbi (London: Bloomsbury, 2018), pp. 179–98. For an analysis of one example of this relation between textual programme and multiple textual instantiations, see Manuel Portela, 'Sentir o sentido: a experiência do código nos "homeóstatos" de José-Alberto Marques', *Texto Digital*, 12.1 (2016), 69–78, online at <https://periodicos.ufsc.br/index.php/textodigital/article/view/1807-9288.2016v12n1p69> [accessed 20 August 2020].

textual algorithms, while developing a generative poetics of his own.[2] This poetics is based on the factorial virtualization of selected syntactic structures and lexicons that he appropriates from other writers through a detailed process of analysis. Deeply influenced by Pedro Barbosa's theorization of virtualized textuality,[3] he practises a systematic form of rewriting that we could relate to current conceptual approaches to writing. However, the randomness and unexpectedness of the factorial permutations are carefully controlled according to a poetic rationale. The range of semantic and metaphorical values that result from the random substitutions of lexical items tend to maintain some kind of constellated structure of relations that prevents meaninglessness. Although liberated from an enunciating self, textual form is tightly constructed so that it can be experienced as a series of evolving variations of a particular syntactic and semantic pattern.

Árvore (2018), an example of his permutation poetics, is particularly relevant for the argument of this essay.[4] Other significant recent works, similarly based on appropriation of earlier texts by other poets, include *Gerador de Homeóstatos* (2015), *Estou Vivo e Escrevo Sol* (2016), and *Fantasia breve, a palavra-espuma* (2016).[5] Besides these programmed explorations for purposes of lyric expression, Torres has also used his poetic engines for deconstructing political and commercial discourses. *PoemAds: Sob o signo da devoração* (2012) is based on the remix of political and commercial slogans, while *a separação:: a(n)estesia* (2016) is a mash-up of propaganda soundbites and advertisement snippets echoing the Portuguese austerity adjustment programme supervised by the Troika between 2011 and 2014.[6] *Árvore* is a multimedia work bringing together textual, visual and sound layers. The text is structured into nine sentences (four groups of two lines plus one final line). Once the first letter by letter animation of the nine lines (from top to bottom) has generated the first full version of the text, individual lines are substituted by other versions of themselves. The text enters an endless process of temporized transformation (Figures 1 and 2).

The asymmetric arrangement of the nine lines, along vertical and horizontal axes, evokes the relationship between branches and trunk of the silhouettes

---

[2] His poems appropriate works by an extensive list of Lusophone writers, including Sophia de Melo Breyner Andresen, Clarice Lispector, Salette Tavares, E. M. de Melo e Castro, António Aragão, Herberto Helder, Fernando Pessoa, José-Alberto Marques, Ana Hatherly, António Ramos Rosa, Ruy Belo, and several others. Most of his works are available on his website: <https://telepoesis.net/poesias.html>.

[3] Pedro Barbosa, 'Aspectos Quânticos do Cibertexto', *Cibertextualidades*, 1 (2006), 11–42.

[4] Rui Torres, *Árvore* (2018) <https://telepoesis.net/arvore/>. For an extended analysis of earlier works by Rui Torres, see Manuel Portela, 'Autoauthor, Autotext, Autoreader: The Poem as Self-assembled Database', *Writing Technologies*, 4.1 (2012), 43–74.

[5] Rui Torres, *Gerador de Homeóstatos* (2015) <https://www.telepoesis.net/homeostatos>; *Estou Vivo e Escrevo Sol* (2016) <https://www.telepoesis.net/estou-vivo-e-escrevo-sol>; *Fantasia breve, a palavra-espuma* (2016) <https://www.telepoesis.net/palavra-espuma>.

[6] Rui Torres, *PoemAds: Sob o signo da devoração* (2012) <https://www.telepoesis.net/poemads/>; *a separação:: a(n)estesia* (2016) <https://telepoesis.net/aseparacao/>.

Torturados e suaves, os abacateiros e as cássias, na encosta do seu alento.
Ergue-se a semente das planícies.

Em desordenados corpos, os vasos libertos das bisnagueiras.
Na minúscula brancura, os campos.

As primaveras habitam o outono, alastram.
No seu bocejo adormecido e nos seus bravos poemas, os limoeiros.

Conservamo-nos como as acácias de uma ilha no canto da lua.
A giesta: adormecida serenidade, alegria recalcada, noite desconhecida e misteriosa.

As plantas não acordam, não sofrem, não suspiram

Simples e calmos, os regatos e as árvores, no verdor da sua primavera.
Sente-se a dor das giestas.

Em desmedidos traços, os gestos solenes dos carvalhos.
Na húmida manhã, os eucaliptos.

As laranjeiras atravessam o inverno, ressuscitam.
No seu silêncio lento e nos seus vagos rumores, as azinheiras.

Tocamo-nos como as oliveiras de uma planície no interior da terra.
A amoreira: lenta reverência, presença adormecida, habitação perdida e encontrada.

Os sobreiros não baloiçam, não irrompem, não se dissolve

Figs 1 and 2. Rui Torres, *Árvore* (2018). Screencaptures of an ongoing textual permutation. Work inspired by poems by António Gedeão, António Ramos Rosa, Fernando Pessoa, Herberto Helder, Miguel Torga and Ruy Belo. txt, html, img, xml: Rui Torres; js: Nuno Ferreira; snd: Luís Aly. Available at <https://telepoesis.net/arvore/arvore.html>.

of the various species of trees and shrubs onto which the text overlaps. The animation of the words evokes the growth of the plants, the movements of the leaves and branches or simply their silhouettes cutting themselves out of the landscape. The nominal evocation of each species through individual referents underlines the perception and the sensation that objectifies the trees and shrubs as objects of perception. At the same time the metaphorical fusions produced by the juxtaposition of concrete and abstract vocabulary results in the animism that seems to blow the spirit into the tree.

The tree is an apt metaphor to describe Rui Torres's approach to textual production because it sustains two sets of metaphorical intersections between poem and tree. On the one hand, the tree is the living expression of its genetic code as the poem is the expression of its programme of permutations. On the other hand, the morphology of the tree and the morphology of the poem have structural similarities in the ways their structures are designed to sustain a multiplicity of combinations of their building blocks: different types of cells evolving into leaves and branches; different types of phonemes evolving into words and sentences (and also lines and groups of lines in multiple configurations). In the fact, syntactic structures have long been described as *trees* precisely because of the hierarchical structures that result from their recursive patterns. Thus *tree* refers both to a particular type of plant and to a diagrammatic representation of a specific structure.[7]

In this kind of procedural work, the text is not only a specific verbal artefact but it becomes a programme for generating variations based on its basic elements — in this case, syntactic templates and lexical lists. In Rui Torres's works, both syntactic templates and lexical lists are generally borrowed from other literary works. As stated in its colophon, *Árvore* borrows from poems by António Gedeão, António Ramos Rosa, Fernando Pessoa, Herberto Helder, Miguel Torga and Ruy Belo. Lexical lists are organized in such a way that the semantic relations between co-occurring words maintain similar metaphoric, metonymic and imagetic relations when permutations occur. Although semantic and lexical fields may change in each iteration, the general metaphorical configuration of the field is maintained. Because changes occur as temporized and sequential substitutions of signifiers in each line, variations are experienced by the reader as progressive semantic shifts that take place line by line along the textual axes.

The syntactic template for the poem *Árvore* can be described as follows:

> Line 1: Adj-pl. e Adj-pl., os N-pl. e as N-pl., no/na N da/do seu/sua N.
> Line 2: V a/o N das/dos N-pl.
>
> Line 3: Em Adj-pl N-pl, os N-pl Adj-pl dos/das N-pl.
> Line 4: Na Adj N, os/as Npl.
>
> Line 5: As/os N-pl V3ªp-pl o/a N, V 3ªp-pl.
> Line 6: No seu N Adj e nos/nas seus/suas Adj-pl N-pl, os N-pl.
>
> Line 7: V-1ªp-pl como os/as N de um/uma N no/na N do/da N.
> Line 8: O/A N: Adj N, N Adj, N Adj e Adj.
>
> Line 9: As/Os N-pl não V, não V, não V.

After defining the nine syntactic units, lexical lists are always organized to

---

[7] Cf. Definition of tree: 1(a): 'a woody perennial plant having a single usually elongate main stem generally with few or no branches on its lower part'; 2(a): 'a diagram or graph that branches usually from a simple stem or vertex without forming loops or polygons.' *Merriam-Webster English Dictionary*, online at <https://www.merriam-webster.com/dictionary/tree> [accessed 20 July 2019].

show not only gender and number agreement but also similar semantic traits so that permutations result in grammatical structures that sustain similar metaphorical intersections. Most nouns belong to the semantic field of plants and natural landscapes (such as names of trees, shrubs and flowers) while most verbs and adjectives relate to human actions, feelings, emotions and values. The textual engine explores the associative dynamics of its source texts in order to make new iterations of each particular phrase or sentence that result in similar intersections between semantic fields. Such textual forms can also be understood in terms of theme and variation. In this case the theme could be defined as both the syntactic template and the semantic template. The syntactic template is used for generating metaphorical associations between signifiers that join features such as animate and inanimate, concrete and abstract, plant and animal, human and non-human through pairs of adjectives and adjectives, nouns and nouns, verbs and nouns, or adjectives and nouns.

Each of the following sentences is the output of successive iterations and permutations of its constituent lists of nouns and verbs:

> As florestas não brotam, não se multiplicam, não suspiram.
> Os vidoeiros não amam, não irrompem, não se misturam.
> As aveleiras não clamam, não ressuscitam, não cismam.
> Os marmeleiros não aquecem, não envolvem, não apaziguam.
> As amendoeiras não clamam, não envelhecem, não se multiplicam.
> As bagas não desabam, não irrompem, não se transformam.[8]

Each new line is generated to replace an earlier version of itself. They are never simultaneously present. Instead, they are experienced as temporal occurrences showing how the text has been virtualized through the endless multiplication of possibilities. Its syntactic matrix accommodates the shifting perceptions derived from the substitution of words. Meaning is revealed as function of that inexhaustible process of substitution which results in this abundant proliferation of language.

Improbable Writing: Syntactic Algorithms and Semantic Music

Topics such as illegibility/unreadability, surrealistic automatic writing and neo-baroque excess have been used in critical readings of Luís Serguilha's works. Acknowledging the challenges of the semantic deformation of his works' proliferative verbal rhetoric, such critical readings are often included by the author as preface or afterword in his books. These readings attempt to provide readers with some sort of key to approach this magma of self-generated language as a monstrous and living organism. E. M. de Melo e Castro refers to 'organic images', 'vitalist' and 'erotic',[9] and also to endless texts based on

---

[8] Rui Torres, *Árvore* (2018) <https://telepoesis.net/arvore/>.
[9] E. M. de Melo e Castro, 'Prefácio', in Luís Serguilha, *Embarcações* (Vila Nova de Gaia: Editora Ausência, 2004), pp. 7–11 (p. 10). All translations of quotations in this paragraph by the author.

'sequential linguistic algorithms' that result in a 'trans-semantic' poetics.[10] Manoel Ricardo de Lima highlights the 'circularity of the hallucinated lines of the spiral' and a 'mobile cosmogony'.[11] João Amadeu da Silva refers to 'a world of hyper-reality in which only images are real'.[12] Victor Sosa describes how the energy of the act of writing calls into question the semantic meaning of language and becomes an orgiastic invitation to enter 'the sexual thickness of language' by means of the 'total engagement of the body'.[13] Luís Adriano Carlos equates Serguilha's writing with the Lacanian psychoanalytic concept of 'lalangue' in order to suggest that it gives expression to the breath of the voice and to the infra-linguistic scream and howl whose vitality shatters the rationality of meaning.[14]

The improbability of lexical and semantic associations in Luís Serguilha's poems reveals the algorithmic nature of syntax. Looking at the meaning of its non-meaning, we perceive how syntactic structures are combinatory and permutative devices, and how the semantic movement intrinsic to language results from permutation and recombination of elements held in place by syntax. The association of lexemes with a low probability of co-occurrence in the pragmatic (or even poetical) uses of language makes it possible to break frequent bonds and remake them in infinitely recursive iterations. The double articulation that allows sounds to generate units of meaning is replicated in the productivity of syntactic structures, which function as matrixes capable of generating new semantic molecules from the more or less improbable association of elements. Too much meaning or even lack of meaning makes syntactic processes more visible as word-sequencing algorithms and as logical-semantic replicators.

The device that generates words from the permutation of sounds finds its equivalent in the device that generates sentences from words. It is this particular device — namely a specific set of sentence structures, already analysed by E. M. de Melo e Castro (2004; 2005) — that is the core of Luís Serguilha's work. In its self-contained automatism, the proliferation of lexical and semantic associations confronts us with the structures of intentionality and meaning as a kind of computational biochemistry and biophysics of language itself. Meaning, like the absence of meaning, is an effect of this internal calculus of language, which is overdetermined by the pragmatics of speech and writing, which also structures them as social acts. Human creativity depends on this proliferative

---

[10]   E. M. de Melo e Castro, 'O interminável texto de Luís Serguilha', in Luís Serguilha, *A singradura do capinador* (Lisbon: Indícios de Oiro, 2005), pp. 10–20 (p. 19).

[11]   Manoel Ricardo de Lima, 'Quando não se sabe dizer', in Luís Serguilha, *As processionárias* (São Paulo: Demônio Negro, 2008), pp. 5–7 (pp. 5, 6).

[12]   João Amadeu Carvalho da Silva, 'A explosão irónica das imagens', in Luís Serguilha, *As processionárias* (São Paulo: Demônio Negro, 2008), pp. 78–82 (p. 79).

[13]   Victor Sosa, 'Sea lo que sea', in Luís Serguilha, *KOA'E* (Belo Horizonte: Anome Livros, 2011), pp. 17–21 (p. 18, p. 19)

[14]   Luís Adriano Carlos, 'A prosódia da prosa', in Luís Serguilha, *Kalahari* (Porto: Edições Esgotadas, 2015), pp. 5–11 (pp. 10–11).

potential which opens up linguistic production to infinite re-association. Without this madness of language there would be no way to make poetry, or to speak, or to think. The world would be mere tautology of pre-given meanings and structures.

This kind of semantic music becomes perceptual and sensorially palpable — the semantic music that, on the other side of the sign, plays its subliminal and surreptitious role of generating in us the meaning of language, the result of differential relations that reconfigure, with each syntactic recombination, the semic identity of the elements in co-presence. The co-presence of improbable elements makes clear the instability of meaning, or rather, the way in which meaning depends on an always reconfigurable set of relations among elements. New combinations trigger term-to-term and field-to-field transfers. The possibility of language itself, and hence of the sayable and the thinkable, arises as a by-product of this metaphoric engine, which is the very essence of the game of naming. The world as representation materializes as a secondary effect of this general transfer and production of meaning inscribed in the DNA of language.

To the pre-given or pre-existing meaning — which results from the constellations of statistically probable and culturally frequent associations — the unintended or unanticipated meaning, that is, the meaning generated by the improbability of the associations, opposes itself. To a certain extent, the modernist and postmodernist poetic experimentation sought to automate writing, that is, to maximize the mechanics intrinsic to the functioning of language and the unconscious in the production of meaning. The Dadaist recipe for producing poems out of random fragments from newspapers is one of the earliest criticisms of the emptying of language by discourse conventions. An equivalent critical function can be found in surrealistic automatic writing, directed at the self-control of the rational subject over his/her own unconscious. In the experiments of the algorithm-driven textual engines, which have automated the combinatorial principles abstracted by the generative analysis of language, it is the linguistic mechanisms themselves that are used to automate the production of language and foreground a critique of the replication of meaning.

In Serguilha's writing the experimental practice of the interpellation of language itself as the space for the poetic act can be recognized. By abandoning referential modes of signification, these poems undo the naturalized transparency of discourse and its merely vehicular function. Syntax is used as a combinatorial engine that allows for the association of words regardless of conventional semantic and metaphorical coherence. The apparent semantic a-grammaticality functions as a machine to produce new metaphors and maximize the improbability of associations, re-semanticizing the terms through the effect of syntactic relations created. Syntactic grids are constructed as recurrences of embedded phrases and sentences whose parallel structures make up the various textual segments. This double syntactic replication (within

HANGAR 14

A cabeça timbrada do gang das intendências belisca
      a pilotagem dos berros dos grilos
como os auditores-saltimbancos a empoleirarem
os calores dos lavatórios na vibração das ferramentas
de baba
      onde os petiscos dos algozes
parecem os focinhos das taras numa forca
(HIPÓDROMO de balões-DE-LARVAS) AQUI os
domicílios do AGUILHÃO do fogo expõem os
refluxos multicolores na estratosfera dos mediadores
de tempestades

As medulas automáticas dos sofás-icebergs condenam
magicamente
      os açaimes do estômago das palavras
entre os esconsos estrados dos eléctricos-refractários
      onde de uma forma possessiva as
espingardas da claridade bronzeiam (CHAFURDAM)
os harpejos dos espasmos dos fósforos
      que escalam os papos alucinatórios
das sentenças cósmicas
A radiância fortificadora dos estilhaços das enxadas
madrugadoras
      embala as fisionomias aceleradas
dos bichos-satélites
      aqui a mutabilidade faunística
apela aos esboços-temperos do glutão

121

HANGAR 15

      Um rio aceso de tigres infinitos é habitado
pelos noivados exaltados dos lenhadores
      que enlaçam os escombros das rédeas
solares nas fracções persistentes das clepsidras
      trabalhadas desamparadamente
pelos grânulos misteriosos

dos tálamos-relâmpagos aqui as profundezas
decoradoras dos fontanários são vaticinadas
      pelos giros convulsivos dos pirilampos
      como os animais
rastejantes a inscreverem-se nas cisões do repertório
das inter-ilhas
      onde os mapas das emigrações
das sementes parecem cristaleiras autografadas
      pelos saltimbancos das bifurcações lunares
      que encaracolam
os sinfonistas-glosadores dos fogos de artifício

      (MIRADOUROS DOS EQUIPAMENTOS
MUSEOLÓGICOS)

      Os alinhamentos das guilhotinas
das aves adelgaçam a dispersão das bocas das
avalanches
      para fotografarem
      o aprisionamento

131

FIG. 3. Luís Serguilha, *Hangares do Vendaval* (2007), p. 121.
First page of 'Hangar 14'.
FIG. 4. Luís Serguilha, *Hangares do Vendaval* (2007), p. 131.
First page of 'Hangar 15'.

sentences and from sentence to sentence) determines both the logical structure of semantic modifications and the syntactic functions of words in relation to other words, as well as the acoustic repetition of verbal music (Figures 3 and 4).[15] It is the generative genesis of the machine of language, characterized by a recursive and feedback dynamics, which we can observe in the syntax-semantics-syntax circuit: 'o/a/os/as... o/a/os/as... o/a/os/as...' 'de/da/do/das/dos... de/da/do/das/dos... de/da/do/das/dos...'; 'que... que... que...'; 'como... como... como...'; 'para... para... para...'; 'porque... porque... porque...'; 'onde... onde... onde...' 'verb + adverb... verb + adverb... verb + adverb...'; 'noun + adjective... noun + adjective... noun + adjective...'; etc... etc... etc... The music of language extends from sound to meaning, as if the semanteme of each term in its relational dynamics could be apprehended in the particular semantic modulation induced by a unique co-occurrence of random associations. An analysis of the syntactic structures shows that the relational productivity of the connectors (prepositions and conjunctions), when used as a permutative grid linking terms from distant semantic fields, makes it possible to question the referentiality

---

[15]   Luís Serguilha, *Hangares do Vendaval* (Évora: Intensidez, 2007).

of the associated terms and the logical inferences contained in the syntactic scheme that binds them together. The schematic nature of language, that is, its abstract character, becomes materially perceptible: meaning is a function of associations crystallized by use in an inherently unstable and chaotic process of semanticization of sounds into words and of words into phrases and sentences.

The possibility of meaning constitutes the core of the criticism of the discourses with which this textual serialism challenges us and frustrates us, due to the high degree of disjunction to which the semantic expectations that govern the daily uses of the syntactic structures and lexical items found here are subjected. Whether in the direction of orality and aurality, or in the direction of writing as an order of representation in itself, confrontation with the grammatological opacity of language becomes inevitable. The experience of non-meaning contains, at once, the experience of the determination and indetermination of meaning. Faced with the possibility of semantic music in experiencing the conceptual and imagetic fluidity induced by permutations, readers wonder about the origin of this music of meaning. A music that seems to resonate in the brain like a laughter of language itself, suddenly disarmed of its own expectations.

Conventional associations, which guarantee semantic coherence and textual cohesion, prevent the fluctuation and semantic instability caused by chaotic and random recombination of words. From this constellation of probable associations depends a social and political world that is organized as an extension or justification of a particular discursive order. The coherence of language also serves to reproduce the coherence of a world that reproduces itself by resorting to a set of syntactic structures and semantic features through which its meaning is producible and thinkable. By taking an anti-discursive discursive form, these poems make it possible to experience in language the perceptual dimension of meaning, that is, the experience of the unique and hypothetical perceptions constructed through language. Its critique of meaning and reference is its particular mode of production of meaning: treated as algorithms to produce utterances, syntactic structures allow us to perceive the materiality of meaning as an asemic–semic continuum from which particular meanings emerge. The statistical experience of meaning as a discursive and cultural pattern is re-contextualized in a probabilistic horizon of combinatorial potentiality. Those syntactic algorithms enable us to listen to the semantic music of the work.

Selfless, Meaningless

Although fundamentally different in their approaches to literary form, these two bodies of work share a common concern with the computational nature of language, that is, with the generative nature that derives from its recursive and combinatorial properties. While the electronic works by Rui Torres are based on the short form (usually on a template that has less than twenty lines), Luís Serguilha tends to use the long form (from a few dozen to more than a hundred lines), very often in the form of long prose sequences of many pages, as in *Kalahari* (2015).[16] In both cases, the proliferative substitution of signifiers is the driving force of their works.

Rui Torres works with a controlled vocabulary extracted from his source texts and turns a particular poem into a programme for generating further poems. Textual transformations tend to maintain the relative intersection between terms and thus keep the overall configuration of the specific metaphorical constellations in each new iteration. In Serguilha's works the improbable association of signifiers is produced through practices of automatic writing that bring together distant semantic and lexical fields. Almost any sequence of two, three or four words will contain unexpected semantic intersections that prevent semantic interpretation. This deformation implies that they can only be apprehended as parts of a written creature in which the living organism of language has taken over its symbolic and representational function.

Perhaps even more significant is the fact that both forms of textual proliferation provide us with an experience of language emptied out of a language-producing self. Even the enunciated 'I' (the 'I' within the text) is almost entirely absent from the syntactic templates used for programming the permutations, in one case, and from the third person and continuous present tense in long endless sentences, in the other. Both works seem to want to ask the question: what happens when language gives itself up to language either through computer-assisted substitutions of signifiers or through automated unconscious associations of signifiers? Through these different but related means of automating the metaphorical processes of language they virtualize the text and open it up to the inner forces of language — the language creating furnaces in which the powerful action of its genetic code can be observed.

Literary art can be described as a reification of language and discourse, either by processes of imitation and parody that recreate certain uses of language (including literary uses) with intentions of mimetic modelling, or by processes of generation and invention that produce new lexical and syntactic combinations. From these, new voices and perspectives emerge that are internal to the materiality of language and which do not yet exist in the previous repertoire of invented meanings. The emergence of a language-mediated worldview depends on a certain relationship between those two modes of reification — imitative reification and inventive reification. In this relationship, the entangled referentiality of language — its referentiality to the world and its referentiality to language itself — plays itself out in multiple ways.

As a language exercise in the second degree, that is, language conscious of itself as language — abstracted from its action in the social semiotics of the world and in the interior monologue of the self — literary art opens up a space

---

[16] Luís Serguilha, *Kalahari* (Porto: Edições Esgotadas, 2015).

for experimentation within the very motions of language. The automation of this experimentation is one of the consequences of the digitization of languages, that is, of the formalization processes that have made natural languages computationally processable at their multiple levels. Permutation involving distant semantic fields is yet another compositional technique for generating improbable associations. Both practices — either in the digital writing by Rui Torres or in the visceral writing by Luís Serguilha — result in a selfless proliferating language, in which the metaphorical music of meaning is an emergent property of the viral replication of its genetic code.

Blood Evocations:
Subversion, Resistance, and Afterimage
in Ana Luísa Amaral's *Ágora*

Paulo de Medeiros

University of Warwick

> Não se distingue
> a quem pertence a quem
> a mão que evoca o sangue
> dessa ferida
>
> [It's hard to tell
> who it belongs to
> the hand summoning the blood
> from that wound]
>
> Ana Luísa Amaral, *Ágora*[1]

In dark times clear vision is as much needed as it is hard to attain. Our present has surpassed even the direst predictions of Guy Debord in his unfailing analysis of the 'society of spectacle' as one in which commodification had absolutely colonized all of social life so that 'we no longer see anything else; the world we see is the world of the commodity'.[2] Ana Luísa Amaral's *Ágora* (2019) is a forceful intervention in that perverted view of reality that offers us alternatives with which to overthrow such illusions. Its thirty-three poems all engage dialectically with a famous painting, or other form of visual art, from the Western canon and with the biblical text behind them, with two exceptions: in one isolated case, with a classical text, the story of Jason and the Argonauts; in the other, with a historical event, the shipwreck of the French frigate *Méduse* off the coast of Mauritania in 1816. One of the most complex, rich, and probing collections by Ana Luísa Amaral, *Ágora* distinguishes itself from her numerous other works, all complex in their own ways, and even from what I have considered as a central elaboration of her poetics, *A Arte de ser tigre* (2003).[3]

---

[1] Ana Luísa Amaral, 'A dor: a outra fala', *Ágora* (Porto: Assírio & Alvim, 2019), p. 57. I am grateful to Margaret Jull Costa for kindly providing all the translations of the poems by Ana Luísa Amaral, only some of which have been published before.

[2] Guy Debord, *The Society of the Spectacle*, trans. by Ken Knabb (Canberra: The Hobgoblin Press, 2002), p. 13.

[3] Ana Luísa Amaral, *A Arte de ser tigre* (Lisbon: Gótica, 2003). See also the first anthology of Amaral's poems in English, *The Art of Being a Tiger*, trans. by Margaret Jull Costa (Oxford: Aris

One is tempted to view it as expressing a 'Spätstil' (late style), or what would be its 'annunciation' in any case, in the sense that Adorno used it to refer to the later works of Beethoven as 'no longer [...] gather[ing] the landscape, deserted now, and alienated, into an image. [Beethoven] lights it with rays from the fire that is ignited by subjectivity, which breaks out and throws itself against the walls of the work, true to the idea of its dynamism. His late work still remains process, but not as development; rather as a catching fire between the extremes [...]'.[4] But that is another matter that cannot properly be addressed now and I merely want to suggest that we view *Ágora*, not so much as inaugurating a completely new phase in Amaral's work, but as one that gathers much of her strength and quiet rage in a way that is more free and bold than ever.[5] That image of 'fire', evoked by Adorno, is one that has also always been a constant in Amaral's *oeuvre*. Although still operative, it has come to be joined in *Ágora* by an image more insistent, more material even: that of 'blood', which forms arguably the book's most important leitmotif.

Neither subversion, nor resistance is new to Ana Luísa Amaral's poetry. Indeed, it can be said that they have always been at the core of all her poems since the aptly titled first volume, *Minha Senhora de Quê*.[6] Similarly, many of her poems refer to visual images and ekphrasis can also be understood as a recurrent device in her writing. Yet, in *Ágora* we are confronted not only with the fact that the entire book, and not just some of its parts, is made of a series of ekphrastic poems, but that often we are given poems that go far beyond the descriptive and actively interfere with the images. In other words, often the poems create alternate images in a sort of double ekphrasis, with significant consequences both for our understanding of the painting at the base of the poem and of the text at the base of the painting. As a result, as I will want to argue, Amaral produces a series of astonishingly beautiful and powerful images that destabilize the painted images with which they engage and create a kind of afterimage that both reproduces and radically alters the original images. Although it really does not make sense to separate subversion from resistance,

& Phillips / Oxbow Books, 2016). In my 'Introduction' to this volume I adumbrated some of the preoccupations I will be developing here, as I noted that Amaral 'addresses, subverts, and continues the hallowed tradition of Portuguese poetry' while 'not being confined to it' (p. 1). My current analysis will, if anything, reinforce the need to read Amaral beyond the 'national' grid and to recognize how important 'subversion' is to her project, no matter how much that may displease some readers for whom either national compartmentalization is still paramount or for whom 'subversion', no matter how flagrant, is always in need of further explanation, which is another, however subtle, form of denial.

[4]   Theodor W. Adorno, 'Late Style in Beethoven', in *Essays on Music*, trans. by Susan H. Gillepsie (Berkeley and London: University of California Press, 2002), p. 567.

[5]   This brief essay is not the place to engage in any sort of overview of Ana Luísa Amaral's works. I have had occasion to discuss a greater panorama of her work and make appropriate references to the accompanying and ever growing body of criticism in a recent article, 'Beauty, Power, and Desire: Notes on Ana Luísa Amaral's Poetics', *Journal of Romance Studies*, 19.3 (2019), 469–85. Here I would like only to call attention to a seminal essay on Ana Luísa Amaral's work: Rosa Maria Martelo, 'O salto do tigre', in *A Forma Informe: Leituras de Poesia* (Lisbon: Assírio & Alvim, 2010), pp. 264–73.

[6]   Ana Luísa Amaral, *Minha Senhora de Quê* (Lisbon: Fora do Texto, 1990).

and neither can one really grasp the power and effect of the afterimages unless seen in the context of the poems' larger strategies for signification, I want to contemplate each in sequence in order to try to make clear how important, in my view at least, *Ágora* is in the moment we are living through right now, how its appeal to tradition, as well as its subversion of the same tradition[7] are inextricably linked to a project of critique that offers alternatives to the ongoing onslaught on culture, a growing normalization of pain, and a gleeful return to widespread forms of cruelty and appalling inequality thought to have been long ago consigned to the dustbin of history. Hannah Arendt, in the 'Introduction' to her edition of Walter Benjamin's *Illuminations*, denounced the specific relation of tradition to authority as circular and self-perpetuating: 'Insofar as the past has been transmitted as tradition, it possesses authority; insofar as authority presents itself historically, it becomes tradition'.[8] Obviously, readers who prefer to read Amaral's poems strictly as beautiful renditions of classical paintings are within their rights and will still have plenty to delight them. They can just ignore that last poem, 'Prece no Mediterrâneo' [Prayer in the Mediterranean], with which the collection closes and imagine it does not really refer to the thousands of migrants who, in recent times, have died trying to cross over to Europe every year.[9] But then the book's title, *Ágora*, will appear to be some kind of odd and not quite explainable homage to ancient Greece as the birthplace of Western democracy, without reflecting on precisely how that evocation is in itself already a critique of the notions of centre, origin, and an unproblematized citizenship, based on systems of exclusion.

Subversion can take many forms. In the case of *Ágora*, however, the kind of subversion I have in mind aims directly at the root of our social organization, that is, patriarchy. It does so in multiple ways, but most obviously by questioning tradition, either in terms of the authority claimed both from scripture and by hallowed custom as expressed through canonical views of art and history and what usually passes for Western civilization or even Christianity. The methods deployed also are multiple, but chiefly involve both a radical decentring of established norms — what one could imagine as a kind of law underpinning the very way in which we tend to imagine ourselves, as individuals and in our relations to others — and a concomitant inversion of related notions such as origin and foundation, hierarchy, authority, and morality. In this perspective *Ágora* presents a fierce critique of present times, the socio-political cesspool

---

[7]   Lídia Jorge wrote a beautiful commentary on *Ágora*, for the book launch in Lisbon on 9 December 2019, which I had the pleasure to listen to. In it Jorge focuses also on subversion, as she refers to the way in which Ana Luísa Amaral subverts myths without destroying them, a view I share and profit from. At the same time, as I hope to make clear, subversion in *Ágora* goes beyond that to aim at the core of the socio-political institutions and practices which rely on myth precisely to legitimize inequality and oppression.

[8]   Hannah Arendt, 'Introduction', in Walter Benjamin, *Illuminations: Essays and Reflections*, trans. by Harry Zohn (New York: Schocken Books, 2007), p. 38.

[9]   The poem has appeared simultaneously — and with an English translation by Margaret Jull Costa — in the December 2019 issue of the *Journal of Romance Studies*, pp. 323–24.

we have come to be mired in, and of a traditional view of tradition, including the arts, as reproducing, and thus enshrining, the principles of oppression, domination, cruelty, and inequality that seem to rule unchallenged. Granted, none of this is completely new, as those in power have always found ways to justify benefiting from the subjugation of others. What is new, perhaps, at least since the dawn of the Age of Enlightenment, is the extent to which it seems the majority has come to resign itself not only to accept domination, but to view it as somehow pre-ordained.

Beyond a critique of our present times though, *Ágora*, I argue, offers possibilities for re-envisioning tradition and our place in it that resist any such resignation and conformity. Subversion should not be conflated with sedition, even though governments usually do so in their attempt to contain and destroy any kind of reasoned opposition. Likewise, *Ágora* does not present any direct threat to established power. This is not to say that poetry cannot be effective, or that thinking cannot bring about change. The subversion effected by *Ágora* is primarily of a different kind: it is directed first of all to art, to the norms that affect our understanding of tradition and the role of representation, even if, of course, one can never totally separate the realm of art and representation from that of social and political reality. At the beginning of one of her Tanner Lectures, on 'Politics and Knowledge in Nihilistic Times' delivered at Yale University on 23 October 2019, Wendy Brown expressed her purpose thus: 'How to understand and plot possibility within this novel present? For me, paradoxically, apprehending the new often involves wrestling with earlier thinkers who were struggling for a cartography of their own time and that is what I want to do with Max Weber [...]'.[10] In a similar way Amaral also thinks the new and plots possibilities in dialogue with, indeed in a dialectical relationship with, past artists, whether poets or painters. And, just as Brown also prefaced her lecture by characterizing our nihilistic present as a time in which vast populations have been 'cast off as waste [...] without access to what we consider the most basic civilizational elements', so Amaral also starts off her book with a reference to the sacrifice of multitudes of nameless slaves for greed and power: 'O *velo de ouro, aquele!* | ele exclamou | E para o possuir | sacrificou exércitos de escravos | sem altura nem nome [...] [*I must have that golden fleece!* | he cried | And in order to have it | he sacrificed whole armies of slaves | lowly and nameless].[11] Those cast off as waste are also the ones to close off the book, as we are faced with another struggle for life and death in the Mediterranean and some of those ancient goals still hold sway, through eternal greed, renewed xenophobic nationalisms, and the sacrifice of thousands.

---

[10] Wendy Brown, 'Politics and Knowledge in Nihilistic Times: Thinking with Max Weber', Tanner Lectures on Human Values, 23 October 2019, Whitney Humanities Center, Yale University, <https://www.youtube.com/watch?v=nG52tEGghTA> [accessed 24 January 2020].

[11] Amaral, 'O velo de ouro (da outra história)', *Ágora*, p. 9. Unpublished translation by Margaret Jull Costa: 'The Golden Fleece (from that other history)'.

Yet, Amaral chooses to end not with images of doom, no matter how dire the present situation is, but rather with the claim, of those cast off, for their common inheritance in a shared humanity, not just in terms of the peace they would have substituted for the fish and loaves of bread, but in affirming their right to both: 'Em vez de peixes, Senhor, | dai-nos a paz, [...] Mas depois da jangada, | da guerra, do cansaço, | depois dos braços abertos e sonoros, | sabia bem, Senhor, | um pão macio, | e um peixe, pode ser, | do mar | que também é nosso' [Instead of fishes, Lord | give us bread [...] But after the raft, | the war, the tiredness, | after the generous, open arms, | Lord, some fresh bread | would be good | and a little fish, if possible, | from the sea | that is also our sea].[12] Already in the juxtaposition of opening and closing poem one can see a deliberate strategy for rewriting tradition. The present-day refugees are the counterpart of Jason's army of sacrificed slaves, as nameless and powerless as they were, more than two millennia notwithstanding. The continued devastation brought on by the thirst for domination and the greed for power was clearly stated already at the end of the opening poem: 'e outro no seu sonho (ou pesadelo) | repetiu: *Aquele!* | Gritando, o reclamou | E a matança ascendeu' [and someone else in his dream (or nightmare) | said: *I must have it!* | And with a cry, he claimed it | and the numbers killed grew].[13] Yet, instead of merely accepting their fate, the newly dispossessed claim their share in the human legacy, and even specifically in that very Christianity the forces of oppression abusively and perversely claim exclusively for themselves: peace as well as bread and fishes. Even such a simple comparison between the two poems — which form a sort of frame to the book as a whole to both anchor and further decentre it — already points to the simple fact that *Ágora* is as concerned with values as with aesthetic questions; that its compelling and forceful wrestling with tradition is not a rejection of tradition but rather its rescue from the forces of oppression that have incessantly, through the ages and even more so in the present, perverted it to justify and legitimize their domination. Seen thus, *Ágora* is a cry against the immensity of suffering but also a voice lent to the oppressed, to all those silenced across time, and a call not so much for justice even, much less for revenge, but simply for compassion. Seen thus, *Ágora* could be said to be fundamentally about values — and here I am thinking again of Wendy Brown's Tanner Lectures already mentioned. Not the values often taken for granted, or worse, brandished as what would keep civilization from falling into barbarism when all that is really meant is that the image, the empty simulacrum, of those values, is what the minuscule minority in power invokes to exclude all others. Brown reminds us that currently, 'one in eight of our species' live in abject conditions. And Amaral does so by other means as she reflects on Géricault's *The Raft of the Medusa* from c. 1818: 'Era esta então | a terra da promessa, | o espaço de fortuna dos eleitos? [...] Feitas de leite e mel | para os eleitos | e de fel e de sangue | para os | outros' [Was this then |

---

[12]   Amaral, 'Prece no Mediterrâneo', *Ágora*, pp. 137–38.
[13]   Amaral, 'O velo de ouro (da outra história)', *Ágora*, p. 10.

the secret land, | the promised | place of good fortune? [...] Made of milk and honey | for the chosen ones | and of bitter gall and blood | for | the others].[14]

Some of the strategies Amaral deploys in order to subvert not only tradition but our own expectations — which all of us, even if in varying degrees, hold with more or less consciousness of it, immersed in that same tradition — are characteristic of much of her writing: inversion, duplication and repetition but always with a significant shift, so that meaning gets accrued across various layers that never completely annul each other, but rather make it impossible to ever accept simple or categorical interpretations. These strategies themselves also reflect the way that her wrestling with tradition is never just a refusal, or an annulment of, tradition but its critique. This can be seen even at her fiercest, say in the words given to Artemisia Gentileschi — or is it to Judith or to both — as Amaral reflects on Gentileschi's painting *Giuditta che decapita Oloferne* [Judith Slaying Holofernes, *c.* 1612]: 'E fomos muitas a rasgar a carne, | em duas partida, | e a outra: elas e eu em conjunção, | como matéria negra' [And we were many rending our own flesh, | myself split in two, | me and the other woman: all of us | conjoined like dark matter].[15] Throughout *Ágora* we are confronted with multiple decapitations, in a total of five. Three of those appear in sequence and all concern Salome and her request, at her mother's injunction, for the head of St John the Baptist. As for the other two, one refers to Judith and Holofernes, the other to David and Goliath. All scenes of decapitation could be read as emblematic of various forms of subversion, against patriarchy, or against the powerful; but they can also be seen as the reverse, as reinscribing the very law they would appear to contest.

The way in which Amaral uses those scenes and in the utterly complex nexus of relations between each image and the poem that goes with it — or the other way around — and between the various images and poems as a whole — part of the larger whole composed by the book itself — there is much more than ambiguity. For they expose and question — and in that both stand in for, and highlight, the book's project as whole — simplistic notions of tradition and legacy, order and violence, gender and domination, language and image. This complex surrounding decapitation then can be seen as essential to the book's project but is not its centre — or even its most significant node. If anything, it serves to reinforce the book's emphatic contestation of both the notions of centre and origin. One is tempted to regard it as a symptom or a phantom. Georges Didi-Huberman in *The Surviving Image: Phantoms of Time and Time of Phantoms* makes a series of observations which, though primarily directed towards an understanding of Aby Warburg, I would like to lean on:

> Might there not be a time for phantoms, a return of the images, a 'survival' (Nachleben) that is not subject to the model of transmission presupposed

---

[14]   Amaral, 'A terra dos eleitos', *Ágora*, pp. 129–30; Ana Luísa Amaral, 'The land of the chosen people, or sermon on the mount', in *What's In a Name?*, trans. by Margaret Jull Costa (New York: New Directions, 2019), p. 171.

[15]   Amaral, 'A dor: a outra fala', *Ágora*, p. 57. Unpublished translation by Margaret Jull Costa.

by the 'imitation' (Nachahmung) of ancient works by more recent works? Might there not be a time for the memory of images — an obscure game of the repressed and its eternal return — that is not the one proposed by this history of art, by this narrative? [...] Might there not be a time for symptoms in the history of the images of art?[16]

Ágora is a 'Museum of Words' (to use the apt expression of James A. W. Hefferman[17]), but also much more. The way in which Amaral uses the paintings included as part of the book, I would suggest, has nothing to do with 'imitation' and all with that 'time for phantoms', which is also always a form of 'survival' and return. More on this in a moment. For now, I would like to point out how, as Maria Irene Ramalho aptly notes, some of the poems included in *Ágora* also represent a way of looking at Amaral's earlier poems. In a text prepared for the book's launch in Coimbra, 'O lírico e o político' [The lyrical and the political], Ramalho remarks on how some poems from *Ágora* — 'Original Pecado', and 'A leste do paraíso' — had already appeared in an earlier book, *Às vezes o paraíso* from 1998, with no, or few, changes, except of course for the images now attached to them: with regard to the latter Ramalho brings together the addition of the painting, 'The Death of Cain' by Georg Frederick Watts, and what she calls a coda 'que aponta sem piedade para a irremediável solidão do marginalizado. Ana Luísa Amaral escreve Ana Luísa Amaral' [pointing without pity to the hopeless solitude of the marginalized. Ana Luísa Amaral writes Ana Luísa Amaral].[18] If I draw attention to this detail it is to stress how, even if a poem has already appeared, the new context, and very specifically, the addition of the paintings, alters the meaning, so that in a sense they become new poems, or at least, if that seems like too much to claim, we have to see them in a new, different, light. And this raises yet other questions I can only signal to here, such as whether the poem or the image comes first. In one sense, all the paintings predate the poems of course; and the way the book is arranged, readers also see the paintings before the poems; and yet, what readers actually see first is the poem's title so that viewing the painting is always already transformed by the poem, even before the poem is actually read.[19] On the one hand, the changes brought about by the re-writing of the poems are crucial as

---

[16] Georges Didi-Huberman, *The Surviving Image: Phantoms of Time and Time of Phantoms* (University Park: Pennsylvania State University Press, 2017), p. 11.

[17] James A. W. Hefferman, *Museum of Words: The Poetics of Ekphrasis from Homer to Ashberry* (Chicago, IL: University of Chicago Press, 1993). Readers interested further in the subject of ekphrasis might want to start with a classic study, Murray Krieger, *Ekphrasis: The Illusion of the Natural Sign* (Baltimore, MD, and London: Johns Hopkins University Press, 1992). With special relevance to Portuguese poetry, see also a special issue of the journal *eLyra*, 8 (2016) on *A Écfrase na poesia moderna e contemporânea*, <https://elyra.org/index.php/elyra/issue/view/12> [accessed 26 February 2020].

[18] Maria Irene Ramalho, 'O lírico e o político: a propósito de *Ágora*, de Ana Luísa Amaral', unpublished manuscript, courtesy of the author and Ana Luísa Amaral.

[19] Ana Luísa Amaral has noted, in a personal message (25 February 2020), that, for her, the poems came first, and only then the images, which she searched out to fit the poems. This is perhaps obvious in the case of those poems previously published. However, I would maintain, none of that really matters if the actual purpose is to disrupt claims of primacy and originality.

they too not only expand but also subvert the poem's meaning. This is clear, I think, when Amaral adds the final question 'Mas com quem?' [But with whom?] at the end of 'A leste do paraíso' [East of Eden].[20] In the new version, it is not only the painting with its representation of a desolate and lonely death for Cain that changes the hopeful tone of the poem in its 1998 version, but that added last line, which makes it more than clear that even though exile might represent a sort of freedom — and especially the freedom to speak about everything — it also means that there is no one to listen to him. And that is much in keeping with Ágora's mood that focuses on resistance rather than merely relying on hope.

This brings me to another form of subversion enacted by Ágora that has to do with its overwhelming, though not total, focus on the biblical tradition and its foundational role for our society. At first glance it could seem that Amaral — in keeping with her trajectory of the last two decades — would want to question religion so as to subvert its hold on our imaginary and practices. Leaving aside that there would be nothing new in that, I think that Amaral's target is not so much religion — which, in Christianity's particular case, at least, would always involve a radical annulment of inequality coupled with redemption — but rather the uses made of religion, more often than not the violent uses made of religion, in order to perpetuate dominant hierarchies and regimes of social and individual control. One way of looking at this might be to say then that Amaral's Ágora does not aim at subverting religion, but the religious, so that its critique of religion is foremost an exposure of its appropriation by those who would deny it while proclaiming to do so in its own — or God's — name. Consider for instance 'Jacob e o Anjo' and its conclusion in the voice of a Jacob conscious of his equality, when he says, 'A leste do Jordão, | naquele dia | *Olhei a sua face, e não morri:* | *não Deus,* | *mas meu irmão*' [To the east of Jordan, | on that day | *I gazed on his face and did not die:* | *not God's face,* | *but my brother's*].[21] Or, perhaps even clearer, Jesus' quiet but firm accusation of the law's sterility when facing the high priest: 'A voz da lei impressa nesse livro | e aquele dedo erguido | quase a tocar a chama | mas sem ponto de luz | que incendiasse' [The voice of the law printed in that book | and that finger raised | almost touching the flame | but with no spark of light | to light it].[22]

Subversion is what enables resistance. It is only because Jesus in 'O Julgamento' subverts the authority of the written — in a beautiful and telling anachronism, 'printed' — law that he can resist its emptiness, its lack of passion. In a recent lecture, Étienne Balibar reflected on our current situation and what would appear to be a return of religion after claims of wide secularization. In part Balibar has in mind fanaticisms of all stripes and his goal cannot be

---

[20]   Unpublished translation by Margaret Jull Costa.
[21]   Amaral, 'Jacob e o Anjo', *Ágora*, p. 50. 'Jacob and the Angel', unpublished translation by Margaret Jull Costa.
[22]   Amaral, 'O Julgamento', *Ágora*, p. 21. 'The Judgment', unpublished translation by Margaret Jull Costa.

confused with any form of apologia for religion — as neither can Amaral's. Balibar is careful to admit, and I can but follow, that one does not really know what would constitute the 'religious' or even if that which we now witness constitutes in any way a return of the religious: 'we are not in a position to tell whether the religious that "returns" is actually the same as the one that had — only more or less, in reality — "departed", like a return of the repressed. That is to say, we don't know, deep down, what the "religious" is, or indeed whether there is such a thing at all, and under what perspective it can be unified, or even compared'.[23] There is much to take from Balibar's analysis but for the moment I will limit myself to an extrapolation that might be more or less justified: if we cannot really know what constitutes the religious, or if the phenomena we see developing every day are linked with a seeming return of the religious, with various fanaticisms, and a general mistrust of the political, it would seem to follow that at some level there would be a separation between religion and the religious much in the same way as there is a distinction between religion and theology. In very basic terms, and to go back to 'O Julgamento', what is being subverted is not so much religion as the law — the printed law — that would seek its authority in divinity.

Now, this might be not just an utter simplification of the question — and of the poem — but also a basic flawed inference. I realize the risk involved, but would like to try a bit further in the hope of clarifying how the poems go from subversion to resistance — and still come to discuss the question of the afterimage in *Ágora*. Take that title. At first glance it refers to the birth of democracy, to the central space in Athens, in other words to the very foundations of Western civilization, to a past that would have been transmitted through millennia to reach the present. Nothing could be more ironic — and of course in Portuguese its closeness to 'agora' [now], only adds to its irony in my view. If Amaral is intent on decentring and subverting tradition and very specifically patriarchy, choosing that term as the title of the book already inaugurates what I think is the book's fundamental critique of established norms. For, romanticized idealizations aside, the 'place of gathering' from ancient Athens was also a place of fierce exclusion — as women, as well as slaves, were not allowed to partake of the discussions that would take place there, would have no place in the governance of the state, would have no voice. As such, to entertain any notion of the book's title referring to a kind of law that would appear more emancipatory than that proffered by religion, and specifically its Judeo-Christian form, should be checked. Moreover, given that the great majority of the images and poems does refer explicitly to that very Judeo-Christian tradition, and only one goes back to an ancient Greek text, it would be seem abusive to think that *Ágora* would represent the book's project, unless one would be so fanciful as to think that the project, would offer a kind of return to the archaic. Conversely, I would suggest, a rejection of the archaic —

---

[23]   Étienne Balibar, 'Critique in the 21st Century: Political Economy Still, and Religion Again', *Radical Philosophy*, 200 (2016), 11–21 (p. 14).

which is not a dismissal of its holding power by any means — is one of the ways that *Ágora* presents us with a model for resistance. For, even as Amaral reaches deep into the tradition, instead of reproducing it she problematizes it, and offers us alternatives that resist oppression. But irony is not all of it of course. If we are to take the title of the book as signalling democracy at all, then we must also be prepared to understand that the version of democracy thus envisioned can be neither a continuation of the present nor a throwback to the past.

Wendy Brown has often commented on the deteriorating condition of democracy in our society and in her most recent book, *In the Ruins of Liberalism*, she presents a long list of actual acute problems encountered as we have fully entered what she calls — and I can only agree — an 'age of nihilism'. Criticizing the failures of the Left to even understand, let alone counter, the widespread rise of the Right in Western democracies, Brown notes that the Left's narrative 'does not register the intensifying nihilism that challenges truth and transforms traditional morality into weapons of political battle. It does not identify how assaults on constitutional democracy, on racial, gender, and sexual equality, on public education, and on a civil, nonviolent public sphere have all been carried out in the name of both freedom and morality'.[24] In *Ágora* Amaral takes recourse to tradition, to the beauty and power of art, in order to resist the current debasement of the political, which perhaps has even gone beyond the realm of the spectacle and into that of a complete negation of any values at all. One way she does so is by taking recourse in desire, as desire, physical and erotic, but also in general, a desire for life, dignity, and beauty, permeates all of the poems and all the images. I think this is crucial to counteract the onslaught of nihilism, which at root expresses not even wrong, misguided, or cruel or abject forms of desire but the simple yet devastating absence of desire. *Ágora*, however, is far from being some sort of wishful thinking exercise or mere game — well, it is a game of sorts but a deadly serious one.

Neither given to undue joy nor unbridled optimism, Amaral's verses confront us time and again with harsh, though human, realities. Take Salomé in the third of the poems dedicated to her, who both affirms her desire and her violence:

> Quantas vezes te vi | e me surpreendi porque te olhava? | Sentindo a tentação de te espiar | e o desejo de amar | o que não tinha [...] Quantas vezes me vi | pensando no meu crime | e na história dos homens | a julgar-me! | Mas o que eu li | na bandeja do crime | foram os olhos com que tu | me olhavas

> [How often I saw you | and felt surprised to be looking at you. | Feeling the temptation to spy on you | and the desire to love | What I did not have [...] How often I found myself | thinking about my crime | and about the history of men | judging me! | But what I saw | on that crime-laden platter, | were the eyes with which you | looked at me][25]

[24]   Wendy Brown, *In the Ruins of Neoliberalism: The Rise of Antidemocratic Politics in the West* (New York: Columbia University Press, 2019), p. 7.
[25]   Amaral, 'Salomé após o crime', *Ágora*, pp. 41–42. Amaral, 'Salome after the Crime', in *The Art of Being a Tiger*, trans. by Margaret Jull Costa, p. 71.

Without the accompanying image, Andrea Solario's *Salome with the Head of Saint John the Baptist* (c. 1507–09), the poem is intensely beautiful, and violent. With the image, the violence acquires yet another meaning as the crime — and especially the platter of the crime, mentioned — no longer can be read just metaphorically but will always evoke the bloody scene depicted by Solario, with St John's head, held by the hand of the executioner, still dripping blood into the platter that will carry it. Yet, as gruesome as the visual depiction may be, it also is beautiful — indeed, one could say that it derives much of its power from the contrast between the seeming innocent beauty of Salome and the shock of the severed head being presented to her as she holds the platter to receive it. The poem in turn renders this if anything more starkly inasmuch as its discourse is above all a lover's discourse — which exceeds the biblical narrative of course. If anything, it was Salome's mother who was the lover and who directed her daughter to request the gruesome gift from King Herod, so as to protect her own lover who was threatened by Saint John. Leaving that behind — not completely of course as the preceding poem, by replacing the name of Salome with that of her mother, Herodias, makes clear — the poem achieves another level of signification as we are made to see Salome not just as the attractive, seductive dancer, but also as a cruel lover capable of murder. Having in mind Brown's reflection on nihilism and the present's abandonment of values, indeed the weaponizing of truth as she puts it, or even, I would say, the annulment of truth altogether, one can read Amaral's poem as going against such debasement of values and their substitution with the empty husk of a pretence of morality. Her Salome is fully aware of her deed and does not shirk responsibility. It is not as if the poem ignores the nature of the crime or the consequences of murder. One could say that the figure of Salome thus presented to us is complex beyond her youth, beauty, and the image passed down by tradition, one that we may even find guilty — the history of men's judgment, as she puts it — but one that is also deeply human and knows both love and desire, and who assumes agency in the act of killing as well as of seeing, instead of only being seen.

Strictly speaking the most visible effect of subversion, both in terms of method as well as result, is the displacement of the very notion of the primacy of origins. Another, that would demand an essay on its own, concerns the absence, the rendering invisible of certain central images such as that of the Crucifixion. Banning those from *Ágora* of course might have a reverse effect, their absence pointing even more stridently to their presence as constitutive of Christianity. Be that as it may be, it seems to me that such effacement or avoidance combines a refusal to entertain any kind of teleological reading with a refusal, or denial, of the notion of sacrifice. To read through all the violence of history, even in such a condensed format as the pages between the covers of this book, is to recognize how human life is so expendable and how an emphasis on sacrifice, docility, and submission, at least outside of the realm of the divine, often just end up further enabling oppression. However, to pursue further the question of displacement of origins: Greek myth, 'the other story', is juxtaposed to the biblical narrative not so much to make them equivalent — besides that opening poem on Jason and the Golden Fleece, classical tradition is untouched — but so as to make us see that in the beginning there might have been the word but the word is always plural, that indeed what has constituted us is that very plurality of narratives that present times, by and by, would either restrict, forbid, or annihilate. Displacement becomes much more than a gesture or device to assume the possibility of resistance as the sequence of poems continuously effects displacement upon displacement, whether it be the various sources of myth, the dialectic between New and Old Testament, or that between images and words. A process that culminates in that final displacement, the clear voicing of a common humanity, claiming its rights, not any kind of charity, in the book's final poem, 'Prece no Mediterrâneo', that actualizes the previous one, 'A terra dos eleitos', and reverses the opening one with its army of sacrificed slaves. That irruption of the present, in all of its grim reality at the closing of the book might come as a bit of a surprise, especially for readers tending to favour aestheticist readings to political ones. And yet, that ending was prepared from the very beginning, indeed, one could say, it is that which gives proper meaning to the beginning, not in any teleological sense, but because of the way in which it forces readers to confront the immediate urgency of a crisis that, rather than being new, has been repeating itself throughout time. The one significant change between the last and the first poems does not reside in the shift it effects as it displaces the hero, Jason, or however he will have been named through the centuries, with the nameless 'rabble' hanging on for survival. Nor in the substitution of the promised loaves and fishes for the gold conquered at such high cost. Rather, the one significant shift, in my view, pertains to the replacement of the docility of the slaves with the affirmation of the right of the refugees to be viewed as human. It is as such that one could see *Ágora* as inscribing itself in the tradition of the oppressed of which Walter Benjamin spoke in his celebrated eighth thesis: 'The tradition of the oppressed teaches us that the "emergency situation" in which we live is the rule'.[26]

If subversion is not to be mired in an endless loop of self-congratulatory illusion, art and beauty serving then primarily to while away our bourgeois evenings and lick the wounds of our bad conscience, it must offer realistic alternatives for the perpetuation of inequality and domination. For Benjamin, that would entail assuming a different perspective on history and actively working towards radical change: 'Then we shall clearly realize that it is our task to bring about a real state of emergency, and this will improve our position in the struggle against Fascism'.[27] Obviously this is not what *Ágora* does or should do. Art that would assume itself as a form of (partisan) politics would

[26]   Walter Benjamin, 'Theses on the Philosophy of History', in *Illuminations*, p. 257.
[27]   Benjamin, p. 257.

in itself be a 'catastrophe', as Adorno reminded us.[28] Besides, so much has changed in the past three-quarters of a century, that even if we wanted to heed Benjamin's injunction it would have to take on different forms. The current rise of authoritarian figures, accompanied by a blatant disregard for the truth and more and more cruelty, bears resemblance to Fascism but is also something else.[29] The last utopian movement in Portugal, expressed with the 1974 Revolution, was quickly quashed by the then incipient forces of neoliberalism that would soon come to dominate Europe. But even those, one could say, have had their day and are in the process of being replaced by something as yet ill-defined but even more violent that would not only co-opt any resistance but would actually commodify it as well. Culture cannot, and never could, escape the very forces it would seek to wrestle with. Amaral is certainly very much aware of this and I want briefly to refer to her take on the story of Jacob and the Angel shortly, but first I want to call attention to the penultimate poem, 'Revelação'. Amaral plays on the dual meaning of the title, both disclosure, revealing, unveiling, that is seeing, and apocalypse as the end of the world. In a sense, this poem closes the book in as much as it closes the wrestling with biblical tradition, contrasting 'comfort' with 'exile' (desterro): 'se os céus aqui: de paz, | e os vossos: livro inteiro | ventos apocalípticos | e nus | saudando tão modernos | cavaleiros' [if my skies are so peaceful | while yours: the very Book | winds apocalyptic | and naked | greeting these very modern | horsemen].[30] As much as Amaral refuses any apocalyptic tone, it is significant that she chooses not to close with that disclosure, but rather to shift her aim to the immediate crisis, that of the refugees struggling to reach Europe, and our immediate present. That jarring bursting forth of the present, a sort of coda to the rest of the book, forces us to see that which so many of us would rather not see at all because it reminds us, if not of our complicity in systematic oppression, then of our impotence to go against it.

The book's cover shows what appears to be a detail — to view the full painting one must see both the cover and the back cover as one — of Bartholomeus Breenbergh's *Jacob Wrestling with the Angel* (c. 1639). This painting, however, does not have a corresponding poem — except if one considers the book as a whole, that is. Inside, the poem that corresponds to the biblical story of Jacob fighting all night long with an angel, 'Jacob e o Anjo', dialogues with one of Léon Bonnat's paintings of the same scene (c. 1876). Without entertaining any pretension at fully addressing the problematics raised by the poem and the paintings, or the biblical text itself (Genesis 32), I want to focus on how this scene has been marked by ambiguity from the start: was it a man, was it an

---

[28]   Theodor W. Adorno, 'Commitment', in *Notes to Literature*, vol. II, trans. by Shierry Weber Nicholsen (New York: Columbia University Press, 2019), p. 76.

[29]   By now there is a growing corpus of discussion surrounding this. As a starting point interested readers may look up Enzo Traverso, *The New Faces of Fascism: Populism and the Far-Right*, trans. by David Broder (London and New York: Verso, 2019).

[30]   Amaral, 'Revelação', *Ágora*, p. 133. 'Revelations', unpublished translation by Margaret Jull Costa.

Angel, or God? The text is far from clear and Jacob himself is said to exclaim afterwards that he has 'seen God face to face'. One point to keep in mind is that even though the Angel would have been far superior in force to Jacob, Jacob is able to hold on to him until morning, when the Angel says that Jacob is actually prevailing and asks to be released. The poem capitalizes on this. Also, looking through the history of the frequent pictorial representations of that scene it is immediately apparent that often the Angel is depicted either in a gender-ambiguous or even feminine fashion. Even though usually the Angel is represented as considerably larger than Jacob, Breenbergh's Angel, but for the wings, appears if anything even smaller or less robust than Jacob, which is already significant, especially as Amaral is intent on presenting Jacob and the Angel as equals: '*Saber das suas asas e das minhas,* | *que as suas pernas junto a mim caminham* | *e o rio que nos separa:* | *um rio igual?* | *A leste do Jordão* | *naquele dia* | *Olhei a sua face, e não morri:* | *Não Deus,* | *mas meu irmão*' [*Aware of his wings and mine,* | *of his legs walking alongside mine* | *and the river separating us:* | *the same river?* | To the east of Jordan, | on that day | *I gazed on his face and did not die:* | *not God's face,* | *but my brother's*].[31]

Bonnat made various paintings and sketches of this scene and the one chosen by Amaral is both the least usual of those I know as well as the most fascinating and modern. In the various versions there is always an ambiguity at play, as to whether the two figures' embrace is that of two wrestlers or two lovers. Usually the Angel is clearly the larger of the two figures and, if not dominant, capable of becoming so if he wishes. While both figures are represented as muscular and beautiful, the Angel is more so than Jacob. The painting Amaral has chosen, although readily identifiable as belonging with the others, has significant differences. For one, the Angel though somewhat larger is not as towering and is shown even more firmly in the grip of Jacob than the others. Also, what separates the Angel from Jacob here is much more the skin colour, the Angel's radiant white in contrast to the darker tints used for Jacob. But the most radical difference between this version and others, I would argue, is that both Jacob and the Angel are faceless. Besides resisting the traditional hierarchy pertaining between Angel and human, Amaral also offers the possibility to resist simple binary gender identifications, continuing and enlarging on the work of Bonnat.[32] In doing so the poem challenges us to see Bonnat's art differently. And seeing Bonnat's painting makes us read the poem differently, adding more layers of meaning to what in any case is already a rich and daring text: '*A percepção sentida por Jacob* | *de que aquele que ali estava* | *não ser só divino,* | *mas feito de matéria tão divina e igual* | *à sua própria carne*' [*Jacob sensed* | *that the being before him* | *was not only divine* | *but made of*

---

[31]   Amaral, 'Jacob e o Anjo', *Ágora*, pp. 49–50. 'Jacob and the Angel', unpublished translation by Margaret Jull Costa.
[32]   For a detailed consideration of the imbrications between a politics of gender and poetics in the work of Ana Luísa Amaral see the essay by Marinela Freitas in this issue.

matter both divine and the same | as his own flesh].[33] Again, I must think of Didi-Huberman's questions already mentioned, concerning a survival or return of images, always phantasmatic, that would have no space for 'imitation', of a time for images as symptoms. This would surely necessitate more reflection. For the moment I would just like to suggest that we consider the possibility of those images as chosen by Amaral, beyond what they already signify — in their specific context and in their place in the history of art — as being symptomatic of a resistance to the dogmas of their respective times, and to the co-optation of art to further drive separating lines between people. How to miss the call for solidarity when the divine is rendered on equal footing to the human, the spiritual to the very flesh, and Jacob recognizes in the Angel, not so much the face of God, but his brother?

What image Jacob does have of the Angel, then, is at the crux of the biblical passage as well as of our interpretations. When, through the hand of Amaral, Jacob affirms having seen, not the face of God, but his brother, what image do we see? Bonnat's one experiment, with the faceless figures — to my mind the one version that manages to surpass its time and inscribe itself firmly into modernity — is a challenging one. And, even if that is not how we might have imagined the face of God ourselves were we to be so tempted, it remains with us. In that sense it too can be said to return, that is resist the dissolution of time, and impose itself on any subsequent attempts we might make to imagine the faces of the Angel or of God. Looking back at other representations of that scene, including the ones by Bonnat himself, will have been forever altered. A simple definition of 'afterimage' explains it as '[a] visual sensation which remains after the stimulus that gave rise to it ceases'.[34] The effect of Bonnat's faceless Angel, I suggest, is then the creation of an afterimage that not only remains after the disappearance of the stimulus, but changes and superimposes itself on previous images. This too is what I would like to claim is an effect of Amaral's poems in their dialectical relation with the paintings. As I already said, as part of a questioning and subversion of origins — a reading of the pair of poems and images of the Annunciation, or of the series of temptations in the Garden of Eden, would leave no doubt as to Amaral's subversive reach — the images evoked by the poems themselves also work on our sensibility so as to create yet another kind of afterimage. A figurative afterimage perhaps, rather than a strictly material one — but then, even in the field of optics, afterimages are, as far as I can understand it, always a product of some photochemical activity in the retina that we may feel but cannot directly watch, not beyond its effects that is. To pursue this line to its logical conclusion is to see *Ágora*, not so

---

[33] Amaral, 'Jacob e o Anjo', *Ágora*, p. 49.
[34] That is the definition provided by the *Oxford English Dictionary*. The earliest recorded example given is attributed to Lady Morgan's *Italy* from 1821 and it significantly already refers specifically to painting and its effects: 'Probably the model lay in the painter's heart, drawn by love's "own sweet and cunning hand" and some beauty, "loveliest in tears", lent a type to the young imagination, which no after-image of loveliness could ever efface'. Online edition, accessed [26 February 2020].

much as a collection of various ekphrastic poems — which it obviously is — and also not just as a kind of continuously renewed double image that lives from the intersection of poem and painting, but as a strong, seductive, and compelling afterimage of our own society that questions our assumptions as much as it directs us towards an affirmation of dignity based on a common humanity. In these cruel and nihilistic times that is a force, a resistance, that may, just may, provide us with the kind of strength, 'um agasalho | interno | para o coração' [a warm coat | to wrap | around the heart],[35] necessary to overcome inertia, our own base instincts, and the ghoulish spirit of tyranny ever more thirsty for blood.

---

[35] Amaral, 'Madalena: Rectificar a História', *Ágora*, p. 89. 'Mary Magdalene: setting history to rights', unpublished translation by Margaret Jull Costa.

Last Will(s):
Withdrawal and Resistance
in the Poetry of José Miguel Silva[1]

PEDRO EIRAS

*Instituto de Literatura Comparada Margarida Losa /
Faculdade de Letras da Universidade do Porto*

Outlining the Problem, 1: Resistance

Born in 1969, José Miguel Silva published his first book, *O Sino de Areia* [The Sand Clock], in 1999, and his sixth poetry volume, *Erros Individuais* [Individual Errors], in 2010. From Camões we learn that poetry can sing 'Erros meus, má fortuna, amor ardente' [My errors, ill fortune, and ardent love]; however, in José Miguel Silva's poetry, the 'errors' seem to lie not so much in the written object as in the very act of writing. I transcribe the opening poem of 'Volta ao Mundo' [Around the World], a sequence that constitutes the 'Preamble', or the first part of *Erros Individuais*:

> Voltemos a isto, à contagem dos erros
> na soma do mundo, à impotência do riso
> contra tudo o que não sabemos mudar:
> a morte, o egoísmo, o levadiço coração
> humano. Porque não há mais nada (ok,
> há o amor — vai-te foder) e no mercado
> do juízo a catequese está em alta.
> Regressemos à toada desta fábrica de luz
> defeituosa, intermitente como a vida.
> Se não há melhor emprego para a culpa
> e os domingos custam dias a passar.[2]

> [Let's go back to this, counting the errors
> in the sum of the world, to the impotence of laughter
> against all things that we don't know how to change:
> death, selfishness, the drawbridge of the human
> heart. For there is nothing else (ok,
> there is love — go fuck yourself) and in the market
> of good sense Sunday school is booming.

---

[1] Translated from the Portuguese by Elena Galvão and Isabel Pedro dos Santos. This article was written as part of research carried out in the ILCML, R&D Unit financed by National Funds through FCT – Fundação para a Ciência e a Tecnologia [Portuguese Foundation for Science and Technology] (UIDP/00500/2020).

[2] José Miguel Silva, *Erros Individuais* (Lisbon: Relógio d'Água, 2010), p. 11.

> Let's go back to the murmur of this factory of light,
> defective, intermittent like life.
> Since there's no better employment for guilt
> and Sundays drag on for days.]

There is calculated negativity in this presentation of a writing project between the dysphoric title and the proposition as 'counting the errors'. The incipit 'Let's go back to this' shows how the five previous books were also 'the impotence of laughter | against all things that we don't know how to change'; we are therefore *in medias* (or *ultimas*) *res*, faced with a negative balance with retrospective effects: this poetry, like all previous poetry, is nothing but a 'murmur of this factory of light, | defective'. However, this declaration of impotence in the very first poem lends the whole book a dysphoric tone, the announcement of an inability. Resisting this diagnosis, there is only love as an indisputable argument — 'amor ardente' [ardent love] in Camões was also a source of anguish, as much as 'Erros' [errors] and 'má fortuna' [ill fortune] — and the resigned decision to write, despite everything.

What can one expect from a book whose opening poem is a metatextual denunciation of the uselessness of all poetry and which admits with difficulty that it is worth writing only when 'não há melhor emprego para a culpa | e os domingos custam dias a passar' [there's no better employment for guilt | and Sundays drag on for days]? The book's first question is, therefore, why write *Erros Individuais*, and why did the author write *O Sino de Areia*, *Ulisses Já Não Mora Aqui* [Ulysses Doesn't Live Here Any More], *Movimentos no Escuro* [Motions in the Dark]?

In his inaugural lecture at the *Collège de France* (2007), Antoine Compagnon starts by asking 'What is literature for?'[3] and points out that this question arises only when the social function of literature is called into question; in other words, the question itself is a symptom of a general malaise. In his historical analysis, which often looks like an apology or a manifesto, he then lists the possible functions of literature. José Miguel Silva seems to be elaborating on the same question: why write a poetry book if writing is but repeating errors? He also looks at the ways in which contemporary literature, painting, and cinema have become ready-to-use commodities (i.e., cultural industry, as Adorno would put it) or an empty celebration of a culture submissive to the status quo, and therefore he does indeed believe that such conservative forms must be 'undermined'. However, *Erros Individuais* does not believe in any epic model of iconoclasm: it despises power-serving art narratives and is suspicious of the power of any wrecking counter-narrative. 'Volta ao Mundo' rigorously fine-tunes the scale of this twofold negative: *neither* acceptance of the world *nor* a sheer rejection of it that might save poetry from the insidiousness of power. Consequently, the question *what is literature for?* or *why write a book of poetry?*

---

[3] Antoine Compagnon, *La Littérature, pour quoi faire?* (Paris: Fayard, 2007).

should not lead to an apologetic manifesto but rather to an anguished work of criticism (or of despair).

The second poem in 'Volta ao Mundo' seeks to explain the reasons why writing may nevertheless be worthwhile:

> Mas na raia do discurso
> o movimento, reconhece, é mais alegre
> e nada passa sem pagar alguma taxa
> de sentido. [...]
> Além disso, quem na poesia busca
> o acicate dum lamento ou esconjuro,
> tem direito certamente à inestética
> dum 'foda-se' canoro quando a sanha
> do martelo lhe rebenta no verniz,
> escurecendo com o dedo o mundo todo.[4]

> [But at the border of discourse
> movement, admit it, is more joyful
> and nothing goes through without paying some tax
> on meaning. [...]
> Besides, those who search in poetry for
> the spur of a lament or an exorcism,
> are certainly entitled to the unaesthetics
> of a loud 'fuck it' when the wrath
> of the hammer strikes their varnish,
> darkening the whole world with its finger.]

After the intense negativity of the first poem, this experience of affirmation seems to now be threatened. The arguments for literature are but a supplement of joy, some meaning, at least the ability to lament, the 'unaesthetics | of a loud "fuck it"', the ultimate possibility of a destructive strike of the (Nietzschean? avant-garde?) hammer, 'darkening the whole world with its finger'. These merits of the poem sound fragile: the only possible meaning is just 'some tax', and, although apocalyptic, the exorcism seems to be singular, short-lived, insufficient. Yet, surprisingly, the author decides to write.

Within the disquiet of these judgements, after the desistance thesis and the writing-after-all antithesis, some synthesis would be expected to emerge at the end of 'Volta ao Mundo'. The third poem describes the arrival of Spring:

> as coisas vão e vêm, e de novo
>
> se levanta o mês de Março nesta era
> da ironia, com seus truques estafados
> e promessas desfolhantes. Juntamente,
> tudo passa e tudo volta, mas diverso.
>
> Só por isso, justamente, tem piada
> estar aqui, abrir os olhos, conferir

---

4   José Miguel Silva, *Erros Individuais*, p. 12.

> ainda e sempre, na vitrina da manhã,
> a produção da Primavera.[5]
>
> [things come and go, and again
>
> the month of March rises in this era
> of irony, with its tired old tricks
> and unleafing promises. Together,
> all things go and return, though different.
>
> Exactly for that alone it's funny
> to be here, open one's eyes, check
> now again and forever, in the showcase of the morning,
> the production of Spring.]

Naturally, the month of March cannot invalidate the 'era | of irony'; but the sight of things 'in the showcase of the morning' seems to be reason enough to go and commit some more 'individual errors', to go back to counting. Even though in minor, ironic terms, with an unpretentious 'it's funny | to be here', the question 'why write?' finally gets a (fragile) answer: in order to 'check | now again and forever, in the showcase of the morning, | the production of Spring'.

Interlude, 1: The Uselessness of Poetry

When *Erros Individuais* argues that writing is merely acknowledging the 'impotence of laughter | against all things that we don't know how to change', it takes away from poetry the possibility of intervening in the world. Responding to the 'Poetry and Resistance' survey organized by the LyraCompoetics international research network, José Miguel Silva answers questions such as 'Is poetry a form of resistance? Always, by default? Or only in specific social, political, cultural contexts?' with painful scepticism:

> um poeta não pode deixar de declarar guerra a todo o género de clichés: verbais, desde logo, mas também políticos, filosóficos, psicológicos, etc. Mas sem nunca perder de vista que, numa era de comunicação de massas, essa sua guerra é tão desigual, e portanto tão caricata, como a guerra que uma sardinha (zangada) decidisse mover a um petroleiro (de aço).[6]
>
> [a poet cannot but declare war on all sorts of clichés: verbal clichés, firstly, but also political, philosophical, psychological, etc. Without ever losing sight of the fact that, in times of mass communication, this war is as unequal and ludicrous as that of an (angry) sardine declaring war on a (steel) oil tanker.]

Paradoxically, even before the impotence of laughter, 'a poet *cannot but* declare war' (my emphasis) on all clichés: 'verbal, firstly, but also political,

---

[5] José Miguel Silva, *Erros Individuais*, p. 13.
[6] José Miguel Silva, answer to the survey 'Poesia e resistência', org. by Joana Matos Frias, Pedro Eiras and Rosa Maria Martelo; see <http://ilcml.com/blog/inquerito-poesia-e-resistencia-portugal> [accessed 20 April 2019].

philosophical, psychological'. Despite its scepticism, this answer signals the ethical and poetical imperative of engaging in combat against the thick tanker of the world.

Such combat requires an awareness of the uses of language: first, there is fight against verbal cliché. In her essay 'Tensões e implicações entre poesia e resistência na contemporaneidade portuguesa' [Tensions and implications between poetry and resistance in Portuguese contemporaneity], Rosa Maria Martelo argues that poetry allows for a 'sabotagem dos discursos dominantes [...] pela derivação crítica' [sabotaging of dominant discourses [...] by means of critical derivation];[7] after evoking Silva's dysphoric response to the 'Poetry and Resistance' survey, Rosa Maria Martelo notes: 'Mesmo assim, há, na poesia, um pensamento que assenta sempre na liberdade que resiste [...]. Essa liberdade não é alienável porque nela se concentra aquela margem de indeterminado sem a qual não nos restariam senão perigosas sociedades orwellianas, de controlo e opressão. Desumanizadas, em suma' [nonetheless, there is in poetry a kind of thinking which is always founded on freedom that resists [...].This freedom is inalienable because it focuses on that margin of indeterminacy without which we would be left with nothing but dangerous Orwellian societies of control and oppression. Dehumanized, that is];[8] and we know how the dystopian societies which Orwell denounces are based on the imposition of a single, universal 'Newspeak'.

If poetry is worthwhile, if laughter is not totally impotent, then perhaps the work of resistance starts with that awareness of language, the invention of one's own language against the language of imposed consensus, an invention of possibilities for debate. Such is the difficulty of a poem: it can neither be subsumed into a collective, acritical language nor remain cryptic, incommunicative, silent. As Jean-Luc Nancy writes,

> the 'resistance' of poetry could be described as language's resistance to its own infinity [...]: the indefinite expansion of language, its constitutive chatter [...] belongs to the order of endless approximation; its other side is exactitude without remainder. This other side is inscribed within language itself; it too is constitutive of language, and this is also the reason why poetry's resistance can just as easily end in silence (which is 'exact' only by default) as become caught in the trap of chatter and measurelessness.[9]

A difficult balance: how to write a poem that neither reproduces insidious, unconscious Newspeak languages nor becomes deleted within the exactitude of silence or of non-communication? How do you achieve a poem that is language-in-process in resistance to language itself?

---

[7]   Rosa Maria Martelo, 'Tensões e implicações entre poesia e resistência na contemporaneidade portuguesa' *eLyra*, 2 (2013), p. 49; see <www.elyra.org/index.php/elyra/article/view/25> [accessed 14 April 2019].

[8]   Rosa Maria Martelo, 'Tensões e implicações...', pp. 49–50.

[9]   Jean-Luc Nancy, *Multiple Arts: The Muses II*, ed. by Simon Sparks, trans. by Leslie Hill (Stanford, CA: Stanford University Press, 2006), p. 21.

Outlining the Problem, 2: Retreat

One year after *Erros Individuais*, José Miguel Silva published a short volume titled *Serém, 24 de Março*. Focusing on the issue of resistance, I am particularly interested in the second part of the book, 'Serém', a sequence of nine poems that narrates the 'escape' of the poetical subject and his companion 'para o interior' [to the hinterland],[10] moving to a house away from the city. I transcribe some excerpts from 'Com o pé no acelerador' [Foot down on the accelerator]:

> O vulcão do paraíso expele vendas de ouropel.
> São os últimos dias do crescimento económico,
> essa mecânica utopia burguesa, os conselheiros
> deitam água na fervura do melhor e o futuro
> retrocede tão depressa que se instala no passado.
> [...]
>
> Resultado: pomo-nos a conjurar uma patética
> fuga para o interior, onde a lixo-dependência
> menos pesa e nos podemos dar ao luxo de ser
> pobres. Assim, vira-se à esquerda na nacional 1,
> depois de novo à esquerda e por fim à direita.
>
> [...]
> Sem descendência, nem vocação para sofrer
> de borla, vou antes tratar (como é que se diz?)
> do meu jardim, solicitado por narcisos, malmequeres,
> amores-perfeitos — em suma: florinhas amorais.
> Então adeus. E boa sorte. Qualquer coisa, telefonem.[11]

> [The volcano of paradise expels tinsel sales.
> These are the final days of economic growth,
> that mechanical bourgeois utopia, advisers
> pour water on the fire of the best one and the future
> recedes so fast that it settles down into the past.
> [...]
>
> Consequence: we start to plot a pathetic
> escape to the hinterland, where waste-dependence
> carries less weight and where we can afford the luxury of being
> poor. Therefore, you turn left onto the N1,
> then again left and finally right.
> [...]
>
> With no offspring and no vocation to suffer
> for free, I will instead tend (how do you say this?)
> to my garden, solicited by narcissi, daisies,
> forget-me-nots — in sum: amoral little flowers.
> Good bye then. And good luck. Call me if you need me.]

[10] José Miguel Silva, *Serém, 24 de Março* (Lisbon: Averno, 2011), p. 25.
[11] José Miguel Silva, *Serém, 24 de Março*, pp. 25–26.

The poem opens with an apocalyptic tone: the 'final days of economic growth', dominated by spectacular, fake, unsustainable capitalism. Although these premises could lead to the development of a poem of resistance and struggle, the result is exactly the opposite: 'Consequence: we start to plot a pathetic | escape to the hinterland, where waste-dependence | carries less weight and where we can afford the luxury of being | poor'. Instead of a dispute, which both consider to be useless, the subject and his companion opt for an 'escape', which is, incidentally, painful and 'pathetic'.

It may be productive to read this 'retreat-to-the-countryside' topic in the light of some paradigmatic models belonging to the Portuguese imaginary. In Eça de Queirós's novel *A Cidade e as Serras* [*The City and the Mountains*], Jacinto's decision to move to Tormes signals the fact that he has lost all hope in the city and indeed in any revolutionary project; as in the case of José Miguel Silva, this is explicitly about escaping: 'Penso, *logo fujo!*' [I think, *therefore I flee*], says Jacinto.[12] Alexandre Herculano's retreat to the Vale de Lobos estate (Santarém) in the 1860s was seen by a number of authors as desistance from political struggles, a sign of scepticism. Ramalho Ortigão, for example, distinguishes the Herculano who was a fighter, an active, much-needed person, from the defeatist Herculano that he later became at Vale de Lobos, 'rescind[indo] a sacrossanta escritura da responsabilidade universal [...]; desdiz[endo] com o seu repentino silêncio todas as afirmações da sua grande voz' [withdrawing from the sacrosanct scripture of universal responsibility [...]; betraying all the previous statements of his great voice with his sudden silence].[13] His individual 'exile' was to have catastrophic collective consequences: 'A isolação de Herculano no remanso estéril do diletantismo bucólico comprometeu o destino mental de uma geração inteira' [Herculano's seclusion in the barren backwater of bucolic dilettantism damaged the mental destiny of a whole generation].[14]

Herculano's retreat was seen as a loss of faith in any change in society; and, although he continued to publish *Opúsculos* till the end of his life, his physical move to the Vale de Lobos coincided with the abandonment of literary writing (which in his case was also a fundamental political, social, and cultural statement). Conversely, the retreat of Queirós's character Jacinto to Tormes is defined as healing, rebirth, the development of a tranquil hedonism, which even includes some progressive initiatives for social development: setting up a school, a library, a crèche, a pharmacy, even a room 'com projeções de lanterna mágica' [with magic lantern projections][15] dedicated to the instruction of the villagers. However, these forms of local intervention could hardly bring to fruition the revolutionary projects proposed in the past by the 'Geração de '70'

---

[12]   Eça de Queirós, *A Cidade e as Serras* (Lisbon: Livros do Brasil, 2014), p. 153.
[13]   Ramalho Ortigão, *As Farpas*, tomo 3: *Os Indivíduos* (Lisbon: David Corazzi — Editor, 1887), p. 7; see <https://issuu.com/carlosduarte45/docs/ramalho_ortig_o_-_as_farpas__v.3> [accessed 22 April 2019]
[14]   Ramalho Ortigão, *As Farpas...*, p. 8.
[15]   Eça de Queirós, *A Cidade e as Serras*, p. 207.

[the generation of the 1870s]: the price for Jacinto's choice is the abandonment of a comprehensive project.

The key problems addressed in José Miguel Silva's poetry include global-scale issues: capitalist exploitation of the workforce, ecological disasters, and conflicts between nations have long ceased to be localized conflicts at country level and have become generalized world-scale problems. In this respect, Ulrich Beck proposes a 'Copernican Turn 2.0', i.e., abandoning a model of thought centred around nations and choosing a cosmopolitan model centred around global risks and threats, as well as global solutions.[16]

One may find merit in Jacinto's late nineteenth-century initiatives at Tormes, but they are certainly not enough if we consider the scale of the problems that face us at the beginning of the twenty-first century, when 'the future | goes back so fast that it settles down into the past'. The closing lines of José Miguel Silva's poem are intentionally cold, as if hiding genuine despair: 'With no offspring and no vocation to suffer | for free, I will instead tend (how do you say this?) | to my garden'. This echoes Candide's last sentence in Voltaire's *Candide* (1759): disillusioned with optimism, neither accepting nor fighting civilization, sheltered in his garden's retreat, tending to his own 'amoral little flowers', the persona in José Miguel Silva's poem is able to depart, not without irony, with a seemingly casual 'Good-bye then. And good luck. Call me if you need me'.

Irony is, properly speaking, self-irony. 'Sinopse', the closing poem in *Serém, 24 de Março*, reads:

> Nem martelo nem bigorna, como sempre
> desejei: as tardes à janela, sem vizinhos nem
> ardis, a injustiça reduzida ao mecanismo
> natural da bicharada, o lavradio do amor
> a tempo inteiro.
>   Só me falta, para tudo
> proteger em cobardia, uma campânula
> de cego na cabeça, aprender a fechar olhos
> e ouvidos ao avanço hertziano da desdita.
> Então serei feliz e integral como um cadáver.[17]

> [Neither a hammer nor an anvil, as I have always
> wished for: afternoons at the window, no neighbours nor
> traps, injustice reduced to the natural mechanism
> of animals, the arable land of love
> full time.
>   I only lack, for everything
> to be protected under cowardice, a blindman's
> bell-jar on my head, and learning how to close my eyes
> and ears to the Hertzian advance of fate.
> Then I shall be happy and whole as a dead body.]

---

[16]   Ulrich Beck, *The Metamorphosis of the World: How Climate Change is Transforming our Concept of the World* (Cambridge & Malden, MA: Polity Press, 2017).
[17]   José Miguel Silva, *Serém, 24 de Março*, p. 36.

The almost cold detachment suggested in other poems is here undone by irony. Against the fake 'paradise' of 'economic growth', this poem seeks to retrieve the most perfect, contemplative, natural, amorous idyll; however, underneath this reencountered paradise, the final lines uncover 'cowardice', blindness, 'fate', and the following balance: 'Then I shall be happy and whole as a dead body.' Any point of comparison with Jacinto or Candide is ruled out; Queirós's and Voltaire's heroes looked upon their gardens as a true Eden or the ultimate refuge, but it always was a vital space. In contrast, in Silva's unsettling lines, only death is the perfect solution.

Interlude, 2: The Usefulness of Poetry

Let me now go back to *Erros Individuais*, part III, titled 'Vozes Apanhadas do Chão na Igreja de San Miniato al Monte' [Voices picked up from the church floor in San Miniato al Monte]: five poems in the first person, testimonies from dead people buried in this Florentine church. These people include a burglar, an actor who has fallen into oblivion, a taxi driver, in a word, the dispossessed[18] who are now left with only a voice, a protestation of hopes forever unfulfilled. The following are some excerpts from the third poem, or dramatic monologue:

> Eu sempre acreditei na aventura. Aos dez anos
> lia o Verne e o Salgari, figurando a volta ao mundo
> [...]
> Comprei um táxi com
> dinheiro emprestado. Iniciei-me nisso a que chamam
> ganhar a vida. Durante trinta anos não saí desta cidade
> [...] E pensar que fiz quilómetros bastantes
> para dar dezoito voltas ao planeta do fracasso,
> e outras tantas neste túmulo de raiva e desconsolo.[19]

> [I have always believed in adventure. At ten
> I used to read Verne and Salgari, and imagine travelling around the world
> [...]
> I bought a taxi with
> borrowed money. I began doing what they call
> earning a living. For thirty years I did not leave this city
> [...] Just think I travelled enough miles
> to go round the planet of failure eighteen times,
> and as many again in this tomb of anger and dismay.]

What is the power of poetry, what can poetry do on behalf of this phantasmagorical voice whose lament goes on forever? There is no place for any compensation because the enunciator is dead. The past tense has a tragic and irredeemable character; even François Villon's 'Ballad of the Hanged Men'

---

[18]   Cf. José Miguel Silva, *Erros Individuais*, p. 21; and Pedro Eiras, *Um Certo Pudor Tardio: Ensaio sobre os 'poetas sem qualidades'* (Porto: Afrontamento, 2011), *passim*.
[19]   José Miguel Silva, *Erros Individuais*, p. 53.

(1489) started from a theological narrative that allowed for the judgement of souls, a spiritual compensation for bodily suffering, divine pardon — 'De notre mal personne ne s'en rie; | Mais priez Dieu que tous nous veuille absoudre!' [Let no one mock our sorry company, | But pray to God that He forgive us all];[20] but this worldview is radically absent from Silva's poetry. However, the voices 'picked up from the church floor' continue to speak to those who visit the church (or who read the poetry volume) and ask: 'Reflecti, vós que passais, na minha história' [You passers by, reflect upon my story].[21] If the deadman's life is irreversibly over, the poem can at least address readers, call upon their empathy; powerlessness in the face of the dead can become the possibility of action for the living.

In her reading of *Movimentos no Escuro*, Joana Matos Frias shows how José Miguel Silva's poetry invokes the torturers and the tortured, the powerful and the dispossessed, and the bad faith of those who believe themselves to be beyond barbarism. Although this exposure will never be able to erase the horrors of the twentieth and twenty-first centuries, it can at least reach contemporary readers, who are directly summoned and interpellated:

> o desconforto que estes versos de imediato provocam no leitor [...] deriva directamente do modo como [...] o poeta consegue 'infectar' o leitor [...] e com isso gerar empatia e torná-lo também uma consciência responsável. Quer dizer: lá onde o leitor sempre manteve, apesar de tudo, uma distância bastante confortável perante a enunciação poética, cria-se agora um vínculo ético — de base interlocutiva — que implica a partilha da consciência infeliz perante o mal-estar da civilização[22]

> [the discomfort that these lines immediately create in the reader [...] stems directly from the way in which [...] the poet manages to 'infect' the reader [...] and thus generate empathy and transform him/her into a responsible consciousness. In other words: there where the reader has always kept, in spite of all, a fairly comfortable distance vis-à-vis poetic enunciation, there is now an ethical bond of an interlocutory nature which includes a shared sorry awareness of the malaise of civilization]

This ethical summoning of the reader may again be found in a distant example. In *Frames of War*, Judith Butler reads *Poems from Guantánamo*, an edition of the very few poems by prisoners that were not destroyed by the US Department of Defense, and comments: 'even though neither the image nor the poetry can free anyone from prison, or stop a bomb or, indeed, reverse the course of the war, they nevertheless do provide the conditions for breaking out of the quotidian acceptance of war and for a more generalized horror and

---

[20] François Villon, *Villon's Epitaph (Ballade of the Hanged Men)*, trans. by Richard Wilbur (2013); see <https://hudsonreview.com/2013/02/villons-epitaph-ballade-of-the-hanged-men/#.XZOZZkZKjIU> [accessed 1 October 2019].

[21] José Miguel Silva, *Erros Individuais*, p. 52.

[22] Joana Matos Frias, *Repto, Rapto (alguns ensaios)* (Porto: Afrontamento, 2014), pp. 101–02.

outrage that will support and impel calls for justice and an end to violence'.[23] Again, what is the power of poetry, or what can poetry do? It cannot prevent the torture inflicted from happening, sealed as it is in the definitive simple past, or immediately change the conditions of an ongoing war; but it can interpellate readers and challenge that 'quotidian acceptance of war', calling for justice and for 'an end to violence' in an urgent future. What can poetry do? Judith Butler responds with firm enthusiasm:

> The poems clearly have political consequences — emerging from scenes of extraordinary subjugation, they remain proof of stubborn life, vulnerable, overwhelmed, their own and not their own, dispossessed, enraged, and perspicacious. As a network of transitive affects, the poems — their writing and their dissemination — are critical acts of resistance, insurgent interpretations, incendiary acts that somehow, incredibly, live through the violence they oppose, even if we do not yet know in what ways such lives will survive.[24]

The enthusiasm of these statements is in contrast with the dysphoric tone of Silva's words; in addition, there are numerous obvious differences between the poetry written by living men who resist at Guantánamo and the voices of the dead in Florence as imagined by a twenty-first-century Portuguese poet. However, there is in both cases a possibility of resistance through the writing of poems, the acknowledgement of past horror, and also the 'incendiary acts' of bringing to the readers the voice of the muted, a censured, fragile, though insurgent narrative.

Outlining the Problem, 3: Testament

Seven years after *Erros Individuais* and six years after *Serém, 24 de Março*, José Miguel Silva published his *Últimos Poemas* [Last Poems]. The title suggests that the poet is renouncing writing poetry forever, and the book's first section, 'Pastéis que sobraram da festa e seria uma pena deitar fora' [Pastries left over from the party and which it would be a pity to throw away],[25] introduces a provocative tone of nonchalance. The whole book is written from an *in ultimas res* perspective, the perspective of one who desists, articulating despair and renunciation. The first poem, 'Lamento e exortação' [Lament and exhortation] reads as follows:

> Que chegámos demasiado tarde ao coreto
> da vida para sonhos e cantigas de libertação
> revulsionária, percebemo-lo aos vinte anos;
> [...]
> Resta-nos perder a última ilusão: a de que haja
> ainda espaço nesta feira popular da mediocracia
> para uma escrita que não seja celebração

---

[23] Judith Butler, *Frames of War: When Is Life Grievable?* (London & New York: Verso, 2016), p. 11.
[24] Judith Butler, *Frames of War*, p. 62.
[25] José Miguel Silva, *Últimos Poemas* (Lisbon: Averno, 2017).

do estridente carrossel publicitário,
[...]
Quando percebermos também isto, saberemos
que a Gloriosa Era da Literatura Ocidental
chegou ao fim, derretida [...]
[...] pelo aquecimento da sandice
global, que não viemos aqui para tentar
reanimar o moribundo, mas alegrar um velório.[26]

[That we arrived too late at the bandstand
of life for dreams and liberation songs of
revulsionary liberation, we understood it in our twenties;
[...]
We still have to lose our last illusion: that there is
still room in this fairground of mediocracy
for writing other than celebration
of the strident carousel of advertisement,
[...]
When we understand this too, we will know
that the Glorious Era of Western Literature
has come to an end, melted [...]
[...] by the warming
of global insanity, that we have not come here to try
and resuscitate the dying one, but rather to brighten up a wake.]

This is not just a metatextual poem which theoretically reaffirms the impotence of poetry at large; it also spells out the project of this *Últimos Poemas* volume: 'to lose our last illusion: that there is | still room in this fairground of mediocracy | for writing'. Writing this book shows that there is no place for poetry anymore, which amounts to a farewell (while writing at the service of 'the strident carousel of advertisement' is steadily thriving). The (fragile though positive) opening balance of *Erros Individuais*, which had justified writing, is now denied. Same question, opposite answer.

In the reference to the 'Glorious Era of Western Literature | [...] melted [...] | by the warming | of global insanity', the issue of the death of literature (or of poetry?) coincides with the issue of ecological disasters in the Anthropocene period, a very rare topic in contemporary Portuguese poetry, albeit particularly poignant in José Miguel Silva. I can only quote some brief excerpts from the last poem in the book, 'Fim' [The End]: the end of the book, of poetry, but also the end of ecosystems. This disillusioned text describes the destruction of 'a nossa casa natural' [our natural home] by a 'sociopatia de narcisos | viciados em picões de dopamina', 'amealh[ando] promessas | de crescer eternamente' [sociopathy of narcissi | addicted to huge dopamine peaks', 'stockpiling promises | of eternal growth] and 'destru[indo] o mundo por dinheiro' [destroying the world for money],[27] leading to the collapse of natural systems: 'o carbono cumulava-se

---

[26]   José Miguel Silva, *Últimos Poemas*, p. 7.
[27]   José Miguel Silva, *Últimos Poemas*, p. 40.

em medusas | de dióxido marinho, rabiscava | "cataclismo" no azul dos festivais | e o metano libertado da Sibéria | preparava o seu discurso de vitória' [carbon accumulated in medusozoans | of marine dioxide, scribbled | 'cataclysm' upon the blue of festivals | and the methane released in Siberia | prepared its victory speech].[28]

The concluding words in *Últimos Poemas* leave no alternative: 'só podíamos seguir | o planograma do genoma e perecer' [we could only follow | the genome planogram, and perish].[29] What can poetry do then? — and, metatextually, what can this book's poetry do? If it is too late now to prevent the end of the world and if poetry has always been impotent 'against all things that we don't know how to change', this last page can only issue a death certificate and refuse to 'brighten up a wake', saying no more.

After *Últimos Poemas*, no other volume of poetry by José Miguel Silva was published; it was probably a genuine farewell. But the author has not stopped publishing texts in his blog — *Achaques e Remoques* <https://eumeswill. wordpress.com/>, although at an irregular, sporadic pace. Generally, these texts are not written by him, but rather transcribed from other authors' works (Gail Tverberg — to whom the last poem in *Últimos Poemas* is dedicated — Tim Morgan, Norman Pagett, Robert Sapolsky, among others). They cover a wide range of topics: from world economic crises to the annihilation of critical thinking, from global warming to the extinction of animal species, from humankind's unsustainable growth to the depletion of fossil fuels. Although these texts are not written by José Miguel Silva, the fact that he quotes them in his blog shows that he shares their worldview. In this essay I can now only add some new questions: why does one give up poetry while continuing to publish prose texts? If poetry is impotent, what kind of resistance becomes possible through a blog? Why does prose still provide the opportunity for a form of combat which poetry has now lost?

(But has it indeed?)

Coda

In a collection of interviews conducted by C. J. Polychroniou, after listing the political, social, economic, and ecological issues of the twenty-first century, Noam Chomsky argues that, in spite of everything, 'We enjoy an unusual legacy of freedom and rights left to us by predecessors who did not give up', which enables us to invest 'in direct activism and pressures in support of significant policy choices, in building viable and effective community organizations, revitalizing the labor movement, and also in the political arena, from school boards to state legislatures'.[30] At the end of the last interview, he considers the

---

[28]   José Miguel Silva, *Últimos Poemas*, p. 41.
[29]   José Miguel Silva, *Últimos Poemas*, p. 42.
[30]   Noam Chomsky and C. J. Polychroniou, *Optimism over Despair: On Capitalism, Empire, and Social Change* (Chicago, IL: Haymarket Books, 2017).

future of humanity:

> We have two choices. We can be pessimistic, give up, and help ensure that the worst will happen. Or we can be optimistic, grasp the opportunities that surely exist, and maybe help make the world a better place. Not much of a choice.[31]

We may agree or disagree with Chomsky (thus confirming the possibility of debate, a fundamental 'legacy of freedom'); we may consider optimism to be dangerously conservative and believe that only informed pessimism will be able to save us; or, on the contrary, we may describe the incapacitating consequences of pessimism and create a strategic, empowering optimism.

However, irrespective of the stand we take, I believe that José Miguel Silva's pessimism is valuable in that it helps us reflect on the threats of our time, the balance of political projects, the function of both poetry and prose, the decision to be silent. Noam Chomsky and José Miguel Silva seem to share the same diagnosis of the most pressing issues of our day; against the background of such an exact agreement, it becomes particularly challenging to ponder the merits and demerits of optimistic and pessimistic narratives. Perhaps — although I cannot develop this intuition on this occasion — pessimism is also a form of resistance, one that is capable of keeping close watch in times of terror.

---

[31] Noam Chomsky and C. J. Polychroniou, *Optimism over Despair.*

'Neither Man nor Woman':
Ana Luísa Amaral's *Queerful* Poetics[1]

MARINELA FREITAS

Universidade do Porto

Nem homem nem mulher,
nem gente nem criança,
mas tudo, e ainda o resto.
do éter e do ar,
da água e fogo, eu sou diferente.

[Neither man nor woman,
neither human nor child,
but everything, and more besides.
I am quite other
than the ether and the air,
than fire and water.][2]

In 2008, Ana Luísa Amaral wrote a playful poem called 'Manifesto Anti-Poetisa' [Anti-Poetess Manifesto], dedicated to Maria Irene Ramalho, who was the first literary critic to write about her poetry, back in 1989, in an article called 'O Sexo dos Poetas: a propósito de uma nova voz na poesia portuguesa' [The Sex of the Poets: Concerning a New Voice in Portuguese Poetry]. In that article, Ramalho raved about Amaral's poetical novelty urging for some publishing house to take a chance on the author, who by now had her first book of poems ready — *Minha Senhora de Quê* [Milady of Me] — but no publisher yet. Ramalho also argued that she would refrain from calling Amaral a 'poetisa' [poetess] because that word was too often associated with what literary critics considered to be minor poets, turning difference into inequality. And Amaral's new voice was indeed different, but not minor. As Ramalho writes: 'Atenta à complexidade do seu existir público e privado, individual e social, e atenta às linguagens em que se diz esse existir, esta é uma voz que **se re-conhece** de poeta — e de mulher' [Conscious of a private and public existence, of an individual and social one, conscious of the languages available to express that existence, this is a voice that **re-cognizes itself** as the voice of a poet — and of a woman].[3]

[1]   This article was written as part of research carried out in the ILCML, R&D Unit financed by National Funds through FCT – Fundação para a Ciência e a Tecnologia [Portuguese Foundation for Science and Technology] (UIDP/00500/2020).
[2]   Ana Luísa Amaral, *Próspero Morreu: Poema em Acto* (Lisbon: Caminho, 2011), p. 29. All English translations of Amaral's poems are by Margaret Jull Costa. Some of the translations are yet unpublished and were kindly provided by the translator, to whom I am especially grateful.
[3]   Maria Irene Ramalho de Sousa Santos, 'O Sexo dos Poetas: a propósito de uma nova voz na poesia

It should be noted that there are two grammatical forms to designate someone who writes poetry in Portuguese — *o poeta* [poet] and *a poetisa* [poetess]. *Poeta* is always used for men, although it can be used to refer to women if preceded by a feminine article ('a/uma poeta'). *Poetisa*, however, is never used for male authors, only for female ones. Since Portuguese is a language with strong grammatical agreement, with a wider variety of gender suffixes than English, *poetisa* is less heavily marked than 'poetess' in terms of its pejorative connotation, as Ramalho shows in that article.[4] However, it still conveys gendered assumptions about poetry and its worth. On the one hand, *poetisa* is often associated with sentimental or love poetry written by women, which might partly explain why many female authors prefer to use *a poeta* (still female, but closer to the canonically validated male term). The only known exception, gender-wise, is the one mentioned by Maria Irene Ramalho, in 'O Sexo dos Poetas', when referring to the anecdote about Teixeira de Pascoaes having called António Nobre 'a nossa maior poetisa' [our greatest poetess].[5] Pascoaes's intention was clearly derogatory, because he used the female form to say that Nobre was a minor poet (only great among women), while at the same time hinting at the poet's homosexuality. On the other hand, *poetisa* may also be applied to signal difference, as in the subversive reclaiming of the suffix made by feminist writers in the 1960s and 1970s, such as Maria Teresa Horta, stressing the centrality of the feminine in their writing. Thus, both 'a poetisa' and 'a poeta' are in a certain sense marked as exceptions, by the excess of femininity semantically attached to them.

Ana Luísa Amaral, who would later co-write with Maria Irene Ramalho a long essay on 'the sex of the texts', entitled 'Sobre a Escrita Feminina' [On Female Writing] (1997), offered her 'Anti-Poetess Manifesto' to Ramalho as an in-joke about their discussion around the cultural meaning ascribed to the word 'poetisa'. In the poem, Amaral uses parody to denounce sexual difference embedded in language by playing with the word 'poet' and its grammatical limits in the Portuguese language. And because in Portuguese there is no neutral 'it' to do away with the question of genderization — as in Emily Dickinson's famous opening line 'This is a Poet — It is that — ', Amaral jestingly offers her own take on this grammatical conundrum:

> MANIFESTO ANTI-POETISA
> Mais fácil é 'a poet — it is that — ',
> que a gramática nossa o não permite

---

portuguesa', *Via Latina* (1989/90), 122–24 (p. 123). Except where indicated, all non-literary translations are my own.

[4] For 'poetess' as an exception in the English language, see Santos, 'O Sexo dos Poetas', pp. 122–24 (p. 123). For a further discussion of this topic, see Ana Luísa Amaral and Marinela Freitas, 'Sorcerers, Prodigies and Meteors: Emily Dickinson's Reception in Portugal', in *The International Reception of Emily Dickinson*, ed. by Domhnall Mitchell and Maria Stuart (London and New York: Continuum, 2009), pp. 127–36 (p. 128).

[5] 'O Sexo dos Poetas', pp. 122–24 (p. 122).

> e precisa dois gumes do estilete
> — o que implicará sempre mais limite.
> Mas, caso a regra for bem aplicada
> (invertendo-se os termos da excepção),
> porque não ler 'poeta', feminino,
> e masculino: ... *vide* conclusão?
> [...]
>
> [ANTI-POETESS MANIFESTO
> How much easier it is to say 'a poet — it is that — '
> which our grammar does not allow
> requiring instead a double-edged sword
> — which will always imply a certain limit.
> But were the rule to be properly applied
> (inverting the terms of exceptions),
> why not read *poeta* as feminine,
> *and* masculine:... *vide* conclusion?]

And the conclusion follows logically, in the last stanza of the poem:

> E na ausência de final dourado,
> tal como na ausência de terceto,
> a **conclusão**: nem homem, nem mulher,
> ou então: a 'poeta' e o 'poeto'.[6]
>
> [And in the absence of a golden ending,
> as in the absence of a tercet,
> the **conclusion**: neither man, nor woman,
> or: *poeta* and *poeto*.]

Amaral's solution comes in the form of a witty transgression: she marks the masculine as an exception instead of the feminine, by endowing it with an excess of masculinity. To do so, Amaral not only uses the traditional definite articles 'a' and 'o' to signal the feminine and the masculine — 'a "poeta" e o "poeto"' — but she also disrupts the nominal inflection that marks the noun by adding the suffix 'o' to 'poeta' (a neutral word in Latin), double-marking it as masculine: '"o poeto"'. The result is that the feminine becomes less gendered, and more neutral by comparison, thus being elevated to a higher stature.

Years later, Ana Luísa Amaral would go back to this line 'nem homem, nem mulher' [neither man, nor woman], rewriting it in her 2011 play, *Próspero Morreu* [*Prospero Died*], this time making it powerfully queer. In Amaral's long dramatic poem, which uses, among others, Shakespeare's *The Tempest* as intertext,[7] Penelope is puzzled by Ariel's identity, and when she asks for clarification, Ariel answers by claiming difference and suggesting an identity even more fluid than the one ascribed by Shakespeare:

---

[6]   Ana Luísa Amaral, 'Manifesto Anti-Poetisa', *Diacrítica*, 22.3 (2008), 157–58.
[7]   Other intertexts are the Greek myths of Theseus and Penelope, as well as Camões's lyrical poetry.

ARIEL   Nem homem nem mulher,
nem gente nem criança,
mas tudo, e ainda o resto.
do éter e do ar,
da água e fogo, eu sou diferente.[8]

[ARIEL   Neither man nor woman,
neither human nor child,
but everything, and more besides.
I am quite other
than the ether and the air,
than fire and water.]

In this case, the expression 'e ainda o resto' [and more besides] points to a meaning outside the boundaries of 'man' and 'woman', an identity that is felt beyond the limits of language. A difference, an otherness, that pushes the boundaries of the possible, exposing the inadequacies of language to articulate it. The line 'Mas tudo, e ainda o resto' [but everything, and more besides] questions and denaturalizes language, pointing to the unthought, the unsaid, what resists being categorized, what is not or cannot be expressed through language — 'the queer remainder', as Noreen Giffney would call it.[9] Or, in the words of Ana Luísa Amaral: 'o reconhecimento de que a linguagem é o espaço de excesso do nosso discurso, sempre ameaçado pelo hegemónico, seja ele cultural, universal ou nacional' [the recognition that language is the space of excess of our discourse, always threatened by the hegemonic, be it cultural, universal or national].[10] In a certain sense, we could say that Amaral's poetry disobeys the rule and goes beyond it, activating the excess, the rest, the 'remainder', rescuing what has been excluded or silenced in hegemonic discourses. She practises a 'rule-breaking creativity' or a 'rule-dissolving creativity', pushing the boundaries of language, expanding and reconfiguring the space of existence, either by subverting it — mining, deforming and destroying it — or by transgressing it, incessantly crossing and re-crossing its limits.[11]

By subverting the traditional balance of gendered assumptions about poetry and creating transgressive or fluid identities, Ana Luísa Amaral reminds us to think differently, in the sense of expansion rather than reduction (which homogenizes and excludes). As Donna Haraway puts it, '[t]he evidence is building of a need for a theory of "difference" whose geometries, paradigms,

---

[8]   Amaral, *Próspero Morreu*, p. 29.

[9]   Noreen Giffney, 'Introduction: The "Q" Word', *The Ashgate Research Companion to Queer Theory*, ed. by Noreen Giffney and Michael O'Rourke (Burlington, VT: Ashgate, 2009), pp. 1–13 (p. 8).

[10]   Ana Luísa Amaral, *Arder a Palavra e Outros Incêndios* (Lisbon: Relógio d'Água, 2017), p. 86.

[11]   For further information on 'the remainder' in language and a 'rule-breaking creativity' or 'rule-dissolving creativity', see Jean-Jacques Lecercle, *The Violence of Language* (London: Routledge, 1990), pp. 11, 49; on 'transgression', see Michel Foucault, 'A Preface to Transgression', in *Language, Counter-Memory, Practice: Selected Essays and Interviews by Michel Foucault*, ed. by Donald F. Bouchard, trans. by Donald F. Bouchard and Sherry Simon (Ithaca, NY: Cornell University Press, 1997), pp. 29–52 (pp. 33, 34).

and logics break out of binaries, dialectics, and nature/culture models of any kind'; otherwise, says Haraway, 'threes will always reduce to twos, which quickly become lonely ones in the vanguard. And no one learns to count to four. These things matter politically'.[12] The political power of Amaral's poetry lies precisely in the way it instructs us to think differently, by questioning the intellectual tradition grounded in the number 'two' underlying Cartesian binary thinking, which reduces the world by establishing violent hierarchies.

In Amaral's lyrical texts, two literary strategies unsettle these hierarchies: the transvestism of the voice and the creation of queer identities. The space of transvestism is the space of the enactment or appropriation of the 'masculine', when Amaral uses male personas and masculine voices spanning centuries and traditions. These male positionings populate her books more explicitly from *E Muitos os Caminhos* [And Many the Ways] (1995) to *Ágora* [Agora] (2019), and are a creative device to subvert and explore the complex negotiations between male and female, self and other, reality and fiction.[13] The space of queerization is accessed when Amaral articulates queer voices or themes, exploring the intersection between both female and male voices, deconstructing dichotomies, disorganizing hegemonic assumptions about sex, gender and sexuality, and resisting categorization through queer transgressions. This takes place most notably in works such as *Se Eu Fosse um Intervalo* [If I Were an Interval] (2009) and *Ara* (2013), but it can also be found in poems scattered across Amaral's many books.

Amaral's poetry has always dealt with the idea of the creation of multiple voices (her 2011 book is, precisely, called *Vozes* [Voices]) and that proliferation of accents, echoes and tones adds a dramatic quality to her diction that is quite peculiar. As the poet writes in the very Pessoan poem 'O Drama Em Gente: A Outra Fala' [Dramatis Personae: Enter Another Voice], from her book *Escuro* (2014), 'O lume que as sustenta, | a estas vozes, | é mais de dentro, e eu não o sei dizer' [The fire that sustains | those voices | comes from within, and I have no words for that fire], reads the poem, 'Mas sempre deste tempo | é o lume que as prende, a estas vozes, | e ao prendê-las as solta | sobre o tempo —' [But it always belongs to this time, | the fire that binds those voices, | and in binding releases them | into time —].[14] Those 'inner waves', as the poet also calls them, bring new perspectives, new fluid or 'transvestistic voices' that allow Amaral, as a writer, to occupy the place of the Other, to (re)create the figure of others,

---

[12] Donna J. Haraway, *Simians, Cyborgs, and Women: The Reinvention of Nature* (London: Free Association Books, 1991), p. 129.

[13] I am loosely using the concept of 'literary transvestism' advanced by Madeleine Kahn, in the sense that 'transvestism' can be used as a literary strategy and metaphor for talking about the 'demands and constraints of gendered imaginations and gendered voices' through the enactment of different gender roles. See Madeleine Kahn, *Narrative Transvestism: Rhetoric and Gender in the Eighteenth-Century English Novel* (Ithaca, NY, and London: Cornell University Press, 1991), p. 8.

[14] Ana Luísa Amaral, *What's in a Name*, trans. by Margaret Jull Costa (New York: New Directions, 2019), pp. 102–03.

thus becoming and (re)creating new Selves.[15] This difficult but necessary task, usually linked to empathy and love in Amaral's work, is at the basis of 'Gramáticas do Olhar' [Grammars of Looking], a poem from *A Arte de Ser Tigre* [The Art of Being a Tiger] (2003):

> Cruzar olhares será tarefa fácil,
> mas não trocar de olhar:
>
> Em foco: um outro ponto, do avesso,
> em avesso: outra luz,
> outra paisagem
>
> Como de um outro azul,
> um brilho outro,
> um céu rasgado a nuvens
> de outra cor
>
> Cruzar olhares será tarefa breve,
> trocar de olhar: uma forma de pôr
> em palco de deserto, antes miragem:
> agora uma viagem
> sem regresso
>
> — que a troca:
> irreversível:
>
> Uma forma de excesso devolvido
> ao espaço inabitado
> por igual
>
> Cruzar olhares: tarefa curta.
> (A outra:
> a mais gramatical
> forma de amar)
>
> [Exchanging glances may be an easy task,
> but not exchanging ways of looking:
>
> To be precise: another place, inside out,
> upside down: another light,
> another landscape
>
> As if it were another blue,
> another glow,
> a sky streaked with clouds
> of another colour
>
> Exchanging glances may be a trivial task,
> exchanging ways of looking: a way
> of putting a desert on stage, or rather a mirage:
> now become a journey
> from which there's no return

[15] Cf. Ben Sifuentes-Jáuregui, *Transvestism, Masculinity, and Latin American Literature: Genders Share Flesh* (New York: Palgrave, 2002), p. 3.

> — for that exchange once made
> is irreversible:
>
> A form of excess restored
> to an equally uninhabited
> space
>
> Exchanging glances: a minor task
> (The other:
> the most grammatical
> way of loving)][16]

To exchange ways of looking is to inhabit 'another place', 'another landscape', seeing things in 'another light' — 'inside out' or 'upside down', dramatized 'on stage' or imagined in a 'mirage' — but always 'a journey | from which there's no return'. To access the space of the Other is to erase oneself and access the excess of another life, a process which will change the self irreversibly. The courage to do so — to imagine what others feel and feel with them and for them[17] — is 'the most grammatical | way of loving'. A similar idea is expressed in the most lyrical passage of *Próspero Morreu*, when Caliban and Ariadne exchange ways of looking as a testament to their love:

CALIBAN	Aí, nesse lugar,
	entrarei nos teus olhos e neles pousarei o meu olhar.
ARIADNE	Entrarás nos meus olhos e neles pousarás o teu olhar.
	E eu irei por teus olhos e neles brilhará a luz do meu olhar.
CALIBAN	Entrarás nos meus olhos e neles brilhará a luz do teu olhar.
	Então, verás o mundo com meus olhos
	e eu, com os teus, contemplarei o mundo.
[CALIBAN	There, in that place
	I will enter your eyes and in them place my gaze.
ARIADNE	You will enter my eyes and in them place your gaze.
	And I will see through your eyes and in them will shine the
	light of my gaze.
CALIBAN	You will enter my eyes and in them will shine the light of
	your gaze.
	Then you will see the world with my eyes
	And I, with yours, will contemplate the world.][18]

This ability to see the world through the eyes of the Other — be it for love, empathy, or a desire to understand — is also at the basis of many of the transvestistic voices Amaral creates. Generally speaking, the male voices explored by the poet are either canonical or historical figures: Amaral writes

---

[16]   Ana Luísa Amaral, *Inversos: Poesia, 1990–2010* (Lisbon: Dom Quixote, 2010), p. 429.

[17]   As Sara Ahmed puts it, '[a]ll of these forms of fellow-feeling involve fantasy: one can "feel for" or "feel with" others, but this depends on how I "imagine" the other already feels. So "feeling with" or "feeling for" does not mean a suspension of "feeling about": *one feels with or for others only insofar as one feels "about" their feelings in the first place.*' Sara Ahmed, *The Cultural Politics of Emotion*, 2nd edn (Edinburgh: Edinburgh University Press, 2014), p. 41 n. 9.

[18]   Amaral, *Próspero Morreu*, p. 33.

poems posing as the poets Dante Alighieri and Luís Vaz de Camões, in her books *E Muitos os Caminhos* (1995) and *A Génese do Amor* [The Genesis of Love] (2005);[19] she impersonates biblical figures such as Jacob, David, Jesus Christ and Saint Paul in *Às Vezes o Paraíso* [Sometimes Paradise] (1998) and *Ágora* (2019);[20] she gives voice, in *Escuro* [Darkness] (2014) to the pioneer Prince Henry the Navigator (in 'Promontório' [Promontory]) or even to the mythological giant Adamastor (in 'Adamastor'), although she also (re)creates anonymous male lyrical subjects such as the soldier from Pessoa's poem 'O Menino da Sua Mãe' [His Mother's Little Boy] (in 'A Voz' [Voice]) or a pageboy (in 'O Retrato' [Portrait]).[21]

Amaral even creates a male alter ego, called Aldo Mathias, whose words she uses twice as epigraph in *A Arte de Ser Tigre* (2003). Amaral's careful construction of this fictional male author is so accurate that she goes as far as to describe him physically — 'um homem alto e magro, sem bigode e de chapéu' [a tall, slender man, no moustache, with a hat] — and to write him a biography: he is a Romanian author, of Jewish and Italian descent, born in 1909.[22] As a young college student of Ethics and Philosophy at the University of Bucharest, he becomes friends with Eugene Ionesco and Mircea Eliade, but during the Nazi occupation of Romania, Mathias is forbidden to teach at the university and is persecuted. He flees to Roussillon, where he befriends Samuel Beckett and joins the French Resistance. He is thought to have written two unpublished collections of short stories and an unfinished novel (whose title is a line taken from one of Amaral's poems), but at the time of his death only some essays and fragments have survived. The portrait of the artist in times of war fits Amaral reflections on love in that book, since Aldo Mathias's words — created by the poet — are a testimony to both the nightmare and the paradise which can be living and loving. As Amaral explains, in her book of essays *Arder a Palavra e Outros Incêndios* [Burning the Word and Other Fires]: 'inventei-o para legitimar essas mesmas reflexões, a partir de um lugar que não era o meu, de um tempo que eu não havia habitado, de uma voz que me não pertencia' [I invented him to legitimate those very same reflections, from a space which was not my own, from a time which I had not inhabited, from a voice which did not belong to me].[23]

[19] For Dante, see '...de uma noite de verão' and 'Dante responde a Beatriz' (Amaral, *Inversos*, pp. 219, 467); and for Camões, see 'Camões fala a Petrarca', 'Camões fala a Natércia', 'Diálogo entre Camões e Natércia', 'Camões fala outra vez a Natércia', 'Fala Camões mais uma vez', 'Última meditação de Camões (I) and (II)' (Amaral, *Inversos*, pp. 461, 462, 468, 475, 477, 478–81).

[20] For Jacob, see 'XVI Monólogo (diz Jacob a Raquel)' (Amaral, *Inversos*, p. 323) and 'Jacob e o Anjo', in Ana Luísa Amaral, *Ágora* (Lisbon: Assírio & Alvim, 2019), p. 49; for David, see 'O Tr(i)unfo de David' (Amaral, *Ágora*, p. 61); for Jesus Christ, see 'O Julgamento' and 'Uma Ceia' (Amaral, *Ágora*, pp. 21, 45); and for Saint Paul, see 'A Conversão' (Amaral, *Ágora*, p. 77).

[21] See in Ana Luísa Amaral, *Escuro* (Lisbon: Assírio & Alvim, 2014): 'Promontório', pp. 36–39; 'Adamastor', pp. 55–56; 'A voz', pp. 57–58; and 'O Retrato', pp. 45–48.

[22] Amaral, *Arder a Palavra*, pp. 256–57.

[23] Amaral, *Arder a Palavra*, p. 257. This invented male persona is so convincing that some critics were led to believe in Aldo Mathias's real existence (see p. 256).

The transvestistic voices of Dante and Camões, mentioned above, are primarily linked to another strategy typical of Amaral's poetry: the rescuing of silent female characters created by male authors. The clearest example is *A Génese do Amor*, where Dante dialogues with his muse, Beatrice, and Camões with Natércia (an anagram of the name of Camões's muse, the court lady Caterina de Ataíde), while Beatrice, Natércia and Catarina dialogue with each other, as well as with Petrarch's Laura.[24] In these lyrical dialogues, the male voices — which literary tradition equates with authority — become more frail in their love and their passion is matched at every step by their female counterparts, thus breaking away from the feudal bonds of courtly love. It is not an unequal relationship between the male poets and their female muses or mistresses, but a relationship between equals — in love and language. A similar strategy is followed when Amaral gives voice to female personas used by male troubadours in the *cantigas de amigo*, as in the four poems dedicated to the Knight and the Dame, in *Vozes*. In this case, a more ironic one, the language of love is revised from inside out: the Dame doesn't want to leave the poem — refusing the authority of the troubadour, which summons her every time. The Knight tries to convince the Dame using Portuguese metrics (*redondilha*), but when he fails to do so, he resorts to French and English language and metrics (*sextinas*), but the Dame refuses: '*Oh, no, Sir, not so!*'. She goes back to her preferred metrics (*redondilha*), controlling the poem and unbalancing the traditional relationship between the *troubador* and the silent, passive mistress.[25]

The biblically inspired male voices in *Ágora* are part of an ekphrastic dialogue between *arte sacra* and the Bible. Many of the poems give voice to the biblical figures represented in the paintings, often subverting the traditional interpretation of the artwork itself. For instance, the two poems featuring Jesus accompany two paintings — Caravaggio's *Supper at Emmaus* (1606) and Gerrit van Honthorst's *Christ before the High Priest* (1617) — and they are both inner monologues in which the Son of God verbalizes his anguish for not being clearly seen or understood — 'Como fui visto | sem ser visto eu?' [How could I be seen | without being seen?] — or his sadness and false serenity: 'Mas eu não estou sereno, | finjo estar || Era então resignado | o meu olhar, | ou de tristeza e infinita pena | por me saber | acima dos mortais?' [But I'm not serene, | I'm just pretending || So, was my gaze then | merely resigned, | or full of sadness and infinite sorrow | knowing I was | above these mortals?].[26] Through his voice, we see the more imperfect side of Christ in its compassionate contempt for humanity.

---

[24]   See, for instance, 'Beatriz fala a Dante', in Amaral, *Inversos*, pp. 465–66.

[25]   Ana Luísa Amaral, *Vozes* (Lisbon: Dom Quixote, 2011), p. 59. For the poems, see 'Mais um sal de memórias: Fala o cavaleiro'; 'Outro sal de memórias: a dama responde'; 'E a memória em sextinas: Fala o cavaleiro'; 'Em trovas de memória: a dama responde' (*Vozes*, pp. 47–59).

[26]   Amaral, *Ágora*, pp. 45, 21.

The embodiment of the masculine is also used, in two other poems, to deal with instances of non-normative sexuality absent from the traditional representation of two different popular figures. The first is the Old Testament story of David and Goliath, in *Ágora*. Written in dialogue with Guido Reni's *David with the Head of Goliath* (1606), David's poem subverts the traditional representation of masculinity: the young David's feat was not so much an act of courage and fierceness, as it was an act of passion and hatred — hating the force with which one loves the thing is the only way to kill it... and relish it, says the poem, evoking the famous line by Oscar Wilde, 'And all men kill the thing they love', from *The Ballad of Reading Gaol* (1896). The notion of passion and hate is interesting when read against the languid homoerotic — almost camp — pose Reni creates for David in the painting and the way David looks at Goliath. The same homoerotic undertones are present in a different book, in a different poem, the one dedicated to Prince Henry the Navigator, in *Escuro*. In 'O Promontório', we find the spectre of the Prince (o Infante Dom Henrique), a central figure in the early days of Portuguese Empire, at the Sagres Point, reflecting on his past life and conquests: his conquests, his uncertainties, his past male lovers, everything is recalled by this tired figure, who only wishes to be set free to dive into the dark.

In Amaral's work, the representation of different ways of loving and being — queer voices or subjects — is frequently linked to a political gesture: calling others to challenge, interrogate, destabilize, resist, transform monolithic discourses, identities and normativities in order to create new spaces of freedom. In a text published in the Portuguese newspaper *Público*, in 2014, with the title 'Co-Adopção: tornar mais curto o mundo' [Co-adoption: Making the World Smaller], Amaral uses one of her poems to comment on a *projecto de lei* [bill] proposed by the Socialist Party (PS) and approved at its first reading in the Portuguese Parliament in May 2013 on the co-adoption of a partner's children by same-sex couples. While waiting for the bill to be ratified by the President of the Republic a referendum was then proposed by the Social Democratic Youth (JSD) and approved by a majority on 29 January 2014. The aim of this unprecedented move was clear: to overthrow the bill previously approved in Parliament by putting pressure on the President to veto it before it became an Act. Quoting from 'Um Pouco Só de Goya: Carta a Minha Filha' [Just a Little Bit of Goya: A Letter to My Daughter], a poem published in *Imagias* (2001), and written in dialogue with Jorge de Sena's well-known poem 'Carta a Meus Filhos sobre os Fuzilamentos de Goya' [Letter to My Children on Goya's Executions of the Third of May], Amaral states the importance of speaking about 'formas de amar todas diversas, | mas feitas de pequenos sons de espanto, | se o justo e o humano aí se abraçam [all the many forms of love, | all made up of quiet cries of astonishment, | if all that is fair and human does there embrace].[27] To

---

[27] For the article, see Ana Luísa Amaral, 'Co-Adopção: Tornar mais curto o mundo', *Público*, 29 February 2014 <https://www.publico.pt/2014/01/29/sociedade/opiniao/coadopcao-tornar-mais-curto-

hierarchize love or ways of loving, continues the poet in that article, is to police sexuality and the free expression of affections, a political option that goes hand in hand with the demonization of difference. For that reason, as the author explains, she wrote that poem to leave her daughter an antidote — made of love and poetry — against the perception that 'those who inhabit the spaces in between lives | have giant's eyes or monstrous horns':

> Lembras-te de dizer que a vida era uma fila?
> [...]
> E o que queria dizer-te é dos nexos da vida,
> de quem a habita para além do ar.
> E que o respeito inteiro e infinito
> não precisa de vir depois do amor.
> Nem antes. Que as filas só são úteis
> como formas de olhar, maneiras de ordenar
> o nosso espanto, mas que é possível pontos
> paralelos, espelhos e não janelas.
> E que tudo está bem e é bom: fila ou
> novelo, duas cabeças tais num corpo só,
> ou um dragão sem fogo, ou unicórnio
> ameaçando chamas muito vivas. [...]
>
> Não sei que te dirão num futuro mais perto,
> se quem assim habita os espaços das vidas
> tem olhos de gigante ou chifres monstruosos.
> Porque te amo, queria-te um antídoto
> igual a elixir, que te fizesse grande
> de repente, voando, como fada, sobre a fila.
> Mas por te amar, não posso fazer isso,
> e nesta noite quente a rasgar junho,
> quero dizer-te da fila e do novelo
> e das formas de amar todas diversas,
> mas feitas de pequenos sons de espanto,
> se o justo e o humano aí se abraçam. [...]
>
> [Do you remember saying that life was a line?
> [...]
> And what I wanted to talk about are the connections life makes,
> About the people who inhabit life beyond the air.
> And total, infinite respect
> does not necessarily come after love.
> Or before. That lines are only useful
> as ways of seeing, ways of giving an order
> to our astonishment, that there are possible parallel
> points, mirrors, not windows.
> And that all this is fine and good: line or

o-mundo-1621433> [accessed 27 January 2020]. For the translation of Sena's poem, see Richard Zenith, *Poetry International Archives* <https://www.poetryinternational.org/pi/poem/9891/auto/0/0/Jorge-de-Sena/LETTER-TO-MY-CHILDREN-ON-GOYAS-EXECUTIONS-OF-THE-THIRD-OF-MAY/en/tile> [accessed 9 July 2020].

skein, two heads on the same body,
or a dragon without flames, or a unicorn
threatening to breathe fire on us. [...]

I don't know what others will tell you in a not-too-distant future,
if those who inhabit the spaces in between lives
have giant's eyes or monstrous horns.
Because I love you, I would like to give you an antidote
like an elixir, that would make you suddenly
grow up and fly, like a fairy, along that line.
But because I love you, I can't,
and on this hot night tearing at the edges of June,
I want to talk to you about the line and the skein
and all the many forms of love,
all made up of quiet cries of astonishment,
if all that is fair and human does there embrace. [...]][28]

When Paul B. Preciado proposes the notion of 'queer multitudes' it is precisely in opposition to the universalist institutional policies that grant 'recognition' and impose the 'integration' of 'differences', denying room for the free exercise of that same difference. For Preciado, this is an example of how sexopolitics is one of the dominant forms of biopolitical action in contemporary capitalism, drawing attention to the fact that there is 'a multitude of differences, a transversality of power relations, a diversity of life powers, differences that are not "representable"', claims the Spanish philosopher, because they are '"monstrous", thus calling into question both the regimes of political representation and the systems of production of scientific knowledge of the "normal"'.[29] It is against this reduction of the world that Ana Luísa Amaral speaks, in her civic intervention, urging others to take action at the end of that article: 'É nosso o dever da denúncia e a revolta. Deles é a indignidade. E a vergonha de querer tornar mais curto o mundo' [The duty to denounce and to rebel is ours. The unworthiness is theirs. As is the shame of wanting to make the world smaller].[30]

Echoes of this discussion can be traced back to a sequence of poems titled 'Discrepâncias a duas vozes' [Discrepancies for two voices], from the book *Se Fosse Um Intervalo* (2009), or traced forward to *Ara* (2013), the first fictional book written by Ana Luísa Amaral and which was the recipient of the PEN Narrative Award for that year. Both texts are created around the idea of dissonance and the creation of a new space to articulate it, dissonant lyrical subjects who cannot find the language to articulate themselves: 'Que se comece a história em nova voz de gente' [Let the story begin in a new voice of people] is a

---

[28] Ana Luísa Amaral, *The Art of Being a Tiger: Selected Poems*, trans. by Margaret Jull Costa, Aris & Phillips Hispanic Classics (Liverpool: Liverpool University Press, 2016), pp. 64–67.
[29] Paul B. Preciado, 'Multitudes Queer: pour une politique des "anormaux"', *Multitudes*, 12.2 (2003), 17–25 (p. 5).
[30] Amaral, 'Co-adopção' [para. 7 of 7].

sentence repeated in both texts.[31] However, *Ara* states the case more strongly. It is a book about difference, about trying to find new 'grammars of looking' and new 'grammars of saying' things that don't fit normativity. It is a structurally dissonant book, not only in terms of literary genre, but also in terms of love and sexuality.[32] *Ara* does not meet the norms of fiction and exceeds the limits of poetry, so it is a difficult book to label. This difficulty of categorizing *Ara* is visible in the different definitions given by several authors who have reviewed it: Maria Velho da Costa calls it 'um romance' [a novel], Maria Lúcia Dal Farra uses the Medieval term '*romanço*' and 'cinema de palavras' [cinema of words], Catherine Dumas talks about 'uma nova modalidade textual híbrida' [a new hybrid textual mode], and Maria Irene Ramalho, in her afterword to the Brazilian edition of *Ara*, considers it, above all, 'um belo *poema*' [a beautiful *poem*], saying: 'Incluo no poético toda a escrita (mesmo que de "romance" se trate) que desassossegue quem a lê através do gesto poético de perguntar aquilo-que-é e de imaginar aquilo-que-deveria-ser' [I include in the poetic all the writings (even if it is a 'novel') that unsettle the person who reads it through the poetic gesture of asking what-is and imagining what-that-should-be].[33]

Asking what-is and imagining what-that-should-be is also applicable to the discussion of non-normative love in *Ara*, particularly in the short narrative called 'Irmãs' [Sisters], which tells the story of the relationship between two women who, years after falling in love, are reunited in a hotel in a foreign country. One of these women, we learn, is married to a man and has children, although she is unhappy in this heteronormative relationship, or, to use *Ara*'s words, in that 'forma de amar conformada' [conformed form of love].[34] The love between these two women — we are later told — is never consummated, never verbalized explicitly.... And yet it lives, breathes, exists, without the right grammar to state it:

> [...] E eu sem palavras para nós cabermos.
>
> Meu amor. Até o termo roubado a outra língua, a única que sei. Com ela criaria, se pudesse, coisas mais insensatas e mais belas que eles jamais fizeram. Com ela dir-te-ia o que não posso em frente dessa gente. O círculo da vida: então nós caberíamos. Não linha periférica, mercadoria andante onde sobramos, mas um círculo mágico com o mundo e nós dentro. Uma língua diferente far-nos-ia — para eles — reais.
>
> [[...] And there am I with no words that we could fit comfortably inside.

---

[31]   Cf. Amaral, *Inversos*, p. 609; and Ana Luísa Amaral, *Ara: Romance* (Lisbon: Sextante, 2013), p. 71.

[32]   Cf. Raquel Ribeiro, 'Língua de Ninguém com Gente Dentro', *Público*, 1 November 2013, section *Ípsilon*, pp. 19–20 (p. 20).

[33]   Maria Velho da Costa and Catherine Dumas's words are quoted from the book flaps of *Ara*'s Portuguese edition published by Sextante. Maria Lúcia Dal Farra's words are taken from the flap of the Brazilian edition of *Ara*, published by Iluminuras, and for which Maria Irene Ramalho wrote the afterword, quoted above. See Maria Irene Ramalho, '*Ara* ou o Desassossego da Poesia', *Ara: Romance* (São Paulo: Editora Iluminuras, 2014), pp. 73–78 (p. 74).

[34]   Amaral, *Ara*, p. 65.

My love. Even the term is stolen from another language, the only one I know. With it I would create, if I could, far wilder and far more beautiful things than they ever did. With it I would say to you everything I cannot say in front of these people. The circle of life: then we would fit in. Not a kind of ring road, moving merchandise where we were surplus to requirements, but a magic circle with the world and us inside it. A different language would make us real for them.][35]

The difficulty in finding a language to articulate this homo-affective relationship exposes the violence of the heteronormative norm, the discomfort and pain of those who do not inhabit normativity, but who are socially forced to live it. The very absence of models to represent this relationship is the result of this cultural silence around forms of love other than those inserted in a reproductive family unit. To break this silence — or to transform this oppressive silence into a creative silence — it is necessary to begin the story 'in a new voice of people', because traditional language is embedded with heteronormative assumptions about love. Take, for example, *Ara*'s critique of the structure of fairy tales, when Cinderella's predominance in popular discourse and imagination is questioned: '*que fascínio nessa pequena órfã a ser sacrificada, e a recompensa depois, o sapato provado, a frase certa, meu amor és tu, vamos casar, e seremos felizes, o teu pequeno pé calçado de cristal? Que fascínio?*' [*wherefore this fascination with this little orphan to be sacrificed, and the reward later, the tried-on shoe, the right sentence, my love, it is you, let's get married, and be happy, your little glass-slippered foot? Wherefore this fascination?*].[36] In order to frame a homoerotic love — which the norm condemns to shame for not following the guidelines of normative existence — it is necessary to destabilize the limits of the norm or, in Sara Ahmed's words, to learn how to '*inhabi[t] norms differently*'.[37] Thus, *Ara* proposes a new litany, a new mantra, a new flow of language that may dismantle the mechanisms of oppression embedded in language and denounce them for imposing feelings of shame:

A quem pertence o mundo? Inventar uma nova litania:

Vergonha: a fome nas crianças, a fome desenhada, omnipresente. Crianças que nem pão, ou gesto, ou um olhar qualquer. Vergonha de haver fome. De olhar fome. Vergonha: só o ver, como estas coisas. A violência de ver, sem mãos para mudar. Essa a vergonha.

Vergonha: amor ausente e lacerado, obrigações de carne e cama, obrigações do resto. [...]

Vergonha: destruir e conquistar sobre terreno alheio. Vergonha é o silêncio, a série de vazio. A quem pertence o mundo? Vergonha é não te amar. Vergonha era fingir que não pertenço.

---

[35] Amaral, *Ara*, p. 74.
[36] Amaral, *Ara*, p. 36.
[37] Ahmed, *The Cultural Politics of Emotion*, p. 155.

[...]

Vergonha é consentir.

[...] Vergonha é não amar.

[Who does the world belong to? To invent a new litany:

Shame: the hunger in children, the clear cut, omnipresent hunger. Children
with no bread, no tenderness, not even noticed. The shame that hunger
exists. Of seeing hunger. Shame: merely its visibility. The violence of seeing,
without the power to change. It's that: that's the shame.

Shame: love absent and lacerated, obligations of the flesh, obligations and
all the rest. [...]

Shame: to destroy and to conquer foreign territory. Shame is the silence,
real silence, fully empty. The world belongs to whom? Shame is not loving
you. Shame would be to pretend I don't belong.

[...]

Shame is consenting.

[...] Shame is not loving.][38]

Reflecting on difference is also one of the touchstones of Amaral's children's
books (some of them chosen by the National Reading Plan), as *Gaspar, o
Dedo Diferente e Outras Histórias* [Gaspar, the Different Finger and Other
Stories] (1998) or *A História da Aranha Leopoldina* [The Story of Leopoldina,
the Spider] (2000), which tells the story of a spider that wanted to knit socks,
instead of making webs ('em vez de teia | só queria fazer meia' [wanted to spin
| but socks were her thing]); the book *Como Tu* [Just Like You] (2012) (based
on the performance *Amor aos Pedaços*, commissioned by the Science and
Development Foundation Educational Service), which reminds us that 'ser
excluído | [faz-nos] sentir sozinhos, || diferentes do diferente' [being excluded |
[makes us] feel alone, || different from different]; or, even, the poem 'Christmas
Carol (Adaptado a Fábula) [Christmas Carol (Turned into a Fable)], from
the book of poems *E Todavia* (2015), which tells the story of a male warbler
(*toutinegra*) who wanted to become a different bird — transitioning to more
female colours (*touti-rosa*).[39]

This political but also deeply ethical gesture of questioning the limitations of
categories and looking for new ways of looking or saying is at the basis of what
we might call Amaral's '*queerful* poetics' or, to use her own words, 'uma poética
queerente'. The term '*queerente*' was proposed by the author, not in her literary
work, but in her essays, when reflecting on how literature can be a weapon of
political and formal resistance to processes of hierarchization and domination,
which operate through sorrow and suffering. For Amaral, destabilizing

---

[38]   Amaral, *Ara*, pp. 77, 78, 79. Translation kindly provided by Claire Williams.
[39]   Cf. *A História da Aranha Leopoldina* (Porto: Campo das Letras, 2000), p. 6; *Como Tu* (Porto:
Booklândia, 2012), p. 45; Ana Luísa Amaral, *E Todavia* (Lisbon: Assírio & Alvim, 2015), p. 113.

fixed boundaries and identities — thinking the dissonant, the disparate, the disjunctive — is a way of looking for alliances in the 'social body (in the space of desire and eroticism)' or in the 'body politic' in order to find new spaces of freedom. In Ana Luísa Amaral's own words:

> Significa habitar uma terra com gente dentro, mesmo que entre espaços de vazio, falar uma língua que efectua uma relação com os mortos e com aqueles que ainda não nasceram. Uma prática não (porque nunca) coerente, mas (e proponho a palavra) **queerente**, aspirando a que as diferenças se possam tornar a indiferença.[40]

> [It means inhabiting a land with people within, even if between spaces of emptiness, speaking a language that makes a relationship with the dead and those who are not yet born. A practice not (because never) coherent, but (and I propose the word) **queerful**, aspiring that differences can become indifference.]

In all her work, the poet celebrates the power of love and common sharing as a form of resistance to the disciplinary processes of dehumanization and marginalization. Her 'queerful' writing is pure power, establishing alliances of sharing and solidarity, channels of affection and communication, hoping to pave the way for a fairer and more humane future. To be human, in her poetry, is to know how to be with others — to feel with, for or about others — who are different and inhabit 'risk zones'. Knowing how 'to be with others', Ana Luísa Amaral would say, is knowing that *Shame is silence. Shame is violence. Shame is consenting. Shame is making the world smaller.*

---

[40] Amaral, *Arder a Palavra*, p. 89.

Poems

Adília Lopes

'A minha casa', 'Um espelho', 'A solidão'

A minha casa
é mágica
como Veneza
onde nunca
estive

Mágica
e mortal

* * * * *

Um espelho
não é
uma janela

Um espelho
não é
um quadro

Quem espreita
por meus olhos
no espelho
sou eu

E eu
sou eu

Não há
enigmas

Le Vitrail la nuit * *A Árvore Cortada* (Lisbon: & etc, 2006)

* * * * *

A solidão
engendra
monstros

A hora
do jantar
é a pior
hora

Os Namorados Pobres (Lisbon: Assírio & Alvim, 2009)

Translated by Richard Zenith

'My house', 'A mirror', 'Solitude'

My house
is magic
like Venice
where I've never
been

Magic
and mortal

*   *   *   *   *

A mirror
is not
a window

A mirror
is not
a picture

I am the one
who looks
through my eyes
at that mirror

And I
am I

There are
no riddles

*   *   *   *   *

Solitude
breeds
monsters

The dinner
hour
is the worst
hour

ADÍLIA LOPES

A Perfeição? A Viagem?

Eva fica sozinha
com as maravilhas
artísticas do mundo
de que lhe servem
as maravilhas
artísticas do mundo
sem os filhos
e sobretudo sem Adão?
Deus e as maravilhas
artísticas do mundo
não lhe chegam
parte a loiça
da dinastia Ming
bate com a porta
(uma porta maravilhosa)
e chora os mortos
o seu sofrimento
não tem leitor
a menos que Deus a leia
mas para que lhe serve Deus
sem Adão
não se suicida
(para quê?)
continua a chamar
Eva precisa de Adão
para se dar bem com Deus

Os Namorados Pobres (Lisbon: Assírio & Alvim, 2009)

Translated by RICHARD ZENITH

Perfection? The Journey?

Eve is left all alone
with the artistic
wonders of the world
what good
are the artistic
wonders of the world
without her children
and especially without Adam?
God and the artistic
wonders of the world
aren't enough
she smashes the Ming
Dynasty porcelain
slams the door
(a splendorous door)
and cries for the dead
her suffering
has no readers
unless God reads it
but what good is God
without Adam?
she doesn't kill herself
(what for?)
she keeps calling
Eve needs Adam
to get along with God

Ana Luísa Amaral

Sintomas e síndromes

Primavera em sintoma repetido.
Estão aí outra vez, intrusos na
manhã. Não me deixam pensar.
O gato quer sair, treme ao vê-los
nos ramos a cantar. Preciso de
pensar. Silêncio em síndrome.
Ruídos de madeira, o tempo a ba-
dalar, são dez e meia. Intrusos
no meu sono de pensar. Preciso
de ar. Mas eles são piores, agora
na manhã já levantada, juntaram
companhia. É ópera de azul.
Um Wagner maior. Navio Real.
O enjoo do ar. Preciso de pensar.
Mas cantam. Cantam. Canção que
não me deixa nem ramo de pensar.
Primavera outra vez e todas as
manhãs o seu sintoma. O gato em
frenesi a tremer mais ao vê-los
a saltar de ramo em ramo. É
primavera e cantam: ligações i-
legais, o ninho em alvoroço.
Só um falcão de asa franjada e
preta que tem casa aqui perto
e que não canta. Só por ele eu
podia pensar. Só por ele o meu
ar, como um telhado. (E o gato
sem ousar-se, viciado, nem
exibindo assim, junto à janela,
estes sintomas de delirium tre-
mens.)

Coisas de Partir (1993), *Inversos* (Lisbon: Dom Quixote, 2010)

Translated by MARGARET JULL COSTA

Symptoms and syndromes

Spring on repeat syndrome. There
they are again, those intruders on the
morning. They won't let me think.
The cat wants to go out, trembling
at the sight of them perched on the
branches, singing. I need to think.
Silence as syndrome. Wood creak-
ing, time tolling, it's half past ten.
Intruders on my sleepy thoughts. I need
air. But they've grown louder now
the day is up and about, they've grown
in number. An opera all in blue. Wagner
in a major key. A Ghost Ship.
How cloyingly sweet the air is. I need
to think. But they keep singing. Singing.
A song that doesn't leave me a single
branch to think on. Spring again and
every morning the same spring
symptoms. The cat is in a frenzy,
trembling ever more to see them
jump from branch to branch. It's
spring and they're singing: illegal
liaisons, the nest all abuzz. Only a
hawk with black, fringed wings
who has his house nearby and doesn't
sing. Only he would allow me to think.
Only he could give me air to breathe,
a roof. (And the cat still not daring
to make the leap, but still, riveted to
that spot by the window, revealing
clear symptoms of delirium tre-
mens.)

ANA LUÍSA AMARAL

Prece no Mediterrâneo

Em vez de peixes, Senhor,
dai-nos a paz,
um mar que seja de ondas inocentes,
e, chegados à areia,
gente que veja com coração de ver,
vozes que nos aceitem

É tão dura a viagem
e até a espuma fere e ferve,
e, de tão alta, cega
durante a travessia

Fazei, Senhor, com que não haja
mortos desta vez,
que as rochas sejam longe,
que o vento se aquiete
e a vossa paz enfim
se multiplique

Mas depois da jangada,
da guerra, do cansaço,
depois dos braços abertos e sonoros,
sabia bem, Senhor,
um pão macio,
e um peixe, pode ser,
do mar

que é também nosso

Ágora (Lisbon: Assírio & Alvim, 2019)

O vento

Vinha de fora
e não era monção, nem vento norte
nem qualquer outro vento conhecido,
vento que lhes dissesse
podem lutar comigo, podem prever-me
de quando em quando as rotas
e por vezes até acautelar-me
os crimes

Este era um novo vento
sem dono e de outra aragem,
sem deslocação de ar que se soubesse,
mas podia, temeram,
destruir muito mais que os outros ventos

E eles trancaram janelas e fronteiras
e cumpriram aquilo que lhes fora ensinado:

Translated by MARGARET JULL COSTA

Prayer in the Mediterranean

Instead of fishes, Lord,
give us peace,
a sea of innocent waves,
and, once we reach the shore,
people who see with their hearts,
voices that accept us

The voyage is so hard,
even the foaming waters wound and boil,
and, during the crossing,
rise high enough
to blind

Lord, let there be no
deaths this time,
may the rocks keep their distance,
may the wind drop
and may your peace finally
spread and multiply

But after the raft,
after the war, the tiredness,
after the generous, open arms,
Lord, some fresh bread
would be good
and a little fish, if possible,
from the sea

that is also our sea

The wind

It came from outside,
neither monsoon nor north wind
or any other known wind,
a wind that told them
you can fight with me, you can sometimes
foresee which route I might take
and occasionally even fend off
my crimes

This was a new wind,
ownerless and not like other winds,
a wind that seemed not even to stir the air,
but that could, or so they feared,
be far more destructive than other winds

And so they closed windows and frontiers
and did precisely what they'd been taught to do:

erguer muralhas contra o que voava mas era rente
ao chão. Como podia um vento voar e rastejar,
ser fome em movimento?

Mas este vento nem se chamava vento, e eles
não sabiam o seu nome. Era um vento
selvagem e com asas, ele mesmo era asa e fogo,
rija e frágil matéria, e tudo
ao mesmo tempo

Por detrás das portadas, os mestres entre si
trocavam coisas várias: saberes e lajes de cimento
e gume para que os muros fossem mais opacos
e chegassem mais alto, combatessem o vento
que não tinha nome, e falavam de ardis
sobre como afiar melhor os seus
ensinamentos

Porque sabiam que este vento chegava
por eles terem lançado as areias
sobre as suas terras

E nele confundidos,
vinham de longe os hóspedes
trazidos nesse vento, donos de nada,
e por muito que os muros
se erguessem contra o vento,
mais o vento se erguia, mais resistente e dúctil
se afinava a matéria
que o compunha

Não se sabe até quando o vento
errou, errou de desacerto e vaguear
por entre as ruas todas, errou sem rumo,
mas com lume bastante para alumiar tudo,
todos os aposentos das casas
que encontrou

e fez arder, de vermelho
insubmisso, os campos e as copas
das árvores mais altas

E conta quem lá esteve,
os filhos dos que tinham chegado com o vento,
os filhos dos escravos por ele libertados,
e ainda aqueles que ainda conseguiam falar com as crianças,
que esse ponto de luz, ínfimo, muito terno,
despertara outra vez –

e eles puderam ver também
a sua cor

Previously unpublished

build walls against this thing that flew and yet kept close
to the ground. How could a wind both fly and crawl,
how could it be hunger in motion?

But this wind wasn't even called wind,
its name unknown. This wild, wingèd wind
was itself all wing and fire,
at once
solid and fragile

Behind closed doors, the masters
traded various things: cunning skills and concrete slabs
with cutting edges so that the walls were higher,
more opaque, and could combat that nameless
wind, and they discussed deceits,
how best to hone their
knowledge

For the masters knew this wind had come
because they had destroyed the land,
turned it into desert

And caught up in that wind,
brought by that wind,
came guests from afar, owners of nothing at all,
and the higher the walls were built
to keep out the wind,
the stronger the wind, the more resistant and pliant
its substance

No one knows how long that wind
spent wandering randomly,
up and down every street, directionless,
but fiery enough to fire up everything,
every room in every house
it encountered

making the fields and the tops
of the tallest trees
blaze rebellious and red

And it's said, by those who were there,
the children of those who had arrived with the wind,
the children of the slaves it had freed,
and even those who could still speak with those children,
that this pinprick of light, tiny and tender,
had reawoken –

and what they could also now see
was its colour

António Franco Alexandre

Moradas — I

9

sentado, meditado, ficarás,
na poeira que os tiros levantaram,
nas ruas devastadas contra o mar;
com a sombra da luz a desenhar-te
o perfil do perfil, imperceptível,
em vasto chão ardido;

a máquina, metálica, movendo
os altos fios do tecto suspendidos
sobre os surpresos dedos, não a pena:
bebendo, pela tarde, o vinho fresco,
o cigarro de sal oferecido
pelo moço mais dócil e sombrio;

ameaçando o céu, secreto, rindo
talvez para poente, aonde vibram
as lanternas do vento sobre a espuma;
à mesa, o mais sereno, acorrentado,
imóvel, mas movendo a mão do tempo,
ausente, respirando a maresia.

Moradas — II

8

estas são as minhas quintas, os meus rebanhos
disfarçados de alcateia,
as azinhagas que dão
para o profundo anoitecer,
aqui os armazéns, cheios de fértil escuridão,
a grande colecção de colinas empacotadas
e minúsculas nuvens que incham com a chuva
dentro, e nenhum sino

perturba este sossego, esta mistura
que os corpos fazem, e desfazem na paisagem,
e ainda as serpentes caminham a quatro patas, sem perigo algum,
e a boca beijada é quente de cordas e laços,
e o grande rio descia para a terra,
o meu amor alimentava-se de pedras e
sopro, possivelmente,
e os filhos nasciam aos molhes, um por um.

por uma fina folha entro na superfície
dos sonhos coloridos,

Translated by RICHARD ZENITH

Dwelling Places — I

9

sitting there, meditated, you'll remain
in the dust that the shots kicked up,
in the devastated streets facing the sea,
with the light's shadow drawing
on the sprawling, burnt ground
your profile's indiscernible profile.

the metallic machine moves the wires
that hang from the ceiling down
to your startled fingers, not your pen.
drinking cool wine in the afternoon
and smoking a salty cigarette offered
by the shyest, gloomiest lad,

in secret you threaten the sky, laughing
perhaps towards the west where
the winds' lights flutter over the foam;
chained to your desk, the calmest of men,
immobile but moving the hand of time,
absent, breathing the smell of the tide.

Dwelling Places — II

8

these are my fields, my flocks
disguised as wolves,
the footpaths that lead
into deep twilight;
here are my storehouses, full of fertile darkness,
my vast collection of packaged hills
and minuscule clouds that swell with rain,
and no bell

disturbs this calm, this medley
made and unmade by the bodies on the landscape,
and snakes still walk on four legs, perfectly harmless,
and kissed lips are warm with ropes and knots,
and the great river flowed down and over the land,
my love fed on stones and
breath, perhaps,
and slews of children were born, one by one.

by a smooth, thin leaf I slip into the plane
of coloured dreams,

os cães açoitados, ladram
aos pés do caçador,
estes são os campos que ardem para quem tem
dois olhos na cabeça,
a mesa, o guardanapo sobre o prato,
o certo limite.

13

ir ser como todos os outros era uma tarefa imprevisível, um labor
minuciosamente distraído,
precisávamos de armas, de bancos, de assaltos
a navios voando com as cores do panamá,
construímos casas, canais
por onde a água se levanta
até à boca dos antepassados,
castelos, moradas

onde as crianças desaparecem para nunca mais, e passam
a vestir bombazina, e a ter
amores perfeitos na gola do casaco, enquanto o ogro os saboreia.
ele dizia, estes são os mais belos animais, o presente a que aspiro
quando for rei. e quando se quebrar
a ânfora, que trouxe ao meu parecer
tão duvidosa eternidade,
serei feliz, generoso com a minha pobreza.

agora fico indeciso
entre um e outro, ou o fantasma de permeio,
o tédio de antigamente.
se vestir gabardine fico de pessoa completo,
civil, esguio, laico quanto baste.
o prazer possível não me deixa viver tranquilo.
vou deixar este negócio de acreditar, não acreditar,
vou ser todo igual, definitivamente outro.

Moradas — III

12

digam que amei, na terrestre toalha,
o tosco amor do corpo. Digam
uma verdade, que o poema não existe.
Digam que arderam mãos, do poder que possui
o prazer de outro corpo. Digam, como sempre,
terra, água, colina.

Virei, depois, envolto em erva doce,
ao inferno que fica atrás da carne. Digam que me conhecem,
assim mudado, a tinta permanente.
Digam-me atlético e subtil, como se fora

the whipped dogs bark
at the hunter's feet,
these are the fields that burn for those
with two eyes in their head,
a table, a napkin on their plate,
the proper limit.

13

to become like everyone else was an uncertain task, a
meticulously oblivious labour,
we needed weapons and banks, we raided
ships flying with Panama's colours,
we built houses, canals
whose water rises
up to the mouth of our ancestors,
castles, dwellings

where children disappear for good, and they begin
to wear corduroy and forget-me-nots
on their lapels, while the ogre relishes them.
he said: these are the handsomest creatures, the prize I want
when I become king, and when the amphora
that brought me the glee of this dubious eternity
is broken, I'll be
content and generous with my poverty.

now I'm undecided
between this or that, or the ghost in the middle,
the tedium of the old days.
if I put on a raincoat I'll be an unmistakable person,
as civil, lean and secular as they come.
what I might have keeps me from enjoying what I do have.
I'm going to quit this business of believing, disbelieving,
I'm going to be completely equal, definitively another.

Dwelling Places — III

12

say that I loved, in the earthly towel,
coarse bodily love. Say
this truth: the poem doesn't exist.
Say that hands burned, so fierce is the pleasure
of another body. Say, as always,
earth, water, hill.

Later I'll come, wrapped in sweet grass,
to the hell that's behind the flesh. Say you know me
in this new version, written in permanent ink.
Say I'm vigorous and subtle, as if I were

o autómato eléctrico que arremessa
luzes miraculantes no lençol aberto.

Digam que usava estrelas nos cabelos,
podem crer.

17

somos um país pequeno, andamos
amarfanhados com a dimensão da boca, aonde não cabe
um peixe. Daí
a construção elíptica, parcialmente nos arredores,
vastas cidades fantasmas que só de noite se deslocam
entre pinhais e faróis,

o sabor a mansão agrícola com maçãs a dormir na mesa,
e o gesto, sempre igual, com que enfeitamos a lapela,
saudamos ao passar, ou oramos ao fim do dia.
Estes costumes, que fazem
o espanto de todos os outros povos,
estas inquietantes maneiras,

são a nossa honra, o nosso suplício. De manhã, mais a norte,
devoram animais vivos; coisa que nunca fizemos.

As Moradas 1 & 2 (1987) and *Terceiras Moradas, Poemas*
(Lisbon: Assírio & Alvim, 1996)

the electric automaton that hurls
miraculous lights in the tousled sheets.

Say I wore stars in my hair,
I swear it's true.

17

we're a small country, dissatisfied
with the size of our mouth, in which a fish
won't fit. This explains
our elliptical expansion, partially on the outskirts,
huge ghost towns that move only at night,
between pine forests and headlights,

our landed gentry air, with apples scenting our kitchens,
and the invariable gestures we use to trim our lapels,
to wave in passing, or to pray at the end of the day.
These customs that astonish
other nations,
these disturbing ways,

are our honour, our suffering. North of us, in the morning,
they devour living animals, something we've never done.

Gastão Cruz

Observação do Verão

Visão do Mundo

Árvores: luz de julho
fez crescer
a folhagem; noto agora
a passagem

da primavera no seu
volume de verdura;
da varanda
revejo

a duração dos
troncos e dos ramos, vida
contemporânea
das que passaram

Observação do Inverno

Árvores de janeiro sem o dom
da folhagem: os seus ramos são linhas
de espessura variável
umas com

outras delas saindo, espinhas
dum peixe irregular ao qual o frio
deixou
somente ossos finos,

e nada noutras folhas se renova
não há cura
para o tempo, ele será o ramo
de folhas diferentes

Observação do Verão (Lisbon: Assírio & Alvim, 2011)

Fogo

1

Há dias em que em ti talvez não pense
a morte mata um pouco a memória dos vivos
é todavia claro e fotográfico o teu rosto
caído não na terra mas no fogo
e se houver dia em que não pense em ti
estarei contigo dentro do vazio

Translated by ALEXIS LEVITIN

Observation of Summer

Vision of the World

Trees: the July light
makes their leaves
grow wide; I notice now
the passing

of spring in their vast
verdancy;
from the veranda
once again I view

their tenacious
trunks and boughs, lives
contemporaneous
with those which have vanished

Observation of Winter

January trees without the gift
of leaves: their boughs are lines
of variable thickness
some with

others coming out of them, bones
of an irregular fish to whom the cold
has left
only the thinnest skeleton,

and nothing is renewed in other leaves
there is no cure
for time, it will be the bough
of different leaves

Fire

1

There are days perhaps when I don't think of you
death kills a little the memory of the living
and yet how clear and photographic still your face
not fallen down to earth but into fire
and if there be a day when I don't think of you
I'll be with you in nothingness

4

The ruffian on the stair

Era uma peça curta, escrita para a rádio:
alguém nela primeiro te temia
num lar inglês da pequena burguesia
mas como no teatro de joe
Orton às vezes sucedia
a vítima seria por fim esse rufia
com um tiro atingido e menos lamentado
do que os peixes vermelhos do aquário estilhaçado

Fogo (Lisbon: Assírio & Alvim, 2013)

Espectros

Restas Dentro da
luz nascido
erraste nas areias que
foram para ti o universo Estás
em tempos diversos onde a ave

que sobrevoa agosto até ao
extremo já não te vê e tu
não podes ver
as asas que te queimam
Mas a vida descobre-te sozinho

tropeçando na carne dos
espectros. E tu
restas
Essa luz é
o nada A praia já entrou

no verão
infinito A aurora eterna
expulsa-te Mas
restas A memória
interpreta-te és a

vítima do dia que te recusa
e exibe Nessa
luz da origem
sobrevives
interrogando o corpo incorruptível

As Pedras Negras (1995), *Os Poemas* (Lisbon: Assírio e Alvim, 2009)

4

The ruffian on the stair

It was a short play, written for radio:
Someone in it was at first afraid of you
in a bourgeois English home
but as sometimes happens in the plays
of joe orton
the victim could be in the end that ruffian
hit by a bullet and less lamented
than the gold fish in the shattered bowl

Ghosts

And you remain Born
within the light
you strayed through sands that
were the universe for you Now you find yourself
in different times in which the bird

that flies across August to its
end no longer sees you and you
can't see
the wings consuming you
But life discovers you alone

stumbling upon the flesh of
ghosts And you
remain
That light is
nothingness The beach has already entered

infinite
summer Eternal dawn
expels you But
you remain Memory
interprets you, you are the

victim of the day that rejects and yet
exhibits you In that
light of beginnings
you survive
questioning your incorruptible body

José Miguel Silva

Na Feira do Livro II

— 'Tem livros sobre o prazer?'
sussurra o desarmado
pistoleiro do amor.
Um deslize do genoma
soterrou-lhe o coração.

Os dentes em balanço,
os olhos de través,
a estopa do cabelo;
sua vida é refutada
pelo cânone festivo
do grego *to kallon*.

Não tem lugar no mundo
dos heróis, aprendeu a soletrar
na escola do revés
e não há quem lhe perdoe
o sofrimento, quando pulsa
na pergunta
entre todas indecente.

A Minha Musa

É mais casta do que eu
e só bebe água mineral.
Furtiva, insolente, caprichosa,
às vezes desaparece-me de casa
durante meses. Apetece-me
bater-lhe. Mas talvez a culpa
seja minha. Passo tanto tempo
a coçar a cabeça ou no terraço
a ver passar os aviões.
É natural que se farte de mim,
raramente estou em casa
quando chega, prefiro dormir
a ver televisão com ela
sentada nos meus joelhos.

Amiúde me pergunto
se compensam os tormentos
a que me força.
Meteu na cabeça fazer
de mim poeta, quando
o que eu gostaria era de ser
aviador. (Mas tenho medo

Translated by RICHARD ZENITH

At the Book Fair II

'Do you have books about pleasure?'
mumbles the unarmed
gunner of love.
A kink in his genome
had buried his heart.

Teeth on edge,
slanting eyes,
hair like tow,
his life has been refuted
by the festive canon
of the Greek *to kallon*.

He has no place in the world
of heroes. He learned to spell
in the school of misfortune,
and no one forgives him
the suffering that throbs
in that utterly indecent
question.

My Muse

She's chaste compared to me
and drinks only mineral water.
Furtive, cheeky and fickle,
she sometimes stays away
for months, and then I feel like
punching her. But it's probably
my fault. I spend too much time
scratching my head or watching
airplanes from the balcony.
Of course she gets tired of me:
I'm rarely at home when
she arrives, and I'd rather sleep
than watch TV with her
sitting on my knees.

I often wonder
if it's worth going through all
the torments she makes me suffer.
She's bent on turning me
into a poet, when what
I'd really like to be
is an aviator. (But I'm afraid

das alturas, e ela sabe-o.
Aproveita-se da minha debilidade.)

Obriga-me a ficar de olhos abertos
durante o sono, a estudar os
caninos que a vida me mostra,
o manual dos elementos, a história
calamitosa dos meus erros.
É preciso ter estômago
para tanta solidão. Não admira
que muitas vezes a traia
com a Helena, com o *bourbon*
dos amigos, com o voo violeta
do jacarandá no Largo do Viriato.
Mas não adianta, não sente ciúmes,
ela própria me empurra
para os braços do mundo.

É tão exigente, tão snob, tão
tinhosa. Por ela, não havia
domingos nem feriados,
não havia verão. Era sempre
toda a vida um quarto escuro
com filmes de série B e
uma banda sonora de tiros, soluços,
gargalhadas de teatro anatómico.
Marca-me duelos — é louca! —
com temíveis espadachins,
à vista dos quais a minha alma
treme dos pés à cabeça. Diz que
me faz bem sangrar um bocado,
que é minha amiga, talvez.

Fria, severa, calculadora,
tenta o que pode para contrariar
a minha natureza ruidosa,
paciente, sentimental.
Diz que é uma porcaria
escrever com lágrimas, recita
Mallarmé, levanta-se de noite
para me rasgar os poemas.
Não é fácil aturá-la.

Só para me irritar, muda
o nome de todas as coisas:
se vê um massacre chama-lhe
acre de terra lavrada,
vê um mendigo chama-lhe
trigo, vê uma porta

of heights, and she knows it.
She takes advantage of my weakness.)

She makes me sleep with my eyes
wide open, studying life's
bared teeth, the manual
of the elements, the disastrous
history of my mistakes.
It's hard to stomach
so much solitude. Small wonder
I've frequently cheated on her
with Helena, with bourbon
amid friends, with the soaring purple
of the jacaranda on Viriato Square.
All in vain: she feels no jealousy.
She herself pushes me
into the world's arms.

She's such a snob, so demanding,
so rude. She'd do away
with Sundays, holidays
and summers. For her,
life could be a darkened room
with B movies and a soundtrack
of gunshots, sobs, and guffaws
of an anatomical theater.
She sets up duels for me — she's
crazy! — with frightful swordsmen
who make my soul shudder
from head to toe. She says
it's good for me to bleed a little,
and that she's my friend. Hmm.

Cold, stern and calculating,
she does her best to contradict
my noisy, patient,
sentimental nature.
She says writing with tears
is crap, she recites
Mallarmé, she gets up at night
to rip up my poems.
It's not easy to put up with her.

She changes the names of things
just to irritate me. If she sees
a massacre, she calls it
an acre of plowed earth. If she sees
a deadbeat, she calls him
wheat. She sees a door

e chama-lhe susto.
Às vezes pergunto-me
se não será parva.

A verdade é que não sou feliz
com ela, apenas um pouco
mais solitário.
Mas sem ela — vejam que
tristeza, que abandono, que.

Ulisses Já Não Mora Aqui (Lisbon: & etc, 2002)

Para Agradar a uma Sombra

Isn't it just like love?
The Psychedelic Furs

Agora que já chorei o meu papel de solitário
posso virar a folha e declarar que, na verdade,
eu nunca estive sozinho. Tive sempre a boa companhia
da minha sombra. E não posso dizer
que nos déssemos mal: uns dias pior, outros pior.
Como todos os casais. Tínhamos (e temos)
a mesma idade, os mesmos gostos musicais,
um amor paralelo por fogo de lenha,
líamos os livros a meias, quase não gastávamos
nenhum oxigénio.

Dos dois era ela quem insistia, às vezes,
para irmos dançar. Mas eu, é claro, detestava
o tremendal das discotecas; amava mais depressa
o movimento descritivo dos romances
do que a luz hipotecada de um corpo distante.

Com o tempo, no entanto, foi crescendo esse litígio.
As nossas relações foram perdendo o vulto
à medida que ela convidava mais gente
para a nossa cama. Até que um dia chegou a casa
e apresentou-me 'o amor da nossa vida; agora
somos três'. E assim a minha sombra,
a minha ingrata começou a dizer coisas lacerantes.
Por exemplo: 'Vai tu ao cinema. Nós ficamos.'
Ou então: 'Bem podemos, de vez em quando,
caminhar separados, ou não achas?' E fecha-se
no quarto com a outra, em colóquios ofegantes.
Altura em que, de raiva, saio porta fora.

Uma vida a três é talvez menos longa do que uma vida
a dois. Há um milímetro agora de distância entre mim
e a sombra. O espaço bastante para um raio de luz.

and calls it fright.
Sometimes I wonder
if she isn't batty.

To be with her doesn't in fact
make me happy, just a little
more solitary.
But without her, see how
sad, how forlorn, how.

To Please a Shadow

Isn't it just like love?
The Psychedelic Furs

Now that I've wept my part as a lonely man,
I can turn the script over and declare that, in fact,
I've never been alone. I've always had the good company
of my shadow. And I have to say
we've done all right together, with bad days and worse days,
like all couples. We were (and are) the same
age, with the same musical tastes
and a parallel fondness for sitting by the fire,
reading the same books, using almost
no oxygen.

She was the one who sometimes insisted
we go dancing, whereas I naturally hated
the scuzziness of discotheques, preferring
the descriptive movement of novels
to the mortgaged light of a distant body.

The tension between us increased over time,
with things going downhill when she started
inviting other people into our bed. Until
one day she arrived home and introduced me to
'the love of our life; now we're a threesome'.
And so my shadow, that ingrate,
began saying the most atrocious things.
Such as: 'You go to the movies. We're staying home.'
Or: 'We could walk separately now and then,
don't you think?' And she shuts herself up in the bedroom
for impassioned [breathless] conversations with the other.
At which point I leave the house in a huff.

A life shared by three is perhaps shorter than one
shared by two. Now there's a millimeter of distance between me
and my shadow. Enough of an interval for a ray of light.
We're not really any worse off than before.

Não ficámos, realmente, pior do que estávamos.
Mas chega a ser enjoativo ver o trevo cor-de-rosa
que semeiam no quintal, felizes como duas estrelinhas
de cinema. Nem sei o que diga. Parecem crianças.

Vista Para Um Pátio seguido de Desordem (Lisbon: Relógio D'Água, 2003)

Ladrões de Bicicletas — Vittorio de Sica (1948)

Mil quilómetros por dia pedalava meu pai, desde
a cama junto ao Douro até à próspera Cerâmica
de Valadares. Se qualquer homem recebe,
à nascença, uns sessenta inimigos por hora,
imaginem a jornada de um operário ciclista.
Tudo são despesas para ele: o rosário de geada
nas giestas, o jornal atropelado pelo vento, o verdor
da Primavera, a poalha do suor em cada mão.

Meu pai, é claro, não se queixa. Ganha um conto
de réis, tem uma casa portuguesa e grandes sonhos
de amanhãs a gasolina. Pelo menos não trabalho
em nenhum matadouro, pensa ele, e com razão,
erguido nos pedais do seu veículo de sombra,
solitário trepador pela encosta de Avintes. Não
trabalha em nenhum matadouro. E nesse reconforto
passa à Quinta dos Frades, alcança o Freixieiro,
sente já o rumor de fumacentos camiões na nacional,
onde tudo, depois, será muito mais plano.

Chuva de Pedras — Ken Loach (1993)

Os desempregados, por definição, não têm
cara. Deve ser embaraçoso não ter cara. Daí
talvez o motivo por que se escondem de nós.
Escondem-se nas ruas, nos bancos de jardim,
nas paragens de autocarro, escondem-se
no pão, no teu porta-moedas, nos poemas
mal escritos ou nos filmes realistas ingleses.
Onde sabem que ninguém os irá importunar.

Movimentos no Escuro (Lisbon: Relógio D'Água, 2006)

But it disgusts me to see the pink clover
they sow in the backyard, happy as two little
movie stars. What can I say? They're like children.

Bicycle Thieves — Vittorio De Sica (1948)

500 miles per day pedalled my father, from his bed
near the Douro River to the booming ceramicware
plant of Valadares. If all men, from birth,
are given some sixty enemies per hour,
imagine a life cycling to and from a factory.
One effort after another: the rosary of frost covering
clusters of broom, a newspaper battered by the wind,
the greenness of Spring, the dusty sweat on each hand.

My father, to be sure, never complains. He earns five
dollars a day and has a small house and big dreams
of gas-powered tomorrows. 'At least I don't work
in a slaughterhouse', he thinks, and with good reason,
standing tall on the pedals of his shadowy vehicle,
a solitary cyclist climbing the slope at Avintes. He doesn't
work in a slaughterhouse. And with that solace
he rides past the Quinta dos Frades, reaches Freixieiro,
and hears the rumble of the smoky trucks on the highway,
where the ride, at last, will be much smoother.

Raining Stones — Ken Loach (1993)

The unemployed, by definition, have no
face. It must be embarrassing not to have
a face. Maybe that's why they hide from us.
They hide in the streets, on park benches,
at bus stops. They hide in your bread,
in your purse, in badly written
poems or in realist British films.
Where they know no one will bother them.

MANUEL DE FREITAS

Tardes de Província

para a Renata Correia Botelho e a Vanda Brotas

Lembro-me muito bem da tarde em que disse ao meu tio José Carlos que a *Paixão Segundo São João* de Bach (que acaba de ser magnificamente gravada por René Jacobs) me agradava mais do que a *Paixão Segundo São Mateus*. O meu tio, que tinha quase sempre razão, deu-me a entender que eu estaria a ser injusto. Havia, na verdade, um problema de base: eu atinha-me então às gravações de Karajan, e não conhecia ainda as de Leonhardt ou Herreweghe. E isso viria, claro, a fazer toda a diferença. Hoje, felizmente, não preciso de escolher — e apetece-me cada vez menos ter razão.

*   *   *   *   *

Sinto, de quando em quando, saudades dessas tardes longas em que o tédio era um luxo possível. Em Lisboa — ou em mim, talvez — o tempo foge, mal chega para o pouco que desejo fazer de cada dia. Persistirão a angústia, o vazio, a ansiedade — mas de modo nenhum o tédio. E Bach, com ou sem Deus, não deixou de me acompanhar. Tem o mesmo exacto efeito da praia rochosa com que a Achadinha nos surpreende, ao virar da curva. E pode também parecer a lezíria, quando entardece. Durante cerca de duas horas, Deus torna-se evidente. Depois, melhor ou pior, continuamos a morrer.

Herança(s)

para a Inês, da Rua dos Sapateiros à Rua Zófimo Pedroso
(que é, literalmente, o fim da cidade e talvez do mundo)

Há fogos visíveis, que ardem pela vida fora. Será, para mim, o caso de Andrei Tarkovsky, de quem revi há poucos dias *Offret* (*O Sacrifício*). Vi pela primeira vez esse filme com dezoito anos. E vira, alguns meses antes, *Nostalghia*. Imaginei muitas vezes o meu suicídio — com gasolina, de preferência, em quase tudo semelhante ao de Domenico — a acontecer no cimo da igreja de Santa Engrácia (onde, curiosamente, nunca entrei). Gosto muito daquele largo, daquela tão clara e inesperada assimetria entre o Panteão e as casas tacanhas mas bonitas que o rodeiam. É como se ouvisse Bach, o pai, a conversar com Irene Lisboa.

*   *   *   *   *

Ver *O Sacrifício* com quarenta e três anos é, fatalmente, uma experiência distinta. Agora também conheço Dreyer, Hammershoi, Nozolino. Estabeleço, como diria Clarice Lispector, «laços de família», assentes num sangue que não é o do mero parentesco biológico. E há, de facto, imagens ou citações (e uma imagem pode ser uma citação, ou vice-versa) que nos ou *me* remetem para Dreyer, no que nele já era plausível evocação de Hammershoi. A Nozolino (e é-me bastante indiferente saber se ele concorda ou não) passei a associar as súbitas imagens a preto e branco que, em jeito de *intermezzi*, nos são oferecidas quer em *Nostalghia* quer n'*O Sacrifício*. Não sou, aliás, o primeiro a sugerir esta aproximação.

Translated by RUI PIRES CABRAL

Country Afternoons

to Renata Correia Botelho and Vanda Brotas

I perfectly remember that afternoon when I told my uncle José Carlos that I liked Bach's *St. John's Passion* (which at the time had just been magnificently recorded by René Jacobs) better than his *St. Matthew's Passion*. My uncle, who was almost always right, suggested I was probably being unfair. There was, in fact, a fundamental problem: I was referring to the Karajan recordings, and was not yet familiar with the Leonhardt or Herreweghe ones. And, of course, that would come to make all the difference. Today, fortunately, I don't need to choose — and I feel ever less keen on being right.

* * * * *

Now and again, I miss those long afternoons when boredom was a feasible luxury. In Lisbon — or in myself, perhaps — time flies, it's hardly enough for the very little I wish to do with each day. Anguish, emptiness, anxiety will persist — but surely not boredom. And Bach, with or without God, has never left me since. He has the exact same effect as that rocky beach at Achadinha, taking us by surprise as we make the turn. And he can also be like the floodplains, as the evening falls. For two hours or so, God becomes evident. And then, better or worse, we go on dying.

Inheritance(s)

to Inês, from Rua dos Sapateiros to Rua Zófimo Pedroso
(which is, literally, the end of the city and maybe of the world)

There are visible fires that last a whole life through. To me, such is the case of Andrei Tarkovsky, whose *Offret* (*The Sacrifice*) I revisited a few days ago. I saw that film for the first time when I was eighteen. And I had seen, a few months before that, *Nostalghia*. I often imagined my own suicide — preferably with gasoline, resembling Domenico's in almost every way — as taking place at the top of Santa Engrácia Church (where, curiously, I have never set foot). I'm very fond of that square, that sharp and unexpected asymmetry between the Pantheon and the modest but pretty houses that surround it. It is like hearing Bach, the elder, chatting with Irene Lisboa.

* * * * *

To see *The Sacrifice* as a forty-three year old man is, inescapably, a different experience. Now I am also acquainted with Dreyer, Hammershoi, Nozolino. I establish, as Clarice Lispector would put it, 'family ties', based on a kind of blood lines that have nothing to do with mere biological kinship. And there are, indeed, images or quotations (and an image may be a quotation, and vice versa) which refer us — or refer *me* — to Dreyer, namely to that part of his work which already was a plausible evocation of Hammershoi. With Nozolino (and I'm entirely indifferent to whether or not he agrees) I came to associate those abrupt black and white images that, as a sort of *intermezzi*, run through both *Nostalghia* and *The Sacrifice*. Besides, I'm not the first one to suggest such a connection.

*   *   *   *   *

Admito que esta questão — que passa, se quisermos, por uma linhagem artística e espiritual — não seja determinante para a leitura ou recepção do filme em si (haverá, em Tarkovsky, esse conceito estrito do filme «em si»?[1]). Mas ela abre, sem dúvida, outros caminhos, sugere diálogos que eu era incapaz de imaginar há vinte e cinco anos (nomeadamente com Tchekhov ou Beckett, embora esses autores nunca sejam explicitamente referidos). Não por acaso, cabe a Erland Josephson incarnar o lado sacrificial em ambos os filmes de Tarkovsky — e passar de uma bicicleta parada (em *Nostalghia*) à bicicleta que (n'*O Sacrifício*) o levará à mais desesperada cena de sexo que até hoje o cinema me deu a ver.

*   *   *   *   *

Quanto a ti, corpo, terei talvez de te pedir desculpa. Não encontrei, em tantos anos, gasolina que me fizesse subir até ao cimo da igreja de Santa Engrácia. Não é que goste particularmente de estar vivo. Mas tudo acaba por ser preferível à morte, à súbita falência dos que nos rodeiam — e foram nossos pais, amigos, pessoas assim. Estamos aqui, onde nem sequer desejámos estar. Um fogo voraz aproxima-se das mãos, destas que ainda temos, para logo e para sempre desaparecer.

Bicicletas

à memória de Joana Dinis

Pedalar — e, se isto vos parecer retórico, faço questão de vos enviar ramos de jacintos, rosas de Santa Teresinha, essas coisas — é, por vezes, a única solução. Desenganados, fomos ver cegonhas, um falcão menos tímido, papoilas cujo rubor nenhum Monet fixou. Havia sobretudo vento, nêsperas ainda verdes, e pessoas que tão próximas ou distantes vão morrendo.

Pedalar contra o vento não é fácil.

Junto ao Chão, Close to the Ground, in Carlos Nogueira and
Manuel de Freitas (exhibition catalogue), Lisbon, Capela do Rato, 2018.

* * * * *

I admit that this matter — concerning what we may call an artistic and spiritual lineage — may not be determinant to the reading or the reception of the film in itself (is there, in Tarkovsky, such a strict notion as the film *in itself*?[1]). But it does open, undoubtedly, new pathways, suggesting dialogues that I could not have imagined twenty-five years ago (namely with Chekhov or Beckett, although these authors are never explicitly cited). Not by chance, it is up to Erland Josephson to embody the sacrificial aspect in these two films by Tarkovsky — and to go from a still bicycle (in *Nostalghia*) to the bicycle (in *The Sacrifice*) that will carry him to the most desperate sex scene I have ever seen in cinema.

* * * * *

As for you, my body, I probably owe you an apology. After all these years I still couldn't find enough gasoline to make me climb up to the top of Santa Engrácia Church. It is not that I am particularly fond of being alive. But ultimately everything seems preferable to death, to the sudden failure of those around us — and they were our parents, our friends, people like that. We are here, where we never even wanted to be. A ravenous fire draws near to our hands — these hands that are still our own –, and just as soon disappears forever.

Bicycles

in memory of Joana Dinis

Sometimes, to pedal — and, should you find this rhetorical, I'll make it a point of sending you hyacinths, roses of St. Thérèse, things like that — is the only solution. Disillusioned, we went out to see the storks, a bolder falcon, poppies whose redness no Monet has ever captured. There was mostly the wind, some yet unripe loquats, and people who, no matter how close or remote, keep on dying.

It is not easy to pedal against the wind.

---

[1] With this I'm suggesting that Tarkovsy has never conceived his cinema as a mere narrative. The poetic side — whether by using seemingly intrusive images, or by resorting to the poetry of his father, Arseni Tarkovsky — often undermines, suspends or illuminates the diegetic aspect. One must also take into account the role of music, a constant element in the great sacrificial moments of his work.

Margarida Vale de Gato

Talvez a Injeção Letal

tão cansada de engolir
comprimidos sem dormir
do meu sexo que se embota
do coração que se esgota
esticado na horizontal
sob uma agulha sensual
e a sopa na panela
embacia-me a janela
e sorvo mas sem palato
sem ter forças para o salto

se há uma falha um abalo
Dickinson Plath Woolf Kahlo
onde foram estavam loucas
queriam coisas eram ocas
queriam chique eram pedras
queriam arte eram merdas
tentando o voo eram estacas
punho em riste eram farpas
fornos hortos seu delírio
nunca foi santo martírio

Mulher ao Mar (Lisbon: Mariposa Azual, 2010)

Translated by MARTIN EARL

Perhaps the Lethal Injection

oh so tired of eating
pills and not sleeping
of my sex made dull
of my heart too full
stretched horizontally
under a tempting needle
and the soup on low
steaming up my window
like a fix, but weak
too delicate for the leap

if anything fails or shakes
Dickinson Plath Woolf Kahlo —
where they went was insane
wanted it all, but were hollow
wanted chic, got a rock
wanted art, were muck
wanted to soar, were stuck
fists on air, were thistles
ovens, orchards, their elation
was no pious abnegation.

MARGARIDA VALE DE GATO

Condições Mínimas

Esta sarça é interdita a matilhas;
há que mudar a pele para comer
o fogo. Não que eu faça render
qualquer talento, ou tenha em vasilhas

semi-intactas ilustres maravilhas:
uma lista de coisas a fazer,
solidão, pedra de isqueiro, um revólver,
e um aparelho já com pouca pilha

e que só uso eu; a nós vontade
basta — e alguma luz: pede-se intensa,
mas sem que obste o brilho à entrega cega,

aceitas? compreendes? aguentas?

no nervo negro desta densidade
penetra só sentindo que sustentas
e me conténs quando eu me desintegro.

Mulher ao Mar Retorna (Lisbon: Mariposa Azual, 2013)

Translated by Ana Hudson and Margarida Vale de Gato

Minimum Conditions

Wolf packs are barred entrance to this bush;
a change of skin must precede the eating
of fire. With this I am not boasting
of particular talents or hush-

ed-up wonders, semi-flawless flattery:
a to-do list, utter loneliness, bristle
cigarette lighter flint, a pistol,
a gadget almost out of battery

for my exclusive use. Willingness
suffices us — and light, hopefully bright,
although not outshining blind surrender

willl you accept? understand? take it in?

pierce the dark nerve of this denseness
but only if you're able to hold tight
and wholly contain me while I fall asunder.

MARGARIDA VALE DE GATO

A Imagem Romântica

Há outras coisas, Horácio,
e a tua filosofia é barata,
na verdade não custa fixar
as coisas ideais à distância:
terás vista panorâmica
mas sempre a visão é polémica.

Gostava que alguém me mostrasse,
mas não terei nunca garantia
de que envelhecer faça sentido.

As pessoas prostram-se, queremos que nos digam
porquê não haver luz nos seus rostos. Crestam
os cravos, antes rubros. Não há modo
de saber se as monarcas
têm memórias arenosas de lagarta.
Tudo sucede dentro de estanques
casulos, a seda é densa,
não se faz ideia
se isto acaba. Estrelas foscas
correm, pessoas morrem, a vida
é breve, impávido o
real se esquiva a designar.
Comparar é colidir: o verbo
talvez nos leve
a mais nenhum sinal.

Mulher ao Mar (Lisbon: Mariposa Azual, 2010)

Translated by RICHARD ZENITH

The Romantic Image

There are more things, Horatio,
and your philosophy's cheap,
it doesn't take much to capture
ideal things from a distance:
you get a panoramic view
but the vision is always debatable.

I'd like someone to show me,
but I can never be sure
there's a meaning to growing old.

People start drooping, we want them to tell us
why there's no light in their faces. The reddest
carnations wither. There's no way
to know if monarchs
have sandy caterpillar memories.
Everything happens in hermetic
cocoons, the silk's wound tight,
we've no idea
if this ends. Dim stars
hurtle, people die, life
is brief, undaunted
reality eludes designation.
To compare is to collide: the word
might lead us
to no further sign.

Margarida Vale de Gato

Termas e Cabaret

Foi preciso furar os poços para se livrar o Kaiser
da cobiça do sal, pois deles jorrou nascente (disse
o piedoso clérigo) numa terra onde a gente era feras
e comia pedra

mandou obra de banhos públicos, à imagem de *domus*
de vila clássica com veredas, pórticos, câmaras
numa planta onde gente ardera, vestindo cinzas
na sua fuga

os líderes nunca param com suas melhorias: o prédio
a seguir era *brique et pierre*, desta feita neoclássico
palácio, com mãos de gente destruída igualmente
por fome e vilania

disparando contra estátuas, sem que voltassem os nervos
ao sítio, onde se instalou o vício, onde vulgares diabruras
emanaram de gente repleta de espírito, involuntárias
judiarias

em caves com pinturas escarlates de medo, a serradura
traçada por foles de luz, relíquias de tabaco onde a trilha
leva os crentes ao fim (disse, de passagem, o platónico)
a gente falha

daqui a anos terraplanarão tipos, raças, onde as raízes
uns dos outros? falareis de nós como dum sonho (disse
Jorge de Sena) com muita calma, querida gente
tão obscena.

(Bad Oeynhausen, 24 de agosto de 2019)

Previously unpublished

Translated by MARGARIDA VALE DE GATO and MARTIN EARL

Baths and Cabaret

Drilling wells was necessary for the Kaiser to appease
his lust for salt, where a source would spring (said
the pious minister) on earth where people were beasts
and ate stone

he had public baths built, in the likeness of the *domus*
of classic villas with lanes, portals, chambers upon
a plant where people had burned, wearing ashes
in their wake

the leaders' improvements are never done: the next
building was *brique et pierre*, a fake neoclassical palace
then from the hands of people who were equally torn
off famine and villainy

shooting at statues, though that wouldn't wire the nerves
back in place, where vice seeped in, and ordinary
pranks oozed from people who were spirited, involuntary
sheenies

in caves with scarlet blotches of fear, with sawdust
scraped off bellows of light, tobacco relics whose trail
drives the faithful to the end (said the passing Platonist)
people fall

in the coming years they will flatten types, races, where
the roots of each to wit? You'll speak of us as of a dream
(said Jorge de Sena) very complacently, dear people
so obscene.

(*Bad Oeynhausen, August 24, 2019*)

RUI PIRES CABRAL

Collage poems from *Oh! Lusitania*

a white
city
changed to grey.

asphalt, gasoline,
the taint of
noise, and

money
atop the corpse of
beauty

everywhere
everywhere

sir,
it's too late
for singing
the long night
is done
and those
left behind
who did not
survive
are waiting for you
in your
cabin.

O! Lusitania (Lisbon: Paralelo W, 2013)

Reviews

Persona. Facsimile edition. 12 volumes in 11 + 1 (Lisbon: Tinta-da-china & Casa Fernando Pessoa, 2019). Print.

Metamorfoses. Edição do Centenário de Jorge de Sena, ed. by GILDA SANTOS (Rio de Janeiro and Belo Horizonte: Cátedra Jorge de Sena para Estudos Literários Luso-Afro-Brasileiros, UFRJ, & Editora Moinhos, 2019). 252 pages + images. Print.

Reviewed by PAULO DE MEDEIROS (University of Warwick)

In her introduction to this number of *Metamorfoses*, celebrating the centenary of the birth of Jorge de Sena, Luci Ruas, its general editor, announces it as a doubly special issue, as it both fulfils the original purpose for which it was started, as the official publication of the Chair of Luso-Afro-Brazilian Studies named after Sena at the Universidade Federal do Rio de Janeiro in 1999, and also represents a unique achievement, managing to include just over a hundred short articles on Jorge de Sena and his works from most distinguished scholars and critics who work in Portuguese Studies, as well as a large number of younger ones, demonstrating not only the sheer vibrancy of the discipline but also myriad connections through the generations. Sena, of course, as controversial as some of his work will always be, not only is indisputably one of the major authors of the twentieth century, but his erudition, sharp critical acumen, and enormous scholarly production make him a key figure to represent the discipline transnationally, as he liked to see himself as at once a Portuguese author, a Brazilian (naturalized) citizen, and a US academic, having held chairs both in Brazil and later in the United States, after he went into self-exile. In her own introductory piece, 'Jorge de Sena entre nós' [Jorge de Sena among us], Gilda Santos, the organizer of this special issue, focuses at once on Sena's period in Brazil and on the way he remains among all who read him now and into the future. It is a Sena both permanently displaced and yet always belonging, always creating possibilities for belonging across national divides, that Santos offers us in this special issue that itself transcends the normal boundaries of a scholarly journal in the multitude of perspectives offered and in the variety of modes of writing it includes, from the analytical to the fictional, from the theoretical to a more traditional close reading, and never forgetting the poetical.

Special as the Sena issue of *Metamorfoses* is, the facsimile edition of the legendary journal of Pessoa studies, *Persona*, under the general editorship of Jerónimo Pizarro, in collaboration with the original editor, Arnaldo Saraiva, is nothing short of a milestone. The first striking feature of this edition is its overall high quality, from the paper stock to the high definition images, the sober yet striking use of Pessoa's effigy throughout, down to the detail of the half-cassette that holds the slim volumes together. But the possibility of once again having access to the articles and documents first published in *Persona* from 1977 to 1985 would have been sufficient cause for rejoicing. Not only are many of those essays pioneering in the study of Fernando Pessoa, but the publication across eight years serves as privileged window on the development of the field, and in particular as the *Livro do Desassossego* [Book of Disquiet], arguably Pessoa's masterpiece, was published for the first time in 1982 in what would begin an editing and publication saga almost as plural as the poet himself. Jorge de Sena, of course, was one of the central figures involved in the development of Pessoa studies and one of the first to recognize the importance and complexity of that most posthumous of all posthumous works, that has caused Alain Badiou to reflect that we might still not have learned to be contemporaries of Pessoa.

The sheer number of senior scholars and highly regarded poets signing individual small articles in *Metamorfoses* cuts across a number of divides. To name just a few, in order of inclusion, we have: Nuno Júdice, Rosa Martelo, Maria Alzira Seixo, Eugénio Lisboa, Ida Alves, Helder Macedo, Fernando J. B. Martinho, Isabel Pires de Lima, Manuel Gusmão, Cleonice Berardinelli, Roberto Vecchi, Jorge Fazenda Lourenço, Onésimo Teotónio Almeida, K. David Jackson, Jerónimo Pizarro, Ana Luísa Amaral, Ana Paula Tavares, and many others. The volume is divided basically into three main sections: first, 'Verbetes e Variações', by far the largest, and internally structured according to Sena's various publications; then a shorter, 'Glosas', apparently more creative and a kind of poetic interaction with Sena's works; and finally, a 'Caderno de Imagens', with a selection of images reproducing well-known works of art that are related to the poems included in Sena's collection with the title of *Metamorfoses*. Although there is nothing to fault in all this, the division between the more critical and the more creative pieces is one that appears unnecessary to me — indeed, I very much think that all the different pieces that variously reflect elements of close reading, structural analysis, commentary, personal observation, testimony, and theoretical reflection, could have been seen as favouring a certain hybridity, to which Sena was no stranger himself. As for the last section, with images, it is of course useful, given that those poems enter in a dialogue — one is tempted to view it almost as dialectic — with famous works of visual art in ways that go beyond the simply ekphrastic. However, I would even have preferred to have them dispersed and interspersed throughout the volume, one to a page if possible; likewise, even though the image that opens the volume, depicting Sena giving a lecture before a large audience at the Universidade de Lourenço Marques in 1972 (a photo by Ricardo Rangel), is very significant, it leaves one wishing for more.

This desire for more is also evoked by the two short, yet very informative articles that make up the additional 'volume' included with the facsimile edition of *Persona*. With the general title of 'A Esquecida e Inesquecível' it includes an entry by Arnaldo Saraiva, 'Para a história da revista *Persona*' and one by Jerónimo Pizarro, 'Em memória da *Persona*'. In a sense, they not only complement each other but also reflect back on each other, as the designations of 'History' and 'Memory' in their respective titles already indicate. Saraiva provides a few, important, contextual facts and dates concerning the creation of *Persona* and the Centre for Pessoa Studies, at the University of Porto, as a consequence of the new air let in by the revolution in 1974. A curious detail for instance, is the announcement that, similar to *Orfeu*, *Persona* was also supposed to have had one more number (in this case the 13th), which existed in proofs, yet never made it to final publication. If Saraiva leaves us with the promise that one day he will tell more — 'Um dia contarei a história' (p. 3) — a reader can only wonder what happened to those proofs and whether it might be possible to retrieve them at some point if they were not lost or published in another venue. Pizarro, in his turn, offers an accelerated overview of some crucial articles and documents that first appeared in *Persona*. Some of these (all reproduced in facsimile, or actually in some cases as facsimile of a facsimile) are merely antiquarian curiosities, such as the polemic between August Willemsen and Edwin Honig; while others, such as the reproduction of Pessoa's youthful notebook in volume 9 (1983), continue to fascinate. Pizarro concludes his homage with a characteristically modest note, stating that notwithstanding Pessoa's canonization and the elevation of his papers to the category of a 'national treasure', there still is no new journal dedicated to Pessoa studies, just as there never was another Centre for Pessoa Studies. Too modest, perhaps, as he leaves out mentioning *Pessoa Plural*, an electronic journal he co-founded and of which he is still the lead editor, which has published a large number of articles and other documents on Pessoa since. And while it is true that no other Centre has been established, this might be more of a reflection of a changed academic landscape, especially in Portugal, where funding requirements have led to the disappearance of many research centres and the consolidation of several into very large units, and also of an exponential growth in the internationalization of Pessoa studies.

For readers familiar with the many works of Sena the present special issue of *Metamorfoses* holds much value, be it through the possibility of comparing reading notes with so many others, be it because some of the readings are frankly original and an invaluable contribution to current scholarship on Sena, be it still because of the testimonial aspect a good number of entries also contains. K. David Jackson, for instance, in '"Cantiga de Ceilão", Com Jorge de Sena em Santa Bárbara' (pp. 204–05) lets us in on the creative process of Sena by relating his visit to Sena in California on March 1974, and sharing some recordings of music as well as some verses, registered on one of his trips to Sri Lanka, which obviously became linked to Sena's poem. Sofia de Sousa Silva brings Sena into relation with Sophia de Mello Breyner Andresen, and at the same time both Camões and Pessoa. The entries that closely mix the personal and the critical bring out unexpected facets. Teresa Cristina Cerdeira, for instance, tells us about her walking through the 'beautiful aristocratic rooms' of the Wallace Collection with one of Sena's poems in her hands to 'confront Fragonard's *L'Escarpolette* with Sena's "O Balouço"' (p. 90). Or consider the fascinating commentary by Roberto Vecchi, on 'Uma sepultura em Londres' [A Grave in London], from 1969, an obvious reference to Marx's final resting place in Highgate (pp. 134–35).

The facsimile edition of *Persona* has all the makings of a collector's item, given the importance and relevance of its contents and the high quality of the printing and graphic presentation. Beyond research libraries one can think of it as tempting for many private buyers, especially given its very reasonable price. Admirable as it is as an object in itself, though, I can only wish that Tinta-da-china would consider making it available in electronic format, at a reduced price, so that it could be much more accessible and not risk, like the original *Persona*, becoming accessible only to the few who might have the privilege of accessing specialized libraries, as was my case, for instance, when at the University of Utrecht. And the same could be said of the special issue of *Metamorfoses* on Jorge de Sena. At the moment past issues of the journal are available online through its own portal <https://revistas.ufrj.br/index.php/metamorfoses>, but with a delay of one year. So, perhaps it is just a question of being patient. Nonetheless, I think that given the nature of this one issue it would merit making it available as a separate ebook through a number of digital platforms, either on open access or for a modest price once that one year is over, as it might thus reach an even wider audience, as it deserves. These two publications demonstrate clearly how vibrant the field of Portuguese Studies is and also how publishing houses and universities are launching projects of very high quality. They each represent a milestone of their own while, if seen in combination, they also reveal some of the interlinked elements that bind poetry and the arts with their critical appreciation and study across generations.

ALBERTO PIMENTA, *Zombo* (Lisbon: Edições do Saguão, 2019). 126 pages. Print.

Reviewed by LÚCIA LIBERATO EVANGELISTA (University of Porto)

Forty-nine years separate Alberto Pimenta's first book (1970) and his latest, *Zombo*.[1] Throughout his vast production, the author has kept away from criticism by going against the strong lyrical tradition of Portuguese poetry, by operating in different media (performance, collage, television shows, review writing and essays), and even more by managing to avoid being categorized. He has always refused labels such as 'experimental writer' and denies being a

[1] This review was written as part of research carried out in the ILCML, R&D Unit financed by National Funds through FCT – Fundação para a Ciência e a Tecnologia [Portuguese Foundation for Science and Technology] (UIDP/00500/2020). Translated from the Portuguese by Elena Galvão. All English quotations are free translations.

'marginal author'. Alberto Pimenta claims to be simply 'unexpected'. There are, however, certain things that his usual readers can expect from him. A book by Alberto Pimenta never misses a trick. Everything is part of the plot: title, front cover, back cover, table of contents, footnotes, prefaces, postscripts, flaps. Everything composes the literary work, everything is tied together, everything is a poetic act.

In *ZOMBO*, for starters, we are immediately attracted by the sound vibrations reverberating both off the title and the image of an ear on the back cover. *ZOMBO*, two syllables: one sibilant, one occlusive. Or: a whisper-buzz and a blow-strike. Or even: idyll and satire, utopia and criticism — all dimensions that Alberto Pimenta's controversial poetry has been exploring from the beginning.

An acrobat playing with senses and sounds, a thinker who encloses himself within concepts, Alberto Pimenta likes to quote a saying by T. W. Adorno comparing poetry to a somersault. The risky flip exists with the sole purpose of challenging the impossible. *ZOMBO* is all about risk and reflection. Risk and reflection, in fact, emerge right away on the book's cover: two characters, one of whom is suspended in the air, jumping, whereas the other is thinking, with both feet on the ground. The book begins even before its beginning. It begins (before beginning) with an epigraph which may be read as a first poem: '*Periandro de Corinto, filho de Cypsélos, disse: "Cala as tuas desgraças, para que teus inimigos não rejubilem!"* | *Alberto do Porto, dito Mínimo, despediu-se: "Estou me cagando para isso!"*' [Periander of Corinth, son of Cypselus, said, 'Hide your misfortunes and your enemies will not rejoice!' | Alberto do Porto, also known as Minimum, took his leave and said, 'I don't give a shit about that!']

That he won't keep silent in the face of misfortune is another aspect to be expected from the author. Pimenta has not remained silent for a very long time. At the age of 82, he is still able to produce a volume whose title consists of a verb conjugated in the first person singular: *ZOMBO*, which may be translated as 'I play, I mock, I joke'. Could the verb *Zombar* then be a form of not staying quiet? The initial verses of 'NÓS, QUE NEXO' (pp. 7–10) [KNOTS or WE, WHAT A NEXUS] read, '*estou exausto deste serviço* | *mais não* | *não peçam,* | *despeçam-me; tanto tempo a contra* | *para quê, para quem?*' [I am exhausted from all this work | no more | don't ask me for more | sack me; so much time narrating | for what, for whom?] (p. 7). The individual *nó* [knot] becomes intertwined with the plural *Nós* [meaning 'knots' or the first person plural 'we']. The subject does seem tired, but he is mostly tired of a civilization which is itself tired — as Maria Irene Ramalho pointed out in her review of this book (*Jornal de Letras*, 2019: 16). It is a civilization which does not yet know where to start, and which does not stop announcing its end. A civilization which plunders time out of life itself — '*estes mártires da Sua Liberdade*' [these martyrs of Its Liberty] (p. 9) — and out of slaves, workers, the indebted — '*vem de longe o nexo, nexus romanus,* | *artigo de luxo, escravo sempre,* | *escravo até que desate o nó, pague* | *tudo o que deve, e a dívida cresce* | *enquanto o tempo corre veloz com ela,* | [...]' [from afar comes the nexus, *nexus romanus,* | luxury item, ever a slave, | slave till the knot is untied, and pays | all that is due, and the debt keeps growing | as time flies by with it | [...]] (p. 10). It is a suicidal civilization that postpones its end.

Alberto of Porto does not hide his misfortunes, but rather makes mockery of them (*zomba*). *Mockery (Zombaria)* arises as the negative side of silence. Words laugh about words, they get angry at themselves. In *RETRATO [PORTRAIT]* 'não era isto! então o quê? | quantas vezes eu ouvi, | não era isto! | então o quê? | [...]' [*this wasn't it!* then what? | how many times have I heard, | *this wasn't it!* | then what? | [...]] (p. 48). Or in *CANTATA PARA AMÉLIA [CANTATA FOR AMÉLIA]*: 'não | nem mais | uma palavra só, não | pobres palavras sós | em si exaustas | ou antes exaustas de si | [...]' [no | not another | word, no | poor lonely words | exhausted in themselves | or rather exhausted from themselves | [...]] (p. 61).

Carlos Drummond, in 'Poema-Orelha' (1959), used to say that the best poetry is a minus sign.[2] And *ZOMBO* displays a great, lonely ear on the back cover.[3] Alberto do Porto, o Mínimo (Alberto of Porto, the Minimum) listens to what is said in Portuguese and dismantles it. And he gets angry at himself and at the readers. The final note of 'SETE PANFLATOS e um provérbio colombiano' [SEVEN PAMPHLATS and a Colombian proverb] (pp. 33–40) reads, 'as eventuais gralhas deste livro são da conta do leitor' [possible misspellings within this book are the reader's responsibility] (p. 40). It is an ironic sound which resonates with Camões and Cesário Verde, but from which it is possible to hear the music scores of social, political, and economic powers — as, for instance, in the poem *METAS [GOALS]* with subjects such as 'ursa mental' [beardgetary][4] (pp. 28–30); or in *PALHINHA [LITTLE STRAW]* (pp. 31–32); or even in LOVE TONIGHT (pp. 79–81), when he mentions the 'Bandas Bolso ignaro' [the 'Bolso ignorant' bands].[5]

In *ZOMBO* there are various forms and themes, each poem defying the next, and those mischievous and introspective verses stage a time which ties up, unties and ties up again — 'teço o que teço | desteço | o que apeteço | e a ninguém peço licença' [I weave what I weave | I unweave | what I please | and I do not seek consent] (p. 113). A time which pertains to a life that inhabits a world, but also to a world that inhabits a life. In this path-labyrinth, Alberto insists on the question, 'Que é isto?' [What is this?] (pp. 93–110). And he asks, from underneath what's visible — '[...] estou de certeza | no subterrâneo do tempo | que anda, anda aqui debaixo | do outro, que anda por cima | [...]' [[...] I

---

[2] Translator's note: despite not being quoted in the original text, 'the best poetry is a minus sign' is from an official translation of the poem in question, by Virgília de Araújo (The Minus Sign, 1980)
[3] Translator's note: this poem by Carlos Drummond de Andrade is a pun on the word *orelha*, as it has a double meaning in Portuguese: 'ear' and 'book flap'.
[4] Translator's note: while the literal translation for *ursa mental* is 'mental bear', the author is punning on the similarity with the word *orçamental*, which means 'budgetary'.
[5] Translator's note: this is yet another wordplay, with *ignaro* meaning 'ignorant' or 'oblivious' and the expression resembling the name of Brazil's president, Bolsonaro.

am certainly | in the underground of time | time wanders, wanders deep down | below the other, who is wandering above | [...]] (p. 96). He asks questions about the life that remains unseen — 'MEMO RIA ou' [MEMO RY or] (pp. 56–90); he also asks questions about what still lies on the other side of history, as in 'A PENÚLTIMA CEIA' [THE PENULTIMATE SUPPER] (pp. 76–77). It is a poetic act that goes from the individual to the collective, from the collective to the individual. 'RESSONÂNCIAS MAGNÉTICAS' [MAGNETIC RESONANCES] (p. 65): a medical exam and an art critic.

Culture is made of omissions, Alberto Pimenta said during the presentation of the tribute-film *O Homem Pycante* (2018), by Portuguese director Edgar Pêra, at the *Cinema Monumental de Lisboa* (6 April 2019). Here is where the words '*I don't give a shit*' from the epigraph poem acquire their full meaning. With its grotesque-satirical topic, *ZOMBO* seems to enable us to see and hear exactly what culture omits. It appears to play with it and with those who take advantage of such omissions. In the illustration on the book's cover and on the colophon, we can see the impertinent image of a fly. 'SETE PANFLATOS' reads, 'Eu sei, eu sei, | não devia matar moscas... | não sei fazer mais nada! e... | não prejudico ninguém. | *prejudicas as moscas!* | sabes lá se elas não estão também fartas dessa merda!... | *não há outra!* | não sabes, a outra | tem muitos crentes, | que só pensam nela, | nesta até jejuam | só para lá ir pousar!' [I know, I know, | I know better than to kill flies... | that is all I do! and... | I do no harm. | *you harm the flies!* | how would you know that they're not tired of this shit, too!... | *there is no other!* | you don't know, but the other | has many believers, | who think of nothing else, | in this one they even fast | just to alight there!] (p. 35). It is important to note that *moscas* [flies] was the derogatory name for undercover policemen during Salazar's dictatorship. Today, one might say that flies are those who live off the *data* of our 'shitty' daily routines — the Internet is the new PIDE (Portuguese International and State Defence Police from the *Estado Novo* regime), Alberto Pimenta explained in an interview (*Jogos Florais*, 2018). The poem 'DOCES MUSAS' [LOVING MUSES] reads, '*olha, lembras-te | d'* "o discreto charme da burguesia", | *lembras-te?* | pois é, mas onde se meteu ela, essa burguesia? || *continua sentada em reunião | concorrencial | no seu trabalho visceral | a produzir investimento | que não aparece à luz, | só na sombra dos mercados:* | *não cheira, o* charme *é dos dados!* | ah! mas dados ou à venda?' [*do you remember* | the 'discreet charm of the bourgeoisie', | *do you?* | right, but where is it, this bourgeoisie? | *still sitting, in a meeting | competing | viscerally working | producing investment | that does not meet the light, | it lies instead in the shadows of the markets:* | *it is unscented, the* charm *is in the free data!* || ah! but free or for sale?] (p. 27). And then I too start imagining a fly who would rejoice at hearing the ruminant speech of everyday life in 'Boa Vizinhança' [Good Neighbourhood] (pp. 44–47).

Alberto Pimenta does not miss a trick. And the path from the singular 'nexus' and the collective 'knots' is entangled amidst risks, misdemeanour, forgetfulness, dismay and long-gone memories — PROLAPSO [PROLAPSE] (pp. 22–24) and POSLAPSO [POSTLAPSE] (pp. 90–92). A pathway with entrance doors but with no foreseeable exit so far. 'PORTA 2' [DOOR 2] (pp. 13–16) describes the pathway to a time with no drama or urgent desire to escape; 'PORTA GIRATÓRIA' [REVOLVING DOOR] (pp. 17–21) describes a western eschatology that collects the interests accrued from our faith in money.

The book's end resumes the dialogue found at the beginning — 'Periandro de Corinto, filho de Cypsélos, disse: "O descanso é uma coisa boa!" | Alberto do Porto, dito Mínimo, observou: "Estou de acordo contigo!"' [Periander of Corinth, son of Cypselus, said, 'Resting is a good thing!' | Alberto of Porto, also known as Mininum, observed, 'I agree with you!']. But it is still not the end. After this, instead of an index, we can read 'DISSE' [I SAID]. We are again attracted by sounds. Even more: the book that announced itself through a verb in the first person, present tense — *zombo* [I mock] — now meets a first person from the past — I said. And this is still not the end. In the book's colophon the fly persists; and on the back cover, lonely and wise, lies the large and venerable ear. The quest for the unexpected continues.

ZOMBO is a book that succeeds in accomplishing what poetry does best: sewing together a singular time with a collective time; sewing together a time that *was* with a time that *is* — read, apropos, the 'SONETO ERRÁTICO com duas caudas (ou codas para pessoas distintas)' [ERRATIC SONNET with a double tail (or codas for distinguished people)] (p. 115).[6] And, along the way, who knows, one may blow away or squash a few flies.

ADÍLIA LOPES, *Aqui estão as minhas contas: antologia poética*, ed. with preface by SOFIA DE SOUSA SILVA (Rio de Janeiro: Bazar do tempo, 2019). 199 pages. Print.

Reviewed by JERÓNIMO PIZARRO (Universidad de los Andes, Colombia)

In 2019, in the Atlântica collection, which 'seeks to present a panorama of the best Portuguese poetry in Brazil', an anthology of poems by Adília Lopes was published. Adília Lopes is a poet who in Brazil has had a very positive reception and has been read by authors of several generations. The anthology, selected and prefaced by Sofia de Sousa Silva, appeared a year after another one made in Colombia and published by a publisher in Medellín: Tragaluz. Adília Lopes's work is being increasingly read and studied outside Portugal, though it remains to be seen whether it will be also within her own country, where it collides with the poetics of other writers, although many defend her — and her 'rather dangerous game', to recall her first book of verses — and she has many devoted readers.

In Brazil, where the 2019 anthology was published, 'Adília Lopes was first published in May 2001, in the 10th issue of the poetry magazine *Inimigo Rumor*', as Silva mentions in her preface. The anthologist adds that in 2002 the São Paulo

---

[6] Translator's note: once more, the author puns on the similarity between the word *cauda* meaning 'tail' and *coda*, 'coda'.

publisher Cosac Naify, now defunct, published, in the collection Ás de Colete, a selection of her poetry, and that in 2018, the independent publishing house Moinhos published *Um jogo bastante perigoso* — and did so with remarkable enthusiasm: 'Owner of a unique imagination, [her] poetry is able to trip up the reader spectacularly, mixing the language of quantum mechanics and encrypted quotes to/from classic authors, with the mental logic of neighbours, old aunts, porcelain dolls, mundane life in Lisbon, and geckos [lizards from Portugal], leaving us helpless — and in love' (see foreword).

The recently published *carioca* anthology contributes to getting to know Adília Lopes beyond 2002 and it is now the best book, for those who live in Brazil, or for those who do not want to begin with *Dobra*, to discover an anti-poet that only those who do not *only* write conventional poetry can read laughing and with passion. In Brazil, where 'the strong colloquialism of Adília Lopes, as well as her *humour*', converse with a 'tradition of the short poem, of the joke poem' (I'm quoting Sofia de Sousa Silva), the admirers are many and will be even more. The anthology does not include narrative poems such as *O poeta de Pondichéry* or *Maria Cristina Martins*, among others, but the former has already been published in *Inimigo Rumor*, and it might even be the object of a re-translation, along with the latter, bearing in mind that these two books have already been published as one in Portugal (and this set is already translated into French by Henri Deluy).

I said, 'for those who live in Brazil', but I could also have said for those who read Portuguese because there are missing anthologies of Adília Lopes, and because this one from 2019 is perfect to get to know, to teach, or simply disseminate the poet who wrote, in *Bandolim* (2016, p. 180), 'Fernando Pessoa invented the Chevalier de Pas, I, who in the end must be Fernanda Pessoa, modesty aside, invented the prosaic Maria Antónia' (see the article by António Ladeira, 'Devo ser a Fernanda Pessoa, modéstia à parte', included in the magazine, *eLyra* dedicated to Adília Lopes, at <https://elyra.org/>). Maria Antónia? Yes, because Adília Lopes, the literary pseudonym of Maria José da Silva Viana Fidalgo de Oliveira, invented many imaginary friends, among them Maria Antónia, and because there are already extensive studies on the subject's figurative experience in her poetry, especially those of the teacher (and poet) Rosa Martelo.

About the anthology as prepared by Sofia de Sousa Silva, it should still be said that it contains, in the final pages, a very useful set of notes (for 'Enterros', for example: 'Tide is a brand of powdered soap, which had as its advertising slogan "Tide washes whitest"') and an indispensable study of some of Adília's poems, or rather, an essayistic attempt to prolong the notes. Thus, for example, Silva dedicates six pages to a poem from *Sete rios entre campos* (1999) — a title that gathers the names of two Lisbon neighbourhoods: Sete Rios and Entrecampos — to illuminate a text that converses at the same time with Camões, Ricardo Reis and 'a jester from Vigo, Mendinho, author of just one known song ("Sedia-m'eu na ermida de Sam Simion")' (p. 169). In a recent text, published in the magazine *A Virada — Literatura e Crítica* <https://a-virada. com/>, I discuss the annotation in poetry (cf. 'O ar lisbonudo e a poesia'). I believe that Sofia de Sousa Silva wisely knew how to transform the exercise of annotating Adília Lopes into a final essay, and that her lesson can be followed by future editors and translators. *Here's my balance* is, in short, an anthology that reveals a part of almost all the books of a great author and that elegantly illuminates her verses.

ANA LUÍSA AMARAL and MARINELA FREITAS (eds), *Do corpo: outras habitações: identidade e desejos outros em alguma poesia portuguesa* (Porto: Assírio & Alvim, 2018). 344 pages. Print.

Reviewed by ANA FILIPA PRATA (Universidad de los Andes, Colombia)

Do corpo: outras habitações: identidade e desejos outros em alguma poesia portuguesa brings an entirely new perspective on Portuguese poetry of the twentieth century (and the first two decades of the twenty-first). Published by Assírio & Alvim, this anthology is organized and presented by Ana Luísa Amaral and Marinela Freitas, who have selected more than one hundred poems, by more than forty authors, all about the representation of non-normative identities. It invites us therefore to consider new interpretations for well-known poems and to read recent compositions within this specific framework and in dialogue with the tradition. This book goes beyond the traditional reception of poetic *topoi* such as love and desire, and stands out for its commitment to subaltern identities and alternative gender performances, as Amaral and Freitas emphasize in their introduction. This is a very significant issue indeed, and it can be considered one of the virtues of the publication, but it is not totally new. This book appeared in 2018 in the wake of the censored editorial project *Antologia de Poesia Portuguesa Erótica e Satírica*, organized by Natália Correia and published in 1966. We are clearly dealing here with different temporal and critical scopes: notions of identity, love and eroticism have changed over time. However, it is very interesting to note that both anthologies share similar social, political and poetic concerns. If identifying deviant experiences of love or groundbreaking discourses on the representation of the self in literature was revolutionary in the 1960s, it is nowadays still urgent and mandatory.

Do corpo: outras habitações opens with Mário de Sá Carneiro's 'Feminina' and closes with Golgona Anghel's 'Vocês até podem não concordar com tudo isto' [You may not even agree with all of this]. Time and space between both poems become the stage for poetical expressions that release identities and bodies from subservience and domination. The first poem, 'Feminina', introduces main topics such as gender role play, identity as performance, eroticism and the female body; these are enunciated by a male subject who desires to be a woman: 'Eu queria ser mulher...' [I wanted to be a woman...]. One century later, Anghel's poem testifies to a contemporary generation of women who, not without violence, subverted conventions and raised their voices intending to be treated as equals. Good stories are for sale where reality is insufficient.

This anthology draws on the creation of a female poetic tradition and, at the same time, on the need to resist conventions. It creates a place for enunciation, while emphasizing the process and not necessarily the product, since subjects continuously strive to be subjects, as suggested in Ana Hatherly's verses, quoted in the introduction: 'A gente | só é dominada por essa gente | quando não sabe que é gente' [We people, | we are only dominated by those people | when we don't recognize ourselves as people]. There are also several male poets or male fictional voices who contribute to place 'num plano justo | e claro | uma razão' [this demand in a fair and clear disposition] (p. 33). António Botto, Pedro Homem de Melo, Mário Cesariny, Armando Silva Carvalho or even Boaventura Sousa Santos, among others, all defy conventional masculinity and/or sexuality. Nevertheless, we still can count (fortunately) many more women than men within this anthology, which is a crucial point that the organizers justify in the introduction underlining their critical and political positioning. This, of course, without sacrificing literary and poetic aspects. Activism is meaningful in times when gender equality has become a widespread concern, but not always under the focus of editorial and critical decisions, Amaral and Freitas affirm.

Including renowned authors such as Florbela Espanca or Sophia de Mello Breyner Andresen side by side with Filipa Leal, Margarida Vale de Gato, Ana Marques Gastão — to name just the youngest — Amaral and Freitas contribute here to the formation of a Portuguese feminine literary canon and present, to both larger and more specialized audiences, a new contribution to the discussion on gender and literature that they have been developing in their academic research. Amaral and Freitas display the fundamental tools, which are the poems, and the possibility to read them in dialogue with others texts and critical perspectives, extending the debate to a wider net of solidarities that must be considered when thinking about marginal voices without totalizing differences.

The introduction by the editors is both a statement of a 'theoretical inflection' and a brief discussion about the importance of gender conventions and poetic representations of (other)sexuality in Portuguese poetry all through the twentieth century. More than a compilation of texts grouped around a certain theme, or from a certain period, this anthology focuses on the reception of the poems, but explicitly proposes new interpretations. *Do corpo: outras habitações* is thus simultaneously a compilation of major poems and poets, but also a political statement that emphatically pushes forward some less celebrated names and, consequently, a majority of female authors, who from their subversive language and poetic strategies are able to problematize and criticize heteropatriarchal discourses, giving a brand new and fresh perspective on a conservative way of reading Portuguese poetry and literature in general. Adília

Lopes sums it all up quite well in 'Poetisa-Fêmea, Poeta-Macho' (cliché em papel couché): 'Sou um poeta-macho | tenho um gabinete | sou uma poetisa fêmea | escrevo na retrete | Sou um poeta-macho | sou um badalo | sou uma poetisa-fêmea | calo-me' [I am a male-poet | I have an office | I am a female poet | I write in the toilets | I am a male poet | I am a clapper | I am a female poet | I shut up].

MANUEL DE FREITAS, *Ubi Sunt*, with an afterword by Mariano Marovatto (Juiz de Fora, MG: Macondo, 2019). 92 pages. Print.

Reviewed by IDA ALVES (Universidade Federal Fluminense, RJ)

Ubi Sunt, by the contemporary Portuguese poet Manuel de Freitas, now in a Brazilian edition, brings together forty-one poems in three sections: 'HIC', 'ET NUNC', 'ET SEMPER'. In the prose poem 'Comovidos a Oeste' [Moved to the West] (p. 37), we find: 'The fundamental usefulness of poetry is, for me, its vocation to approximate people and dilute false borders. Everything else — don't get me wrong — is only history of literature.' The two verbs, *approximate* and *dilute*, may indicate two significant axes in the work of this poet, critic, editor, and translator, who has been, since the end of the 1990s, one of the most interesting poetic and critical voices in Portugal. Over the years, Manuel de Freitas has published anthologies with other poets and more than four dozen poetry books, as well as literary criticism and translations. He is the editor of two valuable magazines on poetry/critique, *Telhados de Vidro* and *Cão Celeste*, and a poet with a keen perspective on current literature, on Portuguese culture and on European urban reality which, due to the forces of globalization, can be experienced anywhere.

Though relatively well known in Brazil, especially in the Rio de Janeiro/ São Paulo circuit, to those who are interested in recent poetry and that follow attentively what is being done abroad, his work in that country was previously limited to two brief anthologies of his poetry: the first one published in 2007 (by Oficina Raquel, Rio de Janeiro) and the second, seven years later (in the *Ciranda da Poesia* Collection of the publishing house of Rio de Janeiro University — EdUERJ), both organized by Luis Maffei. Therefore, this is the first time that a complete book by Manuel de Freitas has been edited among us: *Ubi Sunt*, whose original edition came out in Lisbon, in 2014. Published in Brazil by a recently established contemporary poetry publisher, Macondo, based in the city of Juiz de Fora, Minas Gerais state, this book is the first volume of *A Colecção*, a five-book collection of contemporary Portuguese poetry. The idea defended by the editors is to invite 'their readers to get to know new affective, political and poetic geographies. Books that are like homes. Books that grow like trees', provoking the friction of the poetic Portuguese language (note the non-Brazilian spelling 'colecção'). The work of this Brazilian publisher is similar to that of Manuel de Freitas's own publishing house, Averno, which publishes mainly lesser-known poets in small format books of less than 100 pages, equally small circulation, and discreet or artisanal graphic design, taking into consideration the editorial reality of poetry not having an abundant audience. At the end, the Macondo edition carries an afterword written in fragments by Mariano Marovatto (a young composer, singer, guitarist and poet) dwelling on Manuel de Freitas and the 'feasible disenchantment of Lisbon' (p. 83), with the appreciation of the reader as 'dysphoric accomplice' (p. 85).

But let us go back to the verbs *approximate* and *dilute*. In *Ubi Sunt*, prose poems are predominant, and they approximate, by affection and by the irremediable presence of death, the people who marked the poet's paths in the past and present, places in his life, such as Santarém, Coimbra and Lisbon, with their streets and corners, and human-sized trading: taverns, alehouses, cafes, small bookstores, record stores. With wandering eyes, the lyrical subject evokes reading friends, ordinary people like employees or tavern and café owners, his woman accomplice of so many common projects, Inês Dias, also a recurrently named poet, and his departed father and mother (the book is, in fact, dedicated to his mother's memory). Apart from the closer and more personal companions, poets, musicians and singers, he also evokes characters from other poems (his own or not) and narratives, as well as animals, especially his cats. Thus, the poems are not only directly addressed to companions on journeys and projects (out of the 41 poems, 25 present explicit dedications or epigraphs; in others, it is in the titles that figures and memories are evoked) but also summon, in daily experiences, two forces in friction: the resistance of life and the inevitability of death. 'Poetry sometimes serves to make us feel a little sadder, more lonely and out of place. For it does not ignore, indifferent to the brief look we exchange, the haste in which the afternoon dissolves itself and so do we' (p. 58). It is already commonplace to point out in Manuel de Freitas's writing an agonistic sense of existence, a melancholic diction in the face of the constant presence of death (let us not forget the author has organized an anthology entitled *A perspectiva da morte* [The perspective of death]: *20 (-2) poetas portugueses do século XX* (Assírio & Alvim, Lisbon, 2009). However, when reading *Ubi Sunt*, it is important to highlight his recurring gesture of collecting memories (from friends, from other poets, from people and their common services and, above all, from places where he's lived, from experiences he's shared), a Benjaminian gesture that is configured as a means of survival in a city reality marked by a progressive loss of human interaction spaces, swallowed by a predatory tourism industry supported by a capitalism of indifferentiation and individualism. 'I wouldn't like to appear nostalgic, but there was a time when Lisbon would entice me mainly because of its bookstores, cafes and record stores that allowed us the luxury of postponing death. All of that is lost, obviously' (p. 52). The writing of the poems enables one to keep, to remove from the vortex of indifference, words of others and his own (remains that come from other texts), songs and artists, verses from other poets, human presences that give some meaning to what is lived and lost on a daily basis, frayed daily tissue.

Manuel de Freitas was born in Santarém in 1972, moved to Lisbon in his youth (aged 18) and keeps from that capital, and other cities where he used to live, a map of his own disquiet in modest streets and common welcoming spaces where one could have a drink, talk, listen and see the movement of the world. His poems go on designating people, places, readings and songs, configuring a mosaic of references of which each poem is a tesserae — and let us not forget that *mosaic* comes from the Greek μουσαικόν (mousaikón), meaning 'work of the muses'. But this constant gesture of approximation or reappropriation is also accompanied by the experience of dilution, for everything is crossed by time, by passage, by loss. Not for nothing does the epigraph of *Ubi Sunt* come from Guillaume Apollinaire: 'Passons passons puisque tout passe | Je me retournerait souvent ‖ Les souvenirs sont cors de chasse | Dont meurt le bruit parmi le vent', reminding us of another Portuguese poet, Jorge de Sena, who in the long poem 'A morte, o espaço, a eternidade' [Death, Space, Eternity] (in *Metamorfoses*, 1963), wrote: 'Of natural death no one has ever died | We were not born to die'. In the writing of Sena, whose poetry is often referenced by contemporary poets, including Manuel de Freitas, the verb *to pass* is also recurrent; therefore, the poem testifies, resists and insubordinates.

Poetry readers, as inhabitants of any of today's cities, will know how to recognize themselves in Manuel de Freitas's book, especially in times like ours, when virtual networks make the reality of massification and the acceleration of daily life more evident. They will probably be able to follow the poet's wandering in this Lisbon of today, so transformed by the interests of the tourist market that displaces or ignores people and their simple daily spaces of affection, of shared life, of unrepeatable experiences. Those who will probably most fully understand such poetry are the increasingly urban readers, who see their own cities degraded by the unstoppable political and economic actions that for the most part despise the human factor. And they will share that affectionate gesture (and we think, with Rancière, of a policy of affection) of keeping what inexorably moves on, and of taking care of the words that express the inevitable death that is in everything and in everyone. Freitas's language, in which the rhythm of the poem and the prose of the chronicle are reflexively mixed, approximates his readers, and together we see the fragile things of the world, but we also share memories of beings, of words, of gestures, which give us a possible answer to the question that has echoed for centuries among poets: 'Ubi sunt qui ante nos | In mundo fuere?' [Where are those who, before us, | existed in the world?].

Translated from the Portuguese by BARBARA TANNURI

MANUEL RESENDE, *Poesia Reunida*, 2nd impression (Lisbon: Cotovia, 2020). 280 pages. Print.

Reviewed by RICARDO VASCONCELOS (San Diego State University, CA)

Manuel Resende's *Poesia Reunida*, published by Cotovia in April 2018, and already in a second impression in February 2020, features the author's previously released *Natureza Morta com Desodorizante* [Still life with deodorant] (Imprensa Nacional–Casa da Moeda, 1983), *Em Qualquer Lugar* [Anywhere] (& Etc, 1998), and *O Mundo Clamoroso, Ainda* [The clamorous world, still] (Angelus Novus, 2004). Three other sections are added, namely 'E Mais... (Inéditos e Esparsos)' [And more... Unpublished and Uncollected], the poetry written under the heteronym of Mika Ahtsihaari, and an interesting *hors texte* with the title 'Ar de Cura' — a title literally meaning 'looking like a cure', but also a word play on the Portuguese saying 'o que arde cura', literally 'what burns you will heal you'. The volume also includes an important study on Manuel Resende's poetry by Osvaldo Manuel Silvestre, titled 'A R(e)alidade e as Cerejas'.

It could hardly be said of a poet who has released three books of original work with the distinguished publishing house Cotovia that he is nearly unknown. However, it would seem undeniable that Manuel Resende (1948–2020) came surprisingly close to that situation. Indeed Resende remained on the very fringes of the Portuguese literary field as a poet, despite being well respected for his work as a literary translator of modern Greek and German. As sometimes also happens in the dynamics of the literary field, his rarefied presence also led some to evoke the excellence of his poetry, though; fellow poet, friend and, for a while, co-worker at the *Jornal de Notícias*, Manuel António Pina, for example, recurrently praised Resende's poems, no matter that they were almost always out of circulation.

It would be easy to say that Resende's work was little noticed due to the distraction of critics, or at the very least to a lack of effort to recognize authors that do not gain momentum. And perhaps there is something true in that idea, since we find barely any scholarship whatsoever on books that were indeed published, even if they soon stopped circulating. However, it is more plausible to say that Manuel Resende made a conscious decision to circulate himself very little in the vanity fair of the literary world, and also paid a price for living outside Portugal, for decades, as a translator for the European Union. Be that as it may, Manuel Resende developed a coherent *oeuvre* over the course of several decades, one that is all the more disconcerting to come across given how outstandingly mature and original it is.

When *Poesia Reunida* was released in 2018, in an interview given to Isabel Lucas for the newspaper *Público*, Resende said, regarding the essential elements of life that find their way into his poetic discourse, that 'A poesia é muita rara para ser desperdiçada com porcarias. Essas coisas são o amor, a liberdade...' [Poetry is too rare to be wasted on junk. Those things are love, freedom...], not really adding much more to that list of essentials. Of course, the passage recognizes the value of these things that matter the most in our lives. But it is worth noting the first part of the author's statement, claiming that 'Poetry is rare', because this idea is eloquently reflected in the author's own production. According to this view, *poetry* as a synonym of *high-quality writing* is rarely achieved, and Manuel Resende seems to have been in no rush to compose a vast amount of works, rather being more inclined to preserve a small but highly significant collection of poetry. His *Poesia Reunida* fully matches that description.

For all purposes, this is *twice* a volume of collected poetry, since the various books were already collections of texts written with great temporal distance between them. Fifteen years elapsed between the first and the second book, six years more between the second and the third, and another fourteen years between the third book and this *Poesia Reunida*, which includes previously unpublished poems. The long periods of time that elapsed between each book and the actual texts both show that no single independent title followed an evident plan, nor addressed a narrow specific topic defined ahead of time. This is not to say, though, that the author did not have topics that stand out. These main themes include the celebration of freedom in its various facets, from political freedom to that associated with love; the desire to address the immediately surrounding reality, often in tributes to different cities or places visited or lived in; a consideration of death and mortality; and a strikingly original reflection on the relation of the human being with nature. Many of these topics are discussed against the backdrop of the historical period that Resende experienced first-hand, from the May '68 unrest that the book flap reminds us happened exactly 50 years before its publication, to many other historical events that tested particularly our society's most utopian beliefs. Resende's poetry also establishes a dialogue with numerous other poets, Portuguese, Greek, or otherwise; and several metapoetic considerations — though these are often woven into poems that address other themes. Frequently, the poems take up a disconcerting and humorous tone, many times echoing or denaturalizing popular expressions: 'É como digo | A carne é triste quando a traem a carne é fraca | [...] É como te digo a carne é fraca e a minha então' [As I always say | The flesh is sad when betrayed it is weak | [...] | As I always tell you the flesh is weak and mine particularly]. The author always claimed the influence by Surrealistic languages and practices, something which is clearly visible in the book: 'Há uma grande necessidade de vida | Parem os semáforos todos no lilás' [There's a great need for life | Stop all the traffic lights on purple]. But *Poesia Reunida* illustrates a broad set of poetic strategies that display what the poet also regularly said of his work, i.e. that it was influenced by very different languages altogether.

Given the limited space of this review, I will refer to two different poems from the first and the third books, separated by at least 21 years, that allow us to talk about topics and tones altogether different. In the first book of poems we find echoes of the Portuguese revolutionary process, merging an awareness that certain symbols easily became cannibalized by the political discourse, as well as great hope in the revolution — one that is all the more expected in someone who, like Manuel Resende, always described himself as left-wing. In his masterpiece 'Entre Abril e Junho 74' [Between April and June 74], we hear the disbelieving voice of the underprivileged low-ranking soldier that Resende himself was on 25 April 1974: 'Diz-se que agora o povo escreverá | Aos ministros a perguntar | Pelos lucros e pelas perdas' [They say that the people will now write to | Ministers to inquire | About profits and losses]. This is a voice that, early on, has very few illusions: 'Que caiam os grandes da terra pois é bom ouvi-los fazer o barulho de caírem | E já era tempo de petiscarmos um pouco de ilusão de justiça' [May the lords of the earth fall as it is good to hear the clamour of their fall | And it was high time for us to taste the illusion of justice]. The poem also suggests that the *soldier* has become a positive icon for the Portuguese society, but one whose hardship isn't fully understood. In a relevant parenthesis, it alludes to '(O morteiro 60, o lança granadas foguete | Essas chaimites ameaçando o Carmo) | Teu mero dicionário simbolista' [(The lightweight mortar, the grenade thrower | The armoured tanks surrounding the Carmo barracks) | Your mere dictionary of symbols], recalling the imagery of the day of the coup and the events leading to Marcello Caetano's surrender. Moreover, the passage recognizes early on how the elements of that reality became mostly of a symbolic nature that arguably neutralized their impact. Two main perspectives cohabit in the poem; the first is the presentation of that plight of the soldier, who did not have the same freedom as civilians did to celebrate the revolution: 'não pude ser daqueles que passavam | E não passei, saudando os soldados que ali estávamos, saudando | A queda dum regime odiado' [I could not be one of those passing by | And I did not pass, greeting us soldiers that were there, greeting | The demise of a despised regime]. The second is the approval of the revolution, notwithstanding that the voice that expresses it had never truly mattered: 'Conhecia Lisboa por ouvir dizer e vim aqui ter sem saber ao que vinha | Deixai-me que vos diga aprovo que o regime caísse eu que vivo entre ratos | [...] Que o regime caia pois nos apodrecia' (p. 58) [I knew Lisbon from hear-say and got here not knowing what for | Let me tell you I approve that the regime should fall I who live amongst rats | [...] May the regime fall since it was rotting us].

A very different poem is '1 de Novembro', from *O Mundo Clamoroso, Ainda*. It reflects upon mortality and memory, at the same time considering what makes the poetic word meaningful and relevant, and what in our lives becomes our *history*, beyond our common *History*. Reminding us that 1 November is the 'dia dos mortos' [day of the dead], the poet speaks of the people that left his own past: 'Não recordo, da infância, altas colunas de mármores partidas, | Nem catedrais magníficas, nem ruas históricas, nem tenho onde pôr essas palavras,

| Do passado do mundo, só conheço estas presenças' [I don't remember, from my childhood, tall marble columns broken | Nor magnificent cathedrals, nor historical streets, nor do I have anywhere to put such words, | From the past of the world, I only know these presences]. Greek culture, so important for the author, echoes in the poem, as do other symbols we celebrate collectively, such as historical streets or cathedrals. But Resende reminds us, though, that the past that gains relevance is always personal, marked more by those close to us that may have died than by such historical elements. Particularly striking is the passage that states 'nem tenho onde pôr essas palavras', which alludes to the author's concern with meaningful vocabularies in his poetic discourse, beyond his daily language; a marble column may carry a sense of history, but it will have little meaning for most of us, compared to the people who left their mark on our lives. Certainly there is time to recollect voices silenced with time. In the second tercet of his 'Soneto para o Amigo Morto' [Sonnet for a dead friend], Resende tells again that it is the personal that drives meaning: 'Já sei há tanta morte por aí | Tanta gente morrendo aos pontapés | Mas como tu tão morto nunca vi' [I know there's plenty of death going around | People dying left and right | But as dead as you right now I have never seen] (p. 189). It's the closeness that makes the dead all the more dead; still, the tone is not solemn, resorting to colloquial expressions that become more humorous than dysphemistic, such as 'Tanta gente morrendo aos pontapés'.

I should add that, writing this review more than a month since the moment when a large part of humankind was sent home to slow down the pace of the Coronavirus's spread and the Covid-19 disease, I couldn't help but be startled by the title of a poem by Manuel Resende, which literally tells us the very opposite of the slogans of our day: 'Sai de casa' [Get out of your house], it recommends. Obviously, the poem is not related at all to the current situation of confinement, or any other remotely similar context. Rather, it makes us reflect upon how ephemeral the poetic word is, perhaps even how perishable its message is, like a note for us we may find on the kitchen table and which we tear up after reading. Above all, the poem speaks of the relationship that poetry needs to maintain with the world that, we say, surrounds it, to find its meaning, suggesting that the poem must start coming into being within that same outer world. It is worth quoting the brief stanza: 'Rasga este poema depois de o leres | E depois espalha os bocados | Pelo vasto mundo | Ou então na tua rua, vai à aldeia, à praia, | Atira-o ao mar, deita-o ao lixo, | Para que venha o vento, o sol, a chuva, os homens do lixo, | Acabar com ele de vez. | Passado um dia, | Sai de casa e procura | Encontrá-lo de novo' [Tear up this poem after you have read it | Then scatter the pieces | Through the whole wide world. | Or toss it in your street, go to your hometown, to the beach | Throw it in the ocean, or in the litter bin | So that the wind, the sun, the rain, the men from the garbage truck | May come to finish what's left of it. | The next day, | Get out of your house and try to | Find it again] (p. 171). To be sure, poets will not fail to tear up the poems from which they soon feel distant or which they don't fully appreciate. Even if they don't look for the original street, village or beach, to get rid of it. It remains to be seen in these days, however, which houses poets will invent for themselves to leave, so that they may keep giving voice to the world, as Manuel Resende did in his poetry.

Abstracts

Of Literature as a Composition of the Disparate and its Political Implications
Silvina Rodrigues Lopes

Abstract. This paper aims to study the problem of the indirect relationship between poetry and politics, taking as a starting point a reading of some poems by Portuguese poets (Fernando Pessoa, Sophia de Mello Breyner Andresen, Carlos de Oliveira, Luiza Neto Jorge, and a poet who presents himself under the name Théodore Fraenckel). To this end it constructs a perspective in which the inscription of the other as other is affirmed as a condition for writing and reading from which there flows a persistent dispersal of meaning. An analysis of this dispersion allows us to highlight how reason and imagination unfold each other to move away from the aesthetics of appearance, showing themselves to be inseparable in the poetic establishment of spaces for reply and solicitation that make an imponderable opening of the aesthetic to the ethical-political.

Keywords. Poetry, diversity, dispersion, justice, political implication.

Resumo. Pretende-se estudar a problemática da relação, indirecta, entre o poético e o político, tendo como ponto de partida a leitura de poemas de autores portugueses (Fernando Pessoa, Sophia de Mello Breyner Andresen, Carlos de Oliveira, Luiza Neto Jorge e o poeta que se apresenta sob o nome Théodore Fraenckel). Para tal, constrói-se uma perspectiva na qual a inscrição do outro enquanto outro é afirmada como condição de escrita e leitura de onde decorre a persistente dispersão de sentido. A análise dessa dispersão permite destacar como razão e imaginação se desdobram e se afastam da estética da aparição, mostrando-se inseparáveis na instauração poética de espaços de resposta e solicitação que são abertura imponderável do estético ao ético-político.

Palavras-chave. Poesia, díspar, dispersão, justiça, implicação política.

Some Portuguese Poetry from the Past Fifty Years: A Reading through Images
Rosa Maria Martelo

Abstract. In the past fifty years Portuguese poetry has dealt with images in very distinct ways. There has been rhetorical elaboration of the poetic image; emphasis on poems' iconicity; and the creation of intermedial relations through ekphrasis and media combination. This range of diverse relations between text and image enables us to capture a poetics in the process of transformation. This study proposes some approaches to reading contemporary Portuguese poetry based on these multiple ways of conceiving and working with images.

KEYWORDS. Contemporary Portuguese poetry, image, intermediality, intertextuality, ekphrasis, iconicity.

RESUMO. A poesia portuguesa dos últimos cinquenta anos trabalha a imagem de formas muito diferentes entre si. Da elaboração retórica da imagem poética à ênfase dada à iconicidade do poema, passando pelo estabelecimento de relações intermediais através da écfrase, ou pela combinação medial, a diversidade de relações entre o texto e a imagem permite-nos surpreender uma poética em processo de transformação. O presente estudo apresenta algumas linhas de leitura da poesia portuguesa contemporânea, tomando por referência essas formas de conceber a imagem e trabalhar com ela.

PALAVRAS-CHAVE. Poesia contemporânea portuguesa, imagem, intermedialidade, intertextualidade, écfrase, iconicidade.

The Chant of Images: Fiama and Indifference
JOANA MATOS FRIAS

ABSTRACT. This paper aims to systematize the most characteristic features of one of the most self-conscious writers of Portuguese literature of the twentieth century, with special emphasis on her works *Área Branca* (1978), and *Cenas Vivas* (2000), since these books represent, within Fiama's production but also in the broader field of contemporary Portuguese poetry, spaces of qualitative transmutation of the great issues that have crossed modern and contemporary poetic creation, at least since Romanticism so dear to the poet — language and representation, word and image, memory and imagination, identity and otherness, tradition and individual talent — which in their work were submitted to a dialectical synthesis with surprising reading effects.

KEYWORDS. Fiama Hasse Pais Brandão, Romanticism, indifference, image.

RESUMO. Proposta de sistematização dos elementos característicos daquela que é uma das escritoras mais auto-conscientes da literatura portuguesa do século XX, dando especial destaque às obras *Área Branca*, de 1978, e *Cenas Vivas*, de 2000, uma vez que estes livros representam, na totalidade da produção de Fiama, mas também no campo mais alargado da poesia portuguesa contemporânea, espaços de transmutação qualitativa das grandes questões que têm atravessado a criação poética moderna e contemporânea, pelo menos desde o Romantismo tão caro à poeta — linguagem e representação, palavra e imagem, memória e imaginação, identidade e alteridade, a tradição e o talento individual — e que na sua obra foram objecto de uma síntese dialéctica com surpreendentes efeitos de leitura.

PALAVRAS-CHAVE. Fiama Hasse Pais Brandão, Romantismo, indiferença, imagem.

A Selfless Proliferating Language
MANUEL PORTELA

ABSTRACT. This essay analyses works by Rui Torres and Luís Serguilha as proliferative and de-referentialized expressions of language towards a horizon devoid of self. The factorial permutations that occur in both works — with or without computer assistance — allow us to imagine a literary art whose combinatorial flow, like the passage of time, resides in the pure potentiality and fictionality of its unrepeatability. The reification of language contained in the poetics of expressive singularity, which has so far dominated our practices and concepts of literature, gives rise to an attention to the infinite modulations of the act of saying as an opening to the flow of its becoming, freed from an origin and from a destination.

KEYWORDS. Permutation poetics, automatic writing, generative language, Rui Torres, Luís Serguilha.

RESUMO. Este ensaio analisa obras de Rui Torres e Luís Serguilha como expressões proliferativas e desreferencializadas da língua em direção a um horizonte desprovido de sujeito. A factorialidade das permutações que ocorre em ambas as obras — assistidas ou não por computador — permite imaginar uma arte literária cujo fluxo combinatório reside, tal como a passagem do tempo, na pura potencialidade e ficcionalidade de um dizer-se irrepetível. Nessa medida, a reificação da linguagem contida na poética da singularidade expressiva, que dominou até hoje as nossas práticas e conceitos de literatura, dá lugar a uma atenção às modulações infinitas do dizer como abertura ao fluxo do seu devir, liberto de uma origem e de um destino.

PALAVRAS-CHAVE. Poética permutativa, escrita automática, linguagem gerativa, Rui Torres, Luís Serguilha.

Blood Evocations: Subversion, Resistance, and Afterimage in Ana Luísa Amaral's 'Ágora'
PAULO DE MEDEIROS

ABSTRACT. Ana Luísa Amaral's *Ágora* (2019) is a forceful intervention in a perverted view of reality that offers us alternatives with which to overthrow such illusions. Its thirty-three poems all engage dialectically with a famous painting or other visual art form from the western canon and (in most cases) with the biblical text behind them. Beyond a critique of our present times, *Ágora* offers possibilities for re-envisioning tradition and resisting certain conditions of oppression. Subversion is what enables resistance and in *Ágora* it takes many forms, from a defiance, and inversion, of patriarchal norms, to a questioning of violence perhaps nowhere clearer than in the insistence on images of decapitation. While exploring some of these forms attention comes to rest on the notion of the afterimage that would result from the continuous intersections between poem and image.

KEYWORDS. Subversion, resistance, afterimage, Ana Luísa Amaral, intermediality.

RESUMO. *Ágora*, de Ana Luísa Amaral (2019), constitui uma intervenção decisiva numa certa atual e perversa visão da realidade, que nos permite considerar alternativas para derrubar tais ilusões. Cada um dos seus trinta e três poemas relaciona-se dialeticamente com a imagem de uma obra de arte famosa do cânone ocidental e (na maioria) com o texto bíblico que lhe subjaz. Para além de uma crítica ao nosso tempo presente, *Ágora* oferece possibilidades para re-ver a tradição e resistir a certas condições de opressão. A subversão é o que proporciona essa resistência. Em *Ágora* a subversão assume muitos modos, desde o desafio às (e a inversão das) normas do patriarcado até ao questionamento da violência — bem visível na insistente atenção dada a imagens de decapitação. Da indagação de alguns destes modos, sobressai o conceito de 'afterimage' ou pós-imagem, resultante das contínuas intersecções entre poema e imagem.

PALAVRAS-CHAVE. Subversão, resistência, afterimage, Ana Luísa Amaral, intermedialidade.

Last Will(s): Withdrawal and Resistance in the Poetry of José Miguel Silva
PEDRO EIRAS

ABSTRACT. The first pages of *Erros Individuais* [*Individual Errors*] (2010) pose the question of whether it is worth writing poetry; the answer is rather ambiguous. In *Serém, 24 de Março* (2011), the poetic *persona* decides to retreat to a house in the country, far away from the values of the cities. Very recently (2017), José Miguel Silva published a book called *Últimos Poemas* [*Last Poems*], probably a goodbye to poetry. At the same time, the author has been publishing online texts in which he denounces the dangers of climate change, far-right politics, and the end of democracy. Should we identify a coherent gesture of withdrawal in José Miguel Silva's work? Or is there a sort of ironic resistance in this farewell to poetry and to the world of the *polis*?

KEYWORDS. José Miguel Silva, poetry, withdrawal, resistance, irony.

RESUMO. As primeiras páginas de *Erros Individuais* (2010) perguntam se vale a pena escrever poesia; a resposta é bastante ambígua. Em *Serém, 24 de Março* (2011), o sujeito poético decide retirar-se para uma casa no campo, longe dos valores das cidades. Muito recentemente (2017), José Miguel Silva publicou um livro intitulado *Últimos Poemas*, provavelmente uma despedida em relação à poesia. Ao mesmo tempo, o autor tem publicado textos *on line* denunciando os perigos das mudanças climáticas, da política de extrema-direita e do fim da democracia. Devemos identificar um gesto coerente de retirada na obra de José Miguel Silva? Ou haverá uma espécie de resistência irónica neste adeus à poesia e ao mundo da *polis*?

PALAVRAS-CHAVE. José Miguel Silva, poesia, retirada, resistência, ironia.

'Neither Man nor Woman': Ana Luísa Amaral's Queerful Poetics
MARINELA FREITAS

ABSTRACT. This article examines how the Portuguese poet Ana Luísa Amaral questions gendered assumptions embedded in language and explores new ways of articulating difference. In her work, two literary strategies are often explored to unsettle hierarchies regarding gender, sex and sexuality: the transvestism of the voice, when Amaral uses male voices to subvert the complex negotiations between male and female, self and other, reality and fiction; and the creation of queer identities, which the author explores to dismantle dichotomies and resist the violence of categorization. My contention is that, in Amaral's writings, the representation and articulation of different ways of being has a strong ethical and political component: calling others to challenge and resist monolithic identities by creating new spaces of freedom is at the basis of what the author calls a 'queerful' practice (and poetics).

KEYWORDS. Ana Luísa Amaral, transvestism, queer, difference, 'queerful' poetics.

RESUMO. Este artigo analisa o modo como a poeta portuguesa Ana Luísa Amaral problematiza a diferença sexual contida na linguagem e explora novas formas de articular a diferença ao longo da sua obra. Duas estratégias literárias em particular permitem desmontar hierarquias ligadas ao género, ao sexo e às sexualidades: o transvestimento da voz, sempre que Amaral recorre a vozes masculinas para subverter as complexas relações entre masculino e feminino, 'eu' e 'outro', realidade e ficção; e a criação de identidades *queer*, que a poeta utiliza para desmontar dicotomias e resistir à violência redutora das categorizações. A representação e articulação de diferentes modos de ser ou existir na escrita de Ana Luísa Amaral tem, assim, uma forte componente ética e política, já que o gesto de chamar os outros a desafiar e a resistir a identidades monolíticas através da criação de novos espaços de liberdade está na base do que a autora chama uma prática (ou poética) 'queerente'.

PALAVRAS-CHAVE. Ana Luísa Amaral, transvestimento, queer, diferença, poética 'queerente'.